On Rue Tatin

ALSO BY SUSAN HERRMANN LOOMIS

The Great American Seafood Cookbook

Farmhouse Cookbook

Clambakes and Fishfries

French Farmhouse Cookbook

Italian Farmhouse Cookbook

SUSAN
HERRMANN LOOMIS

Broadway Books
NEW YORK

On Rue Tatin

LIVING AND COOKING
IN A FRENCH TOWN

Designed by Jennifer Ann Daddio
Title page illustration by Robert Hunt

The Library of Congress has cataloged the
hardcover edition as follows:

Loomis, Susan Herrmann.
On rue Tatin: living and cooking in a French town /
Susan Herrmann Loomis.—1st ed.
p. cm.
1. Cookery, French—Normandy style. 2. Normandy (France)—
Social life and customs. I. Title.
TX719.2.N67 L66 2001
641.5944′2—dc21   00-060836

ISBN 0-7679-0455-9

12 14 16 18 20 19 17 15 13 11

I dedicate this book first and foremost to my partner in life, Michael, and to our two wonderful, humorous, and, above all, adaptable children, Joe and Fiona.

I also dedicate this book to Louviers and its inhabitants, for making room for us.

Contents

Acknowledgments

Before I thank anyone I must turn to Edith and Bernard Leroy, friends who are like family, for their part in the adventure we call our life.

Thank you to our dear friends Christian and Nadine Devisme, Patrick Merlin, Bernadette Brière, Chantal and Michel Amsalem, Babette and Jean-Lou Dewaele, Marie Odile and Marie Claire Bunel, André Taverne, Brigitte Tois, Dalila and Sala Boufercha, the staff at Chez Clet and La Maison des Simples, Monsieur et Madame Richard, and all the others in Louviers who make it the special place that it is.

Thank you, too, to Patricia and Walter Wells and to Martha Rose Shulman for friendship, spice grinders, and more! And thank you to Marion Pruett for her careful testing of the recipes in the U.S., and to Kurt for helping out!

I cannot thank Angela Miller, my agent, enough for her support, generosity, and keen sense; my once-upon-a-time editor, Harriet Bell; and my current and very much appreciated editor,

Jennifer Josephy, who goes right to the heart of things. Thank you to everyone at Broadway Books, including Anne Resnik, for making the process so pleasant. And finally, thank you to my editor at epicurious.com, Betsy Beckman, for her excellent editing, encouragement, and enlightened nature.

ONE

The Beginning

THE STORY OF OUR ADVENTURE, our move to Rue Tatin, began some thirteen years earlier, when I first went to live in Paris. Of course back then I had no idea that I would fall hopelessly in love with Michael Loomis, and then with France. Nor did I ever imagine longing so heartily for the French countryside, the French language, the thousands of things that make French life what it is, from dozens of varieties of bottled water to the sweet cream butter. There wasn't any way to know then how deeply and irreversibly seduced I would be by the markets, the restaurants, the French lifestyle that takes its cue from the meal and the table.

THE SUITCASE WAS BIG, and it was heavy. It had everything I thought I would need for a year in Paris, including a little wire contraption that worked on 220 current and would boil water in-

1

stantly, my favorite earthenware Melitta coffee maker, and a *Le Petit Robert Dictionnaire de la Langue Française* French dictionary, the best I could find.

After months of planning, applying for and getting a student loan, packing, and moving, I was finally in Paris for a year's experience as a *stagiaire*, or apprentice, at a cooking school for English-speaking students. It sounded like a dream—working all day at the school, taking cooking classes at night with French chefs, and living in Paris to boot. I was beside myself with excitement. And fear. I didn't know a soul. I'd only been to Paris once before, for a short week when I was barely twenty. I'd studied French for years in school but had never really spoken it.

Already concerned about just how I was going to make the $2,500 loan I'd gotten stretch for a year, I decided on arrival to take the metro rather than a cab from the airport to the city. That meant heaving the suitcase up and down stairs, through archaic turnstiles (all of which have been modernized since to accommodate luggage), in and out of metro cars. It was several very rough hours before I arrived at the apartment where I was to stay with a young woman who had just started working at the cooking school and had offered me her spare bedroom. The apartment was in the ninth *arrondissement*, not far from Montmartre. I would stay there just long enough to find a place of my own.

No one was at the apartment and I was in a hurry. I dropped my bags, took a deep breath, and immediately ran back out the door to renegotiate the metro and report for work.

The apprenticeship was set out in six-week stages, the first being that of school receptionist, which meant sitting behind a desk, answering the phone, greeting visitors, and dealing with mounds of paperwork. My ideas of a romantic, food-filled year hadn't included such stultifying work; the only thing that kept me going was peeking at the cooking classes going on in the adjacent room and knowing that two nights a week I would join the other *stagiaires* for cooking classes.

I could hardly wait for the first class. When my workday was finished and the door to the street locked, I followed the other *stagiaires* to the kitchen. They explained the system to me, which sounded too good to be true. There was a list of perhaps a hundred required recipes to work through during the year, calculated to teach the basics of classic French cuisine and to prepare us for the year-end exam. All we had to do before each class was to choose the recipes we wanted to work on, in a certain order that went from simple to complex. All of the ingredients would be ordered so that on the night of the class we simply had to run downstairs to the *cave*, or cellar, where they were kept, and bring them upstairs. We paired up to work and kept the same partners throughout the year, to the extent everyone's staggered schedule would allow.

Once I had traded my phone and typewriter for a chef's knife and covered my street clothes with a long white apron, I was in heaven. Hours to cook, good company to cook with, fabulous ingredients. Never had I imagined produce so gorgeous, so intense in both appearance and flavor. Though my culinary education was relatively broad—I lived in England and Germany while growing up and had a mother who was endlessly creative in the kitchen and rarely made the same dish twice—it was not sophisticated.

My personal interest in cooking had come rather late in life. It

THE BEGINNING

wasn't until I was in my last year of high school when both of my sisters, who seemed to spend hours in the kitchen baking cookies, were out of the house that I realized I had a passion for cooking. That year and all through college I cooked whenever I had free time. When I wasn't cooking I was reading about it, planning my next meal, designing my next dinner party. After earning a degree in communications and working at newspapers and in public relations, it dawned on me I could incorporate food into my professional life, which is what had led me to La Varenne. I wanted to be a food writer, but first I had to learn how to cook.

So here I was in 1980 in a two-hundred-year-old building in Paris, near the Place des Invalides, basking in the world's best butter; the fattest, most pungent pink garlic; spinach whose leaves were so firm and meaty they stood up on the table instead of lying flat; brown eggs whose yellow yolks tasted as rich as they looked. I thought I knew good apples, fragrant strawberries, juicy pears. But never had I tasted the likes of the *fraises des bois* I had on a tart at La Varenne, and the pears I sniffed made me want to fold them into cakes, slather them with chocolate, poach them in fragrant herbs and spices.

The food was so *whole*. Chickens came with head, feet, and pinfeathers, and so did the pigeons and quail; the fish looked at me with big, dreamy eyes as I took them from the cooler; the lettuce still had soil clinging to it.

Once my onerous receptionist stint was finished I moved on to washing dishes at cooking demonstrations, a job I much preferred. At least I was in contact with food. I lived in a blessed cloud of ecstasy about the food, the flavors, the techniques I was learning. I jumped at the chance to run errands to the market, the cheese

4

shop, the bakery. When I wasn't at La Varenne I took jobs cooking for embassy families, catering bar mitzvahs, making canapés for special occasions. Anything to be with food. Whenever I could I went to spend a day at a bakery or *pâtisserie*, often getting up at 1 A.M. and arriving when the baker did, so I missed nothing and could still get to work on time.

The chefs on duty with us for our evening classes—all of them terribly handsome in their crisp whites and with their Gallic attitudes—would yell, scream, cajole, flirt, pinch, and generally try to pummel us into cooks of some merit. After several hours of cooking we would sit down late in the evening to sample and critique our creations. I always raced through whatever my required dish or dishes were so that I could jump ahead and make something else from the list, usually in the dessert category. I always toyed with these extra recipes, embellishing and transforming them by adding ground walnuts to a *gâteau Breton*, for instance, and *pâté sablé* to a chocolate charlotte. It was more fun than I could have imagined.

Being a *stagiaire* at La Varenne was a unique experience, not always easy but invaluable, a sort of boot camp for cooks. All those long days doing the bidding of the chefs and the hours spent in the basement peeling garlic for a cooking demonstration, or in the office writing or rewriting something for one of the school's books that were produced there, were ideal training for the life of a freelance food writer.

I had expected, while doing my apprenticeship, to travel on weekends. Before arriving in France, I'd joined an organization called SERVAS, which is set up to further international goodwill by supplying travelers with names of host families in countries where

THE BEGINNING

they want to visit. The idea is that the traveler stays with the host family free of charge for up to three days and must, in exchange, be willing to participate in whatever the family is doing, be it harvesting grapes, taking care of children, or touring the countryside.

I looked through my list and found a family that wasn't too far out of Paris and called to see if I could come out the following weekend. They were busy but their daughter, who lived nearby, said a visit would be just fine. Early Saturday morning I climbed on a train at Gare St-Lazare and was on my way to my first weekend in the French countryside.

When I arrived at the train station in Normandy I was met by a tall, thin, harried-looking woman who drove me to her large stone house. We entered a huge courtyard with its sculpted privets and riotous dahlias and I saw the image of all I love in France. Solid and square with graceful proportions, it was a *maison bourgeoise*, its façade a parade of tall windows each hung with a different antique lace curtain. Geraniums and pansies spilled out of window boxes, an antique bicycle leaned against the wall, the wicker basket on its back fender overflowing with petunias.

She said something to me I didn't understand, pointed to her three chubby, gorgeous golden-haired children, and took off in the car. I was alone and the children immediately started fighting. I searched frantically for words like "be quiet" and "go to your room," but of course, nothing came out. I finally yelled *"Arrêt."* They stopped, looked at me with their big, wide eyes, and all started to giggle and point their fingers. I searched in the cupboards looking for something to give them to eat and found only one box of organic biscuits (I now remembered that the description of this family included "vegetarian"). What else had it included, I wondered, as I chased the children through the freezing, massive, stone-floored house.

My hostess finally returned, fed the children, giving each a heaping plate of steaming noodles with Gruyère cheese, and put them all to bed. They were crying, but she simply shut their doors and went downstairs. We had a quick lunch of the same pasta, with the most delicious green salad I'd ever tasted, then she indicated I follow her out to the garden. There we worked in almost complete silence, carrying wheelbarrow after wheelbarrow of soil, weeds, and stones from one part of the garden to the other. I was delighted, eking out bits of conversation as we worked.

I learned that the woman, Edith Leroy, who was just a few years older than I, and Bernard, her husband, had just bought the house. She was by profession a painter; Bernard had recently started his own company, and they were stretched very thin. The conversation was slow going. Edith didn't make eye contact, didn't talk much, and never smiled. I was in heaven. I had always heard the French were cold and somewhat austere. I found Edith's behavior gratifyingly exotic.

We worked for hours, then Edith got the kids, gave them a snack (those organic biscuits), piled them into the back of her green Deux Chevaux and indicated I get in beside her. She flew out of the driveway and we careened through the village and down a winding road to the next town, where she had an errand to run. She left the children with her parents—older, more austere versions of Edith—and off we went.

We ended up at an *herboristerie,* or herb store, that smelled like lavender, rosemary, and fresh thyme, and was so calm and peaceful I wanted to set up camp there. Edith bought bread, organic cookies, and a *cajot*, or crate, full of soil-covered carrots, leeks, potatoes, and cabbage, all organic, then we piled back into the Deux Chevaux, picked up the kids, and careened back home. The kids were flying around in the backseat screaming and hitting each other, themselves, the car seats. Edith was perfectly composed. I was a wreck, imagining an accident and a little sturdy ball of a child hurtling through the windshield. We arrived home safely, however, and the kids piled out of the car and went to play in the yard. Edith and I went into the house and she began to prepare dinner. It was about 7 P.M. An hour later her husband, Bernard, a stocky man with fine brown hair and large brown eyes, arrived. He set down his brief-case, shook my hand, and offered to give me a tour of the house. He spoke decent English, and we could understand each other perfectly. It was a huge relief. He showed me the small bathroom off the master bedroom upstairs with a pastoral mural painted on the walls, Edith's work. It was lovely, and freezing. "You may want to take a shower before dinner," he said, waving to the small bathtub which had a shower attachment. "I know Americans like to be very clean." Nothing in the world would have induced me to bathe—I could barely keep my teeth from clattering.

Bernard was the picture of civility, as calm and warm as Edith was tense and cool. I started to relax and almost immediately began to understand a bit of French. Edith fed the children and put them to bed, and sometime later the three of us sat down at a candlelit table in the kitchen next to the fireplace, the only warm spot in the house. Bernard explained that the house had an old coal furnace, which Edith had to fill several times a day. Even when full it didn't offer much comfort. Some day they would change it.

Edith had made a simple meal—*carottes râpées*, a mound of *sar-*

rasin (buckwheat groats), with a garlicky, lemony vinaigrette and braised leeks, a huge garden salad, a Camembert so creamy it melted in my mouth. Dessert was an apple *clafoutis*. I had felt close to starvation during the afternoon, accustomed as I'd become to my daily La Varenne snacks of *baguette* slathered with butter, and the edge of hunger made the meal taste even more delicious.

The following morning everyone rose early. Bernard was vice-mayor of the village, so he was off to some function. Edith had more plans to work in the garden. The children took care of themselves. I headed for the wheelbarrow, and together and in silence, Edith and I worked until lunchtime. We had soft-boiled eggs; I watched the children as they stuck little sticks of toasted, buttered bread (*mouillettes*) into their eggs, and did the same. I easily made my way through two eggs, the most delicious I'd ever tasted. I reveled in the intensely garlicky, tart salad, had more Camembert slathered on the hearty whole wheat bread Edith had bought the day before at the health food store, then enjoyed another *clafoutis*, this time with pears instead of apples.

My train back to Paris was mid-afternoon, and Bernard arrived home just in time to drive me to the station. I bade Edith good-bye; there was a flicker of warmth from her, but not much. The kids yelled "*au revoir*." At the station Bernard bid me a safe journey and told me I was welcome to return any time, and if I needed anything all I had to do was call. He kissed me on each cheek, then was gone.

I was completely charmed by the whole experience. I'd finally gotten the soil of France on my shoes in a beautiful little village, stayed in a three-hundred-year-old *maison bourgeoise*, frolicked with (and yelled at) three darling French children, and been inspired by the simple foods I'd eaten. I was walking on air.

9

THE BEGINNING

On returning to the school the next day I suddenly found my French much improved; it was finally emerging from my head. My comprehension was better, and I dared to say a few things. My fellow *stagiaires* gaped at me.

That was the only weekend trip I took. I was too captivated by my life in Paris and five-and-a-half-day school week to leave. I lived in a *chambre de bonne*, or maid's room, with a bed so narrow I had to carefully maneuver my body to turn over. My few clothes hung in a small *armoire*, and I had a sink and small window that let in a flood of light. I loved it. My life was whittled down to the essentials. I showered at a friend's apartment, used the toilet down the hall, had virtually no housework to do, and the only bills I had were my monthly *carte orange*, or metro pass, and the seven hundred French francs (about $175) I paid each month for my room. I had no phone and didn't miss it, no kitchen to mess. The biggest problem with my lodging was its location on the sixth floor, without an elevator, and that was a problem only when I'd forgotten my pen and notebook upstairs. Usually, I just bought new ones.

I subsequently moved into two other *chambres de bonne*, each one slightly better equipped. The best one was in the sixteenth *arrondissement* above the apartment of the American cultural ambassador. The size of a small studio, it had an elevator and a washing machine and a bathroom I shared with one other person. After months of traipsing down a dark hall to the toilet it was pure luxury to have one at hand and be able to stretch and not touch a wall on either side. I traded occasional cooking services. Another *stagiaire*, Roscoe Betsill, my cooking partner at school and now a food stylist, lived down the hall and together we were expected to prepare food for dinner parties when the ambassador and his wife entertained. It was a fine situation except that the ambassador's wife would call us at the last minute to prepare a meal, and there was never any food in her house. We learned to bring ingredients home from school that would otherwise have gone to waste—fresh herbs, for instance—and we had certain staples on hand. We became expert at making little canapés from canned tuna and fresh bread that seemed to delight our employers.

But a small cloud had formed over my experience. My French, which I discovered was extremely literary and terribly impractical, wasn't improving. I was tongue-tied, and even with the chefs I had to concentrate so hard to catch what they were saying that I would fall way behind in classes. I desperately wanted to translate a cooking demonstration for the English-speaking guests, banter with the chefs and the delivery people, have a conversation with a French person that lasted more than two seconds. As it was, I didn't really know any French people besides the chefs, since everyone who worked at the school came from an English-speaking country. For a while I traded conversation with a Frenchman who wanted to improve his English. With him I discovered that even though a person is French and speaks English with a sexy French accent he can be a crushing bore. My most childish romantic fantasies about Frenchmen were shattered, and my French didn't progress either.

The month of August, when all of France goes on vacation, approached. The school would close. Paris was already empty, the weather was stifling, most of the *stagiaires* had exotic vacations planned. I was scheduled to work through the month, though there was really nothing to do but type up recipes. Then one day, Edith called. Bernard had had a terrible accident and would be laid up for three months in bed, at home. She wanted to paint, and she needed

THE BEGINNING

someone to come out for the month of August to cook and help around the house. The children would go to day care. Did I know anyone? Without hesitation I said I'd do it, and we made arrangements. I had to check with the head of the school to see if I could get time off, something I was certain would be granted. To my surprise she refused. I begged. She relented, though not without letting me know that she wasn't happy. Evidently, the typing was more important than I'd realized. Nonetheless, a week later I was on the train to Normandy.

Edith was friendlier this time when she came to pick me up. She told me right away that she couldn't believe I had wanted to return after she'd been so rude. She explained to me that she had been completely exhausted and that, frankly, she really didn't feel like welcoming an American who lived in Paris, and didn't know why she had said yes when I called. It was several years before I admitted that I had thought it was perfectly normal.

I arrived to find Bernard in a wheelchair surrounded by friends, drinking chilled hard cider and expounding on something. He'd fallen some 45 feet off a ladder while pasting up a campaign poster for a friend. Despite the fact that his back and legs were a mess, his spirits were high, his greeting warm.

I joined the circle around him long enough to drink some cider, then went in to see what I could do for dinner. That evening began one of the most memorable months of my life. Edith turned out to be funny, filled with energy and up for anything. I had already glimpsed Bernard and knew he was easygoing; he turned out to be more than that. Brilliant, always searching to learn, he immediately set up a schedule of daily French and English lessons with me. Edith and I worked it out that I would cook two meals a day for the family, and after my first few dinners she began inviting all of their friends, so that each night there were eight to ten people for dinner. I was in heaven, cooking exactly what I wanted within a vegetarian diet—which was fine with me, since I had been a vegetarian for nearly ten years.

Edith, who was supposed to be painting each day, instead decided it would be more fun to show me around, and we roamed the countryside going to *brocantes* (combination junk and antique stores) and markets, visiting her friends, nearby Rouen, and pretty villages in the area. She wanted me to see everything, so each day unfolded with a new project.

Throughout the month, which sped by, I got to know Bernard's parents, who lived on a very modest farm, and two of his three brothers. I met each of Edith's seven brothers and sisters, all of her friends, many of her numerous other relatives as we traveled here and there, once as far as Amiens in the north to visit her favorite aunt. I kept urging Edith to paint, to take advantage of my being there, but she preferred instead to amuse herself taking me places, proposing long bicycle trips, or sewing. She made all her own and her children's clothing, and soon I was wearing her vivid, clever creations, too.

The days followed a certain pattern. I would prepare breakfast, Edith would get her children off to day care, Bernard and I had our English/French lesson, then the day would speed by while we either ran around the countryside or stayed home and she sewed while I cooked. In the evenings Edith put the children to bed and I prepared the evening meal; and she, Bernard, and I, and whoever else had been invited, usually sat down to dinner somewhere around nine o'clock. I made everything from asparagus soufflé to peach and yogurt tarts, from Asian tofu soups to layered vegetable terrines to classic *œufs florentine*. I discovered that the lady across the street,

13

Madame Dancerne, had a huge herb garden and raised lettuces, rabbits, and chickens. She became my supermarket, and I got plenty of good cooking lessons from her in the bargain. Everyone called me Suzanne and I became something of a novelty.

For the first two weeks at Edith and Bernard's I was physically present at the dinner table, but the conversation rolled on too rapidly for me to participate, and I would find myself battling sleep halfway through the meal. No one had any mercy, least of all Edith, who spoke like a *mitraillette*, or machine gun. About the middle of the third week I responded to something someone said. Bernard and Edith looked at me and laughed. "It's coming Suzanne, it's coming," they said.

As the end of my stay approached my spirits drooped. I had come to love the family and this turbulent, fun life. They, too, were loath to see it end and offered me a room and the price of a commuter ticket to Paris if I wanted to stay on. I was tempted, but the train schedule didn't match my long hours, and besides, I was ready to return to the city.

We said tearful good-byes—I was part of the family by now and couldn't quite imagine how their life would proceed without me. Bernard was relatively mobile in his wheelchair and was now going to the office, which was in the village center within walking distance. The children would be starting school, so Edith would have some time to work. I would re-enter my five-and-a-half-day-a-week routine. They made me promise to come visit often.

I was delighted to be back in Paris, in yet another *chambre de bonne* in the seventeenth *arrondissement* just over the border from the chic eighth *arrondissement*. It was small but had a tiny balcony. The family who rented it to me were sweet and gave me free use of their shower. School was beginning anew and it was good to see all the *stagiaires,* each of whom had gone in a separate direction for August.

I stunned everyone with my French. Now the chefs couldn't indulge in rude teasing because I understood them. I was capable of translating and couldn't wait to do it. From living with Edith and Bernard I'd picked up a very casual, current French, so that my *repartie* was rapid, and I felt perfectly comfortable. I knew I could avoid even the worst pitfall. And it came my way during my first translation. One of the students asked about preservatives in food. I turned to the chef to translate, and was just about to ask him about *préservatifs,* when I caught myself—a *préservatif* is a condom; *produit chimique* is the term used to describe food additives, and I remembered it just in time!

That fall a reporter for the *New York Times* who lived in Paris came to speak at La Varenne. She decided later to do a piece on young Americans who cooked for their living in Paris, and I fell into the category. She arranged to meet with all of us at a café, and we had a wonderful time. Later she called me to see if I would like to work for her. Her name was Patricia Wells, and I became her assistant.

I would race to her apartment after work whenever I had a free evening and do whatever job she'd left for me. My favorite one, and the one she and I still laugh about, was testing a cake called the *marjolaine,* a stunningly rich confection of layered hazelnut and almond meringue with pastry cream and *ganache.* I would spend the evening making it in Patricia and her husband Walter's apartment while they were out to dinner, then leave the finished product on the kitchen counter before going home to fall into bed. Patricia would taste it, make some comments, and I'd go back to the drawing board. I think I tested it four times over the course of a couple of weeks. Finally one day Patricia called me. "These cakes you leave us are gorgeous—why don't you ever take a piece for yourself?"

It had never occurred to me to do that. I loved leaving a perfect-looking, perfectly frosted cake in the middle of a clean kitchen. I'd sampled all the elements as I cooked, so I knew the flavors. And I honestly had no appetite. I'd spent almost a year eating more food than most people eat in ten years, and when my workday was done, my appetite was gone.

The year at La Varenne came smoothly to a close. I passed my final exam—preparing *consommé* with a garnish of *brunoise* (vegetables cut in tiny dice), roast beef with watercress and freshly made pasta, and *mille-feuille* for dessert, all made under the piercingly critical gaze of head chef Fernand Chambrette—and earned my *grand diplôme*. I was ready to move on, but hated the thought of leaving France. By now, I was a regular visitor at Edith and Bernard's; I'd gotten to know Paris well; I had my favorite markets, bakers, restaurants, and pastry shops, where I would do day-long *stages*, or visits, whenever I could. I couldn't quite imagine returning to the United States, but I couldn't simply stay on, either. Most of the other *stagiaires* were leaving, so my base of acquaintances would soon disperse.

I got a call from a woman who was looking for someone to open and cook for a *salon de thé* in the sixth *arrondissement*. It was to be part of an English-language bookstore, and she wanted the food to be American. I went to be interviewed and landed the job. Whew! I could stay on for at least another year. I had a month before the job would begin so I went back to the United States to visit my family. While there I met my future husband, Michael Loomis.

Tall, lean, and achingly handsome, he had been invited to a party to meet my older sister, and I knew that so I stayed clear. But circumstances were such that we couldn't seem to avoid each other. Before our first date I checked in with my sister who waved her hand and said go for it. Within a month, Michael and I were engaged.

I returned to Paris to begin my job. My bosses—two Parisiennes, each of whom had lived in the United States for extended periods—showed me the café bookstore, very much a raw space, a piece of which was destined to become a kitchen. One of my employers, Odile, turned to me and said, "It's yours, do what you want with it."

That started a month of hunting out the best appliances and fixtures I could find. It was July and burning hot; my memories of that time are infused with soaring temperatures, exacerbated by the heat generated by arguing to get everything I needed as I learned the French rules of commerce.

Buying an electric mixer stands out as one of my most memorable lessons. I walked into a kitchen supply store and saw the mixer I wanted, which at that time was hard to find in Paris, high upon a shelf. I asked the *vendeuse* for it by name, and she said they didn't carry them. I told her they did and pointed to it on the shelf. Without turning to look, she said, *"Ça n'existe pas ici,"* "This doesn't exist here." I was dumbfounded. I pointed to the shelf again, but she wouldn't look. I wanted to grab her head and swivel it around, but instead, feeling my face get very hot, I raised my voice and said, *"Madame, j'insiste. Je veux cette machine, vous l'avez, donnez-la moi."* "I insist. I want that machine, you have it, give it to me."

Startled, she turned, climbed up a ladder, got the machine, and hefted it onto the counter. I examined it, paid for it, and walked out with it under my arm. *"Au revoir, madame,"* said the *vendeuse* with her musical accent. "Not likely," I thought, but went on my way, hot, drenched, and still angry. But victorious. Or at least I felt victorious. I'd gotten what I wanted. She undoubtedly felt victorious, too. After all, she'd made me suffer. It took me awhile to cool off. But when I plugged in my mixer back at the *salon de thé* and made my first batch of brownies, I forgot it all and put the lesson I'd learned to good use. I wasn't brought up to argue, raise my voice, or object. Doing business in France taught me to do all three.

After choosing ovens and mixers, cook tops and sinks, I was ready. I tested my recipes and fed them to my employers and their families. Finally, in early September we were ready to open. *Le tout Paris* had been invited. I had prepared pans of my mother's sticky brownies, chocolate chip cookies, spice breads, molasses cookies, and other traditional American foods which, at that time, were novelties in Paris.

Opening night was a stunning success, and it began an intensely busy year, as my weeks sped away in a flurry of early morning shopping at the nearby Marché-St-Germain, where I became friends with the chicken lady and her *pâté*-making husband. She delivered chickens—heads, pinfeathers, and feet attached—whenever I had chicken salad or stew on the menu, and she was always giving and asking for recipes. I took my work seriously and put in long hours, trying to live up to the tradition of what I'd learned. The customers loved the food, from the hearty chili to the green-flecked zucchini bread (which I called spice cake, or no one would have eaten it). My saucer-sized chocolate chip cookies were the biggest hit. One day I stuck my head into the dining room and saw a properly dressed woman eating one with a knife and fork!

Michael, a sculptor in the mood for an adventure, had decided to join me in Paris. Before he'd met me he had been making plans to take a year off, live in Europe, and work on his drawing, so moving to Paris fit in with his plans. Four months after I returned he arrived. He was eager to study French, since he spoke not a word, and he couldn't wait to strike up an intimate relationship with the museums of Paris. While I was at work he would spend the day in museums or sitting in a park drawing, or attending French classes. In the evenings we would go to movies, or walk along the river eating Berthillon ice cream, the best in Paris, or simply wander the city streets. We were living on practically nothing and loving it.

I loved my schedule—early mornings at the market, cooking for hours in a music-filled kitchen, filling baskets with buttery cookies and slices of cake, stirring pots of spicy soups, and rolling out pounds and pounds of pastry dough. The bookstore became a destination for Parisian literati. The *salon de thé* was successful. The duo who had begun the enterprise began having problems, however, which made the working atmosphere unpleasant, and after a year I was ready to move on. I missed writing, too, and needed time to do it. I had already given my notice and Michael and I had decided that we would go back to the States when Patricia Wells came in for lunch one day. In the course of the meal she offered me a job as assistant on her first book, which was to be called the *Food Lover's Guide to Paris*. I refused. I knew how much Michael wanted to go back to the United States and his sculpture studio. Patricia persisted, however, pointing out the advantages of working with her.

I was tempted, and when I told Michael about the job he insisted I take it. He would manage for another year and a half, he said. I was thrilled, and grateful to Michael. I knew it was a sacrifice for him. He loved Paris, but needed more room than our tiny studio allowed. And he had discovered something he had already known about himself, but forgotten. Drawing was all right, but manipulating large pieces of wood, metal, plastic, and stone were lifeblood for him.

At about the same time I accepted the job, a friend of mine wanted to know if Michael would be available to help shore up disintegrating buildings at her cousin's farm in the Dordogne. He jumped at the opportunity. He didn't care that it was five hours south of Paris. It didn't faze him that the farm family spoke no English and that he himself spoke virtually no French. He didn't mind that the job would begin immediately. He wanted out of Paris, and he wanted to work with his hands. I saw him off at the Gare d'Austerlitz a few days later, not sure when I'd see him again—either he would return to Paris, or I would go down to visit.

Meantime, I started working with Patricia. Ours was a good match, and we spent an intense, concentrated, happy year walking the streets of Paris, sampling every bit of food the city offered. We developed a rhythm. Patricia would choose addresses to visit during the day, and I would plot them on a map at night. We would meet at a café that we wanted to test in the morning, and go from there. Our addresses included *boulangeries*, *pâtisseries*, kitchen stores, *brocantes* (many of these secondhand stores carry food wares), or anything at all to do with food. We would go until about 1 P.M., then stop for lunch and start out again when the shops reopened, around 3 P.M. Our day ended around 7 P.M., when we would separate for the night to prepare for the following day.

I was in heaven. I was also planning Michael's and my wedding and couldn't imagine being happier. We were married in a very simple ceremony in Le Vaudreuil, presided over by Bernard, in his role as vice-mayor. Patricia and her husband, Walter, brought the champagne, and Michael and I prepared the lunch we served to our twelve guests. One of our friends supplied the flowers, another loaned me a silk petticoat, and Madame Dancerne, Edith and Bernard's neighbor, contributed her homemade cider and *calvados*. It was a gorgeous misty Saturday. Bernard gave a short speech about the appropriateness of the wedding and how it continued the tradition of the Anglo-Saxon communion with France, so prevalent throughout the ages in Normandy. Our lunch of cream of watercress soup, *cannelloni à la crème*, salad, and Camembert was rich and satisfying. Our wedding cake was a *marjolaine* that I had made the day before in Paris, and which was transported to the wedding on Patricia's special silver *marjolaine* tray.

After the meal, we borrowed Edith's Deux Chevaux and drove to the nearby village of Bec Hellouin. We wanted to attend mass in the abbey's twelfth-century chapel on Sunday morning, to hear the renowned Gregorian chants. We spent our wedding night in a small *auberge*, or inn, went to mass the next morning, toured the village, then drove back to Le Vaudreuil, returned the car, and took the train to Paris. On Monday, Michael returned to the farm and I picked up work again.

Living separately was hard now that we were married. We missed each other so much that we decided I should spend my three-day weekends on the farm, where Danie and Guy Dubois raised geese for *foie gras*. Right after work each Friday I got on a train that arrived at Brive-la-Gaillarde in the Dordogne just before midnight. That first time was magic; Michael picked me up and we drove through the night to the farm, down winding, inky black

THE BEGINNING

roads. At the farm the kitchen light was on and the table was set with a bottle of the farm's wine, some fresh *rillettes* (shredded pork and goose meat cooked in goose fat) that Danie had made that day, a loaf of gorgeous bread, and some fresh cheese. Though everyone was asleep, it was a very warm welcome, and that midnight snack began yet another phase of my culinary education.

Not only did I get to see Michael every weekend, but I became, along with him, part of the extended Dubois family. I already knew them from Michael's stories—there was Danie, who did everything including cooking the most delicious meals Michael had ever tasted, which she served to her family and to paying guests who spent the night on the farm, and Guy, who had terrible eyesight and was a little loopy but sweet and a very good farmer. He always went off half-cocked, though, doing wheelies with his tractor as he took corners too fast, occasionally bashing a trailer into one of the walnut trees on the property, leaving his tools everywhere, and spewing corn all over the farmyard when he unloaded the trailer. Gilles, their teenaged son, was in cooking school and would return home now and then to stir up the kitchen, and Cathie, their daughter, was a moody adolescent who loved to eat anything and everything. She was skinny as a rail, which frustrated her slightly plump mother no end.

Danie and Guy's life was a throwback to medieval times. Danie married Guy and, through obligation, went to live with him at his parents' house. As the daughter-in-law she was expected to do all the work around the house, yet she had no rights and no money of her own. Within their first year of marriage she gave birth to Gilles, who cried all the time. She was still expected to do

ON RUE TATIN

all the work and keep the baby quiet. She was, she once told me, a slave.

Danie is short and solidly beautiful with wavy dark brown hair, soft, intense brown eyes, and a rare determination. She chafed at her position. She worked with no modern conveniences, so her solution was to do what farm women have done throughout the ages. She bought a few geese and fattened them up for *foie gras*, which she sold to earn money of her own. With it she bought an iron, so she didn't have to heat irons in the fireplace any more. Then she bought a washing machine.

Her *foie gras* was of such high quality that she soon made a name for herself. She convinced Guy they should build their own house down the road from his parents. They enlarged their by now substantial flock of geese, and their family, too—Cathie was born.

Danie continued making *foie gras*, which she sold locally, doing all the butchering, preparing, and preserving with the help of several women from the village. Guy did the field work and helped with the geese. Danie, who loves people and activity and had always felt isolated in their tiny village of less than one hundred inhabitants, began taking in paying guests. She devised a program where a group would come for the weekend and they would all butcher and prepare a pig together. She cooked sumptuous meals for the group, regaling guests with dishes she'd grown up eating. Everyone would leave happily on Sunday with parts of the pig preserved for their own use. Danie also did weekends where guests prepared their own goose and all the meals revolved around luscious, silken *foie gras*. She became even more successful, her *foie gras* renowned.

23

Danie's food was simply the food she learned to make growing up, but it was the most intensely, purely flavorful food I'd ever tasted. Her potato *galettes* were crisp and perfectly seasoned with garlic, her meaty *magret de canard* so tender you could cut it with a fork, her baked stuffed tomatoes the essence of tomato. She made her own cheese, which was creamy and light; her *rillettes*—a staple on the table—were rich and succulent.

Every weekend was an intense culinary learning experience for me, redolent of garlic and goose fat, filled with freshly butchered rabbits, wild mushrooms, greens harvested in the fields for flavorful salads and vegetables fresh from the gardens. There was always a crowd for meals—whether paying guests or the postman, Hubert, who timed his daily visit at lunchtime—and we were always racing to get everything done in time. Danie took to showing me once how to do something—like slicing potatoes paper-thin with her incredibly blunt paring knife for *galette de pommes de terre*, or trimming a goose breast, or cutting butter into feathery thin slices (with the same dull paring knife) for her tender, crisp pastry. Then she would disappear, leaving me to prepare meals, showing up to do the finishing touches.

Danie and I became comrades. We worked around the clock either preparing meals, gathering ingredients (which meant going to the nearby village to pick up fresh milk from the dairy farmer, walnuts from the Dubois barn down the road, lettuces from the garden outside the house), or cleaning up.

I loved every minute of being at the Dubois farm, especially those consecrated to food (which were most of them). Each process on the farm had its own gastronomic ritual, so that goose-butchering time meant *foie gras* straight from the bird, served on bread grilled over the coals. It also meant *demoiselles*, the goose carcasses after the breast meat has been removed, which are highly seasoned with salt and pepper and grilled over the fire. There isn't a great deal to eat on a *demoiselle*, but it is considered a rare treat and so tasty that we would all dive in with our fingers. Butchering a pig meant fresh blood sausages and roast pork, and during bean season we had mounds of green beans tossed in garlic and Danie's own walnut oil. Spring meant fresh wild mushrooms and tiny dandelions tossed in a walnut oil vinaigrette and golden sweet walnut meats from the orchard across the street.

Michael stayed at the Dubois farm for six months. His relationship with the family was a love affair. He never really did become comfortable speaking French, but it didn't matter. He was raised on a farm so he knew what to do without asking, and during his six-month tenure he repaired farm buildings and fixed anything that was broken (and had been broken for years), helped Danie or Guy when he could, amused the children, ruffled the ears of the dog. Now and then he would strike out from the farm across the fields, up and over the rolling hills, which were covered in snow in winter and in wildflowers from the first sign of spring. Stone farmhouses and ancient fortified chateaux dot the region, and Michael spent a good deal of time investigating and studying the stonework used to build them, for he wanted to learn the techniques and apply them to his sculptures. The archways of golden stone were of particular interest, and on one of my visits he took me to a spot on the farm where he'd built one, from stone he'd gathered off the land. It looked as though it had always been there.

Michael's stay ended at the same time that Patricia and I finished the book. Michael and I took stock and decided that we would move back to the States. We thought we needed to get serious about our careers, and the United States was the best place to do that. We packed up, gave up our studio, and shipped our things home. I left with a very heavy heart.

I returned to France at least once a year after that and dreamed of moving back. Finally, ten years after we had left, with the signing of a contract for a book that would celebrate French farmhouse cooking, it could happen.

DANIE'S STUFFED TOMATOES
TOMATES FARCIES

When tomatoes are fat and juicy this is the perfect way to serve them, as I learned from Danie Dubois so many years ago. Our family loves them so I make at least two per person; with a green salad, bread, and a simple dessert they make a filling summer meal. Use tomatoes that are ripe and firm and not too soft, so they hold up in cooking.

2 slices fresh bread (about 2 ounces/60g each)
½ cup/125ml whole milk
4 pounds/2kg juicy tomatoes
Sea salt and freshly ground black pepper
2 tablespoons/30ml extra-virgin olive oil
1 medium onion, minced
2 garlic cloves, green germ removed, minced
8 ounces/250g button mushrooms, trimmed, wiped clean
    and diced
1¾ pounds/875g lean ground pork

¼ cup/10g fresh tarragon leaves
1 cup/10g loosely packed flat-leaf parsley
2 large eggs

1. Preheat the oven to 425° F/220° C/gas 8.

2. Tear the bread into bite-sized pieces and place it in a small bowl. Cover it with the milk, press the bread down so it is completely covered, and let it sit until it has absorbed all the milk, about 30 minutes.

3. Slice the top off of each tomato and reserve it. Remove the seeds and most of the inner pith of the tomatoes and discard. Lightly season each tomato inside with salt and pepper.

4. Heat the oil with the onions and garlic in a medium skillet over medium heat. Cook, stirring, until the onions are translucent, about 8 minutes. Season with salt and pepper and transfer the onions and the garlic to a medium-size bowl. Add the mushrooms to the pan and cook, stirring occasionally, until they have given up their juice and are tender, 5 to 6 minutes. Transfer the mushrooms to the bowl of onions and garlic.

5. Add the bread and milk to the ingredients in the bowl, along with the pork. Mince the tarragon and the parsley together and add it to the bowl along with the eggs. Blend the mixture thoroughly, using your hands. Season with salt and pepper and blend well. Cook a teaspoon of the mixture and taste it for seasoning—adjust if necessary.

THE BEGINNING

6. Evenly divide the stuffing among the tomatoes, pressing it firmly into them, and mounding it above the edges of the tomato if necessary. Place the tops of the tomatoes atop the stuffing and bake until they become a deep gold, the stuffing is completely cooked, and the tomatoes are tender, about 1 hour. Remove from the oven and serve, drizzling the tomatoes with the cooking juices in the pan.

6 TO 8 SERVINGS

THE DORDOGNE POTATO CAKE
LA GALETTE DE POMMES DE TERRE DORDOGNE

This is the potato galette *I learned to make from Danie Dubois, on her farm in the Dordogne where Michael spent six months. She serves it often and always with roasted goose or pork. It makes a fine first course or an accompaniment.*

6 garlic cloves, green germ removed
1 cup/10g loosely packed flat-leaf parsley, plus additional
    for garnish, optional
5 tablespoons/75g fat such as lard, goose, or duck fat
3½ pounds/1.75kg waxy potatoes, peeled
Sea salt and freshly ground black pepper

1. Mince the garlic with the parsley and transfer it to a small bowl. Add 3 tablespoons (45g) of the fat and mix thoroughly, to

make a sort of paste. You may make this ahead of time and re-frigerate it, covered.

2. Melt the remaining 2 tablespoons (30g) of fat in a large, non-stick skillet with sides that are about 3 inches (7½ cm) high. You will need to slice the potatoes paper-thin for this dish and the best way to do that is to use a European-style vegetable peeler. "Peel" (or slice) the potatoes right into the hot fat, stirring them occasion-ally so they don't stick and seasoning them regularly with salt and pepper as you add them to the pan. It will take about 20 minutes to slice all of the potatoes into the pan, and the potatoes will cook evenly as long as you remember to stir them from time to time. They will stick together somewhat, so gently break them apart as you stir.

3. When all of the potatoes are sliced into the pan, season them one more time with salt and pepper and stir so they are all coated with fat. Add the garlic and parsley mixture and stir so that it melts evenly throughout the potatoes, then cook until the pota-toes are deep golden on the underside, a generous 10 minutes.

4. Carefully invert the potato *galette* onto a large plate, then slide it back into the pan, golden-side up, and cook until the under-side is deep golden, about 15 minutes. To serve, place a serving plate on top of the pan and invert so the *galette* falls onto the serv-ing plate. Garnish with flat-leaf parsley leaves if desired, and serve.

6 TO 8 SERVINGS

THE BEGINNING

TWO

House Hunting

I FLEW TO FRANCE on my own for two weeks to find a house for us to live in. I had dreamed of returning, hankered after the life I had known, my friends, the fragrance of golden butter, fresh bread, and coffee that is so much a part of the French way of living.

By now Michael and I had our two-year-old son, Joseph, a chubby, curly-red-haired bundle of sweet energy and constant motion, and we thought it would be wonderful for him to grow up bilingual. Moving to France to live while I researched a cookbook would give him that chance. Michael was personally less enthusiastic about the idea of going to France, because he had no inherent passion for the country. But doing creative work and being with his family is what's important to him, and France, he decided, would offer him that.

After poring over the map of France and considering every region we knew and some we didn't, Michael and I had decided we would live in Normandy. We wanted to be near Paris and near friends, and we'd grown to love the Normandy coast on earlier trips. So on arriving I took the train to Le Vaudreuil, where my by now dearest friend Edith Leroy met me at the station. She was delighted at the idea that we were moving back, and had not only asked if I would stay with them while I looked for a place to live but offered her help.

After making coffee and toast, which we enjoyed with her homemade blackberry and red currant jelly, we began plotting how I should go about looking for a house. I decided to consider anything within a thirty-minute drive of Edith and Bernard's village. We didn't care if we lived in the village, but we wanted to be close to it, since we knew almost everyone who lived there and were comfortable with its rhythm. After our breakfast I went out to the village café and bought newspapers, brought them back to the house, and checked the ads. I made several appointments to see houses, and the following day set out early to look.

Mostly what I looked at were contemporary bungalows, which didn't fit my romantic notion of a house in the French countryside. I spent another day looking, going all the way to Vernon in the east, to Houdan in the southeast, and Honfleur in the northwest, though that was getting pretty far afield. I didn't find a thing.

After two days, I regrouped. A friend of Edith's, Christine, said I was going about it all wrong and offered to accompany me the next day. "I'll show you how we rent houses here," she said. The next morning we headed off into the countryside, stopping to ask everyone we saw if they knew of anything to rent, including hailing a tractor and asking the farmer. We discovered a few places but nothing fit my criteria. I was looking for space—both Michael and I worked at home—proximity to a choice of schools for Joe and shopping (so I didn't have to live in the car), charm, and a low price.

I decided to try the realtor in Le Vaudreuil. Edith, out of curiosity, came with me. The man had nothing to rent but as we flipped through his book of available properties he pointed out two houses for sale, both in nearby Louviers. Michael and I had no money to buy, so I discounted them. Not Edith. "*Allez*, Suzanne, let's go look, it'll be fun. I've always wanted to see what these places looked like inside." I decided I could take a break from my house search, and away we went in the realtor's car.

We arrived in Louviers, a mid-size town whose center is a tasteful blend of ancient and postwar architecture. It was badly damaged during World War II—burned by the Germans on their way through—and, like so many towns throughout France, it had to rebuild itself quickly afterward. The rebuilding was done with style—capacious shops and lodgings, cream-colored stuccoed buildings with sharply sloping slate roofs. A boulevard surrounds the center of town, with small streets leading off of it into the heart of the town where a central cherry-tree-lined square serves a multitude of purposes. Mostly it is a parking lot, except on Saturdays when it hosts the farmer's market that transforms Louviers into a vibrant, colorful fête. The square is also used for special presentations: go-kart races; a twice-yearly, town-wide garage sale where individuals set up stands and sell everything from antiques to children's trading cards; a spring plant and flower sale.

Another large, grassy square, which is about a five-minute

walk from the main square, is bordered by homes and the police and fire stations. It is here where, regularly, huge stages are built and theater performances and concerts are held, and big tents are erected for traveling circuses.

The River Eure runs through Louviers, and it is in the midst of being rediscovered. The current mayor and his administration want to resurrect its banks, which are mostly wild and overgrown, making it a focal point of the town. A kayak club is already based on it at one end of town, and there are a few paths alongside it that are pleasant to walk along, though they eventually peter out into wild growth. The river was long ago diverted into several canals that once powered the textile mills. Houses built along these canals are generally large and prosperous, and they have private, often fanciful wooden bridges across the water.

The streets of Louviers, which are generally very busy during the day and empty quickly after 8 P.M. when shops close, vary from wide—the main boulevards—to extremely narrow, winding, and cobbled. There are many ancient buildings in Louviers, mostly on narrow, cobbled streets, and many are three stories high and just the width of a single room.

Louviers also boasts the remains of cloisters from a Franciscan convent, which was built in 1646, supposedly the only cloisters built over a canal.

Unlike in many old French towns there are decently wide sidewalks throughout most of Louviers, though occasionally one is obliged to walk single file and on tiptoe to avoid being squashed by a speeding car—speed limit signs are merely for decoration rather than serving any practical purpose, it seems. Parking places have been inserted wherever there is room for a car, and still many people park on the sidewalk, or angle themselves into impossibly tight spots.

We wound our way through a maze of streets and stopped in front of one of the tiny, room-wide houses. Outside it was charmingly derelict. Inside it was a complete wreck and smelled like the bowery. Piles of clothing and rags in a corner showed that it was a way station for homeless travelers. We sped out of there.

The second house was another story. It was across from the lavish Romanesque/Gothic church right in the town center, which is so large and imposing that everyone refers to it as a cathedral, though it isn't, since it is not the principal church of the diocese. The house had been a convent for three hundred years, and before that it was purportedly owned by an artist. For the past twenty-five years it had been the property of a Parisienne who had purchased it to live in, and to transform the ground floor into an antiques shop. It was dry and didn't smell at all. The old walls were timbered, the clay tile roof sported a tiny bell tower, the windows were paned with old, wavy glass. Inside, it was all blue and gray. And a wreck. The downstairs looked like an archeological dig—big holes, mounds of rubble, a total mess. The walls were in terrible shape, their pale blue paint streaked with grime. Dust covered everything. But the house was filled with a palpable, warm presence.

We followed the realtor and his stiff gray pompadour up the beautiful staircase, which curved gently around a corner, and emerged onto a landing awash in clear, soft light. As he babbled about the attributes of the house I looked out the window and caught my breath—the church was near enough to touch. I was transfixed. We proceeded through the house and Edith kept whispering to me, *"C'est fabuleux, cette maison. Elle a besoin de la pein-*

ture et un peu d'électricité, c'est tout." "It's fabulous—all it needs is a few coats of paint and some electricity."

The house must have been a perfect convent for it rambled on and on, up and around short stairways, in and out of rooms, yet it wasn't vast. It was very human—the rooms were quite small, the staircases short, the floors old wood, worn in many places.

The rooms were in varying states of decay. Some had graffiti scrawled on the walls and ceilings. "The owner allowed squatters to come, she is very open," said the realtor. "She is very *spéciale*." *Spéciale* is a word that means many things, from strange to difficult. I was beginning to get a notion about the owner.

On the third floor was a long, furnished room. A coal stove sat at one end, its pipe jury-rigged out a window. A single bed sat against a wall, with a large chunk of plaster in the middle of the bedspread. At the opposite end was a small kitchenette with garish orange and yellow flowers painted on the wall. A lovely old buffet filled with dishes sat along another wall.

The realtor explained that this is where the owner, a single mother of grown children, lived when she came to stay. As I looked at the room, which had lovely proportions, I was amazed she hadn't asphyxiated herself with the rigged-up stove pipe. Apparently the woman was an antiques dealer who, for whatever reason (the realtor hinted at a family tragedy), hadn't been able to fix up the house and install her antiques shop downstairs. She instead stripped it of everything valuable, from fireplace mantels to the crystal ball that had once graced the stairway. She seemed to have become somewhat *folle*, crazy, according to the realtor, leaving the doors unlocked, living in these makeshift conditions, letting the house tumble down around her.

Our final stop was the cave underneath the house, a fascinating vaulted dungeon filled with bottles, cobwebs, and mystery. I wanted to inspect it further, but the realtor shooed us out with his wavery flashlight.

I was captivated. I didn't say much on the way back to Le Vaudreuil. When we said good-bye to the realtor Edith was vibrating. "What a house," she said. "You have to buy it. Michael could fix it up in no time. All it needs is paint, some work here and there, a little rearranging." I listened with half an ear, discouraged beyond measure, seeing our romantic sojourn in France spent in one of the new bungalows I now knew were the preferred rentals in the area. I had loved roaming through the old house, but it just wasn't possible.

Edith, who is passionate and high-strung by nature, wouldn't stop talking about the house. She remembered as a child growing up in Louviers passing the house and seeing, inside a window right on the street, an elderly nun in her bed. "We always looked in on her. It is a sweet memory," she said. Her chatter about the house went on all day. When Bernard came home she told him about it. I'd been thinking about it too—the quality of light inside it was unforgettable, as was that warm feeling within its walls.

Bernard fixed me with his gaze. "What do you think of the house, Suzanne?" he asked, seriously. I faltered. I thought it was beautiful, but it was a mess. And we didn't have any money to buy it anyway. I told him so. He wanted to go look at it, so I made an appointment for the next day.

I allowed myself to dream, just a little. Imagine not just renting but owning in France. Imagine such a beautiful house. The location was perfect—right in the center of town, in proximity to shops and schools and everything. I didn't know Louviers at all, but it was a big enough town that nearly everything was available.

As I thought about the house and the town I remembered spending an afternoon there on my own many years ago when I'd been visiting Edith and Bernard. I remembered walking around the ancient cloisters. I remembered the finely manicured public garden, which looked like a tiny version of the Jardin du Luxembourg in Paris. The more I thought about it, the more memories surfaced. There was a wonderful store there filled with herbs and potions and organic foods of all sorts. The city hall and the museum were in a lovely old brick building surrounding a garden with a fanciful concrete-made-to-look-like-wood pergola in the center. From what I'd seen today, Louviers bustled, traffic sped through it, the sidewalks were crowded with people.

Louviers comprises twenty thousand inhabitants, making it the largest town within about thirty miles. It is the commercial center for farmers in the immediate area, who go there for banking and business. It has the rollicking Saturday farmer's market, another smaller farmer's market on Wednesday, and its own collection of boutiques and food shops.

I called Michael that night to give him a report. I told him about the house, downplaying Bernard and Edith's interest in it, simply describing it to him. He said nothing. Then he said, "Go look at it again, get more information." I couldn't believe my ears. "But we don't have any money," I countered. "We can't buy a house."

"Go get more information" was all he would say. I am hopeless when it comes to money. My department is dreams. I rely on Michael to see the truth, so when he said get more information I figured that buying the house was somehow possible.

HOUSE HUNTING

The next day Bernard saw the house and loved it. He thought it was an *affaire*, a deal. He said that if we decided to buy it he'd loan us the down payment if we needed it and cosign the loan. Bernard is a very successful entrepreneur who started a quality control company almost two decades ago, well before anyone else in France had the idea. The company has done nothing but grow, so that now it does business in most countries of the world. Bernard sold it not long ago, making him a very wealthy man. He is still the director, however, and spends most of his time traveling to distant points on the globe. When Bernard says something is "interesting" it pays to listen. I suddenly started to get very excited.

I called Christian Devisme, a friend, talented architect, and Edith's brother, and asked him to come inspect the house and give me his professional opinion. He and his partner arrived and spent at least an hour poking, prodding, and snooping around like detectives. They finished in the back garden, where I joined them, and we all gazed at the exterior wall, which was so full of holes it looked like lace. I asked Christian what he thought. He slowly cleared his throat, shook his head, then looked at me sideways. *"Il ne faut pas sousestimer le travail,"* he said, gravely. "You must not underestimate the work." That sent a chill through me.

Then he swiveled to look at the little brick building behind the house, which belonged to the church. "You should try to buy that, too," he said. "It would add a lot of value to the property."

"So you think we should buy the house?" I asked.

"If I were younger I might think about buying it," Christian, who was then forty-five, said. "At this point in my life it's too much work, but it's a beautiful house."

I understood Christian's point. He and his wife, Nadine, had bought an old farmhouse nearly twenty years before when they had three tots, and had lived in a tent in front of it for a year while they made it livable. It is not an experience he would want to repeat and he is convinced he accomplished it only because he was young. Yet he obviously thought this house in Louviers was full of potential.

"Its walls and roof are solid," he said. "If you have to pay someone to fix it up you can't afford it. If Michael can do it himself, you should seriously think about it."

I took that for encouragement.

Edith came to pick me up and before we left we went through the house again, deciding what should be where when it came time to decorate the rooms. I could just imagine all the *soirées* we would have there, in the shadow of the church, L'Église de Notre Dame. That night I reported everything to Michael, who knew all the protagonists and could judge their responses. He seemed excited, too. I thought the world was turned upside down.

I called an engineer, a plumber, a roofing specialist to come see the house. I got estimates for installing electricity. I took photographs, pasted them together, and FedExed them to Michael, along with the estimates and every shred of information I could find about Louviers. I talked at length with Bernard, who assured me that there were no complications for a foreigner buying property in France. He said he would introduce us to his banker, and that would help expedite matters should we decide to buy it.

Michael and I talked, we debated, we each agreed we didn't have the money to undertake the project. And then, with Bernard's help, we decided to buy it.

HOUSE HUNTING

I was beside myself. With excitement. With dread. With panic. With desire. My dream to own property in France—a dream I had never actually articulated, even to myself—had come true. It didn't matter that we were moving to France on a wing and a prayer. It didn't matter that we were always seeming to scrape by. It didn't matter that life in France was bound to be more expensive than life in the United States with sky-high prices for everything from gasoline to farm-raised chickens. And it didn't matter that we would be so far from our families and American friends. Never big on paying attention to reality, I definitely put on my soft-focus lenses this time. If Michael thought we could do it, then we could.

We made an offer on the house, which was immediately accepted. I met the owner, who was a small nervously sad woman, and signed the *compromis de vente*, or the contract to buy the house. Bernard was true to his word, taking time to help with all the paperwork and signing where necessary. On my last night before going back to the United States we celebrated. Christian and Nadine came for dinner bringing a dish of richly flavored braised pigeons from their farm, where they raised eight hundred of the squeaky birds for local restaurants.

Edith and Bernard opened champagne. Christian made a toast. "To Suzanne and to Michael, who have just bought a house in the Marseille of the north," he said with an evil smile. "That your car doesn't get stolen nor your windows broken." My heart stopped. Marseille, a lovely city, nonetheless has a reputation of being full of *voyoux*, hoodlums. Was there something I should know? They all burst out laughing. "He's just trying to scare you," Nadine said.

I left the following morning for Paris, where I was to spend a few days before returning home. I met an American friend for coffee and showed her the picture of the house. "It's gorgeous. I've lived here fifteen years and always wanted to buy a house," she exclaimed. "How did you find the perfect house in one week?" I told her I didn't know. I was in a dream, pinching myself. We were really going to do it, I thought.

I returned home and Michael and I prepared for our move. We loved our house in Maine and decided not to sell but to rent it. After all, we imagined, after two to three years in France we might return and, meanwhile, it was a good investment.

We were busy packing and organizing, trying to decide what to take and what to leave. After doing comparative studies of moving costs, we decided we would bring the bare minimum— my kitchen equipment, which included a collection of heavy copper pots I'd amassed over the years, knives, baking dishes, scales, and dozens of other small necessities in the life of a cook and food writer. We would also bring my office chair (a luxuriously comfortable one), file cabinets, and computers. We would bring Michael's most essential tools, a futon couch, Joe's stuffed animals, and as many of his toys and treasures as we could fit. We decided to send our Subaru station wagon over and gave it a complete overhaul.

An American friend of mine (also a food writer) was moving back to the States from Paris and she made a list of things she wanted to sell, which included lamps and bookcases, chairs and a table, and an impressive array of coffee grinders that she used to grind spices. We bought what we thought we would need and she threw in many things she didn't want to sell but didn't want to ship back either, and arranged to have it all moved out to Edith's. Yet

HOUSE HUNTING

another friend, warning me of how expensive everything was in France, listed all of the things in her attic that she was planning to give away but that she would save for us if we needed them. With all of that we figured we could get to work immediately. What we didn't have we would gradually acquire.

We sold or gave away just about everything we weren't going to take with us, which accentuated the feeling that we were embarking on a huge adventure, a new life. Joe observed all the activity and it made him nervous. Children don't generally like change and he likes it less than most—I had to scheme to get rid of anything belonging to him, for the minute he would see something leaving he'd say, in his two-year-old English, "I love that, I just love it!" and try to grab it.

Meantime, Edith and I talked regularly. She described the garden, the size of the apples on the gnarled old tree in the yard. The hydrangeas turned out to be purple, one of my favorite colors, the roses were pink, red, and white. She and I planned the garden and talked endlessly about the house. I would report what she'd said to Michael, and then he and I would plan and scheme some more. He spent a lot of time with paper and pencil sketching out ideas for the house, all based on the photographs I'd taken. We never talked about the financial aspect of it, which seemed daunting. Our attitude was "It will all work out."

We spent the month of September 1993 visiting our families and our friends on the West Coast as a sort of farewell, then we embarked for France, landing at Charles de Gaulle/Roissy Airport where Edith met us. We piled into her VW van and she flew down the *autoroute* toward Louviers at 150 kilometers an hour, the equivalent of about 100 mph. I looked at Michael who raised his eyebrows. It was great to be back in France!

Both Michael and I were so excited we could hardly sit still. Joe, a boy who doesn't like to miss anything, had been awake for days, it seemed, as we took him to and fro to see family and friends. He hadn't slept much during the twelve-hour plane trip either, but once the van started moving he conked out, draped over his father's knees. I looked at his pale, chubby, toddler's face. We knew he was upset at the move because he didn't quite understand what was happening. We hoped it wouldn't take him long to adjust.

Our first stop was Louviers and the house, for Michael's first look. He extracted the still-sleeping Joe from his knees and laid him tenderly on the backseat. Edith passed the house keys over to him and waited in the car with Joe while Michael and I went to look. The house was as beautiful as I'd remembered. A large red and white *vendu*, sold, sign hung over the door, physical proof that the *compromis de vente* still held good. It gave me a sense of ownership, which helped override the sense of panic I felt as I approached the front door.

Michael opened it. I held my breath as I walked with him through the rooms. We didn't talk. We were both too busy looking. I breathed a little easier as I looked at the curved staircase in the foyer—it was still as graceful as I recalled. Michael walked through the door into what I supposed had been the kitchen, a high-ceilinged room with a big window overlooking the back garden, an angled back wall, and a graceful fireplace—it was so filled with dusty antique furniture and piles of newspapers, buckets of stones and wood and other rubbish that it was hard to get a real sense of it. We poked our heads in the other rooms on the ground floor, all of which looked as if small bombs had exploded in them.

Michael banged on walls, scraped surfaces, looked in nooks and crannies, wiggled doors, opened and closed windows, all things that wouldn't have occurred to me to do. At the best of times Michael is a man of few words. He was absolutely silent, intent on his inspection.

I'd truly forgotten what a mess the house was in. I'm not sure I ever really noticed. Even now, as I stumbled over chunks of stone, tiptoed around holes in the floor, and realized that there wasn't one single room out of the fifteen in the house that could really pass for livable, I felt an excitement bubbling inside. It was a blank slate, ours to re-create.

The crisp fall weather outside meant the house was cold inside, and as I focused on the holes, the grit, the lath showing through the walls, it seemed worse than I'd remembered. What had I been thinking? What if Michael hated it? What if I'd made a huge mistake? These were questions I was to become extremely familiar with over the next years, as I watched Michael struggle not only with learning the French vocabulary involved in building, but with unfamiliar materials, dimensions, customs, and traditions.

As we emerged from the last room, the one above the curious little "apartment" that the owner kept, which was even shabbier than it had been the first time I'd seen it, and made our way down the many sets of stairs, Michael's blue eyes absolutely blazed with excitement.

"I love it," he said. I let out my breath. We walked hand in hand into the garden—it was overgrown and messy, but the old

ON RUE TATIN

apple and pear trees that graced it were unmistakably charming, and the church loomed over all.

While we stood there looking at the house with its boarded-up window on the ground floor, its lovely timbering, and the bell tower, an elderly lady parked her bicycle by the front door and went off to do her shopping. Pigeons cooed from under the eaves. We were caught up in the magic of owning such glorious real estate, of having a concrete project to work on. I was in a state of bliss to think that for the foreseeable future we would be in France, would come to understand its rituals and traditions, would no doubt make new friends and deepen the wonderful friendships we already had. And the thought of the food and the flavors that would be ours! I couldn't wait for the adventure to begin.

We drove on to Le Vaudreuil, for we were staying with the Leroys for our first few days. As I walked inside I was enveloped with the familiar aroma of lavender and fresh thyme that has always pervaded her house, and I felt I was home.

We hauled in our baggage and settled Joe to sleep on a couch in the living room, which doubles as Edith's painting studio. Finished and half-finished portraits and still-lifes in Edith's characteristic vibrant colors, as well as a collection of paintings by other artists, provide the decor; the pleasant scent of oil paints the ambience.

While Edith built a fire in the kitchen fireplace I made coffee, got out butter and honey, and cut the *baguettes* we had stopped to buy in the village into lengths for *tartines*. Edith's children were in school, Bernard was at work in his office across the street, the house was quiet. All was right with the world, I thought, as I dipped my butter-and-honey-slathered *tartine* into my bowl of stiff black coffee before

45

HOUSE HUNTING

biting into it. We talked over our strategy for the next few days, then simply enjoyed this taste of France. Michael relaxed in an easy chair and fell asleep, while Edith filled me in on the local gossip.

That evening we had a celebratory dinner with Edith, Bernard, and their now four children, and the following day Michael went to the house to poke around and I took Joe to look at the little house in Le Vaudreuil that I'd rented over the phone from the town mayor. We figured we'd need it for two to three months, the time it would take Michael to install enough electricity and plumbing to make the house in Louviers livable.

Set on the back boundary of the mayor's garden, it looked like a little timbered doll's house. Its main room downstairs had a picture window looking out at the languidly flowing river Eure. The corner kitchen was adequate, the small bathroom functional, the two bedrooms upstairs charming. The only thing it needed was a telephone.

I spoke with Florence Labelle, the mayor's wife and our landlady, about the phone. I had asked her if we could install it before we arrived, but she couldn't see the necessity for that. "We'll do all that when you get here." True to her word, she called the phone company directly. No doubt because she was the mayor's wife they arrived later that day, but the news wasn't good. They couldn't install a phone in the back building because it wasn't a legal residence. To Florence, this didn't seem a problem. "You can use my phone when you need to," she said kindly, not realizing how vital a phone is to my work.

I panicked, just a little, explaining to Florence why I had to have a phone, how I had a great deal of research to do not just for the cookbook I was about to write, but for all the articles I had contracted to do. She had a private conference with the France Telecom representative, and the next thing I knew a date was set to install the wiring and hook up the phone. "So it will be all right?" I asked. "It's not illegal?" She looked at me. *"Bof!"* she said, pushing back her hair. "All we have to do is trim a few tree limbs and not mention anything."

Michael returned from the house in Louviers with stars in his eyes. He'd spent the morning giving it a closer look. "It's so beautiful," he said. "It's incredible." For the rest of the afternoon he sat at a table in Edith's house making drawings, chewing on his pencil, calculating.

Our third day in France we signed the papers which made us the legal owners of 1, rue Tatin, in Louviers. We did this in front of the *notaire*, a sort of lawyer who handles real estate deals. A portly, officious young man, he greeted us in the waiting room and showed us down a long, wood-paneled hallway to his large, stuffy office. He abstractly shuffled papers on his desk while we awaited the owner. Michael and I gazed around at the stuffed game birds high atop his bookcases that looked as if they'd been there a hundred years. So did the stacked books, for they were covered with a thin veneer of dust. I knew a lot about him for he was Edith and Bernard's *notaire*, and his father had been Edith's parents' *notaire*.

The owner and her daughter finally arrived, breaking the silence. We shook hands all around then sat formally while the *notaire* handed us each a copy of the mortgage contract. He called us to attention and proceeded to read it aloud in a slow, excruciatingly formal manner. My thoughts wandered to all I had ever heard about *notaires*, who are incredibly powerful figures in France. No one could ever tell me what they actually do, but I did know they spent a lot of time and made a lot of money doing just this sort of thing, drawing up lengthy contracts then reading them aloud.

His drone became mere background noise. My eyes were crossing. I looked at Michael and his were almost shut. Suddenly, the *notaire*'s voice came alive.

"You must pay special attention to this part," he said. We sat up. He began reading a passage about the church's easement of our property. "You are sure you understand this part?" he asked. I hadn't really been listening, so I asked him to repeat it. It had to do with the right of the priest and his domestics to walk through our property to get to his house, which was behind ours. The *notaire* stared at us. "I just want you to understand that this is a condition of buying this house," he said. "You cannot change this. It is immutable." He said it gravely, pushing us to understand the implications of it. I looked at the owner. "Oh," she said quickly. "It's not a problem, no one ever walks through." Reassured, Michael and I told the *notaire* we understood and wanted to go through with the purchase. We would have many occasions in the future to think back to that moment and wonder if the *notaire* was trying to protect or warn us.

Finally he finished reading the contract. We all initialed each page of each copy, then signed it in several different places. Above each signature we had to write *lu et approuvé*, read and approved, and a whole paragraph of other words all of which were intended to slow us down, I assumed, in case we suddenly got cold feet and didn't want to buy the house, since it took forever. It seemed so old-fashioned and gracious to be writing things by hand on a cold, formal mortgage.

We finally finished and the house was ours. We shook hands all around again, agreed to let the owner store her furniture in the house until she could have it removed, took our keys. The *notaire* said he was at our disposal if we needed him, then we shook hands again and walked out into the chilly sunlight. We stopped at a café for a celebratory *café exprès*, then hurried to the house.

We stood for awhile in the garden, just looking. The sun shed a lovely, golden glow on the house. I breathed deeply for the first time since we had agreed to buy it.

A young man who worked at the *aumônerie*, or parish hall whose property abuts ours, emerged from the building and came up to us. "Are you the new owners?" he asked. "Yes," I said, expecting a welcome. "Well," he said dourly, "if you decide to sell the house the church wants to buy it. They had hoped to buy it. They didn't realize it was sold." Then he walked away. Nice greeting. Michael and I looked at each other and promptly forgot him as we went inside the house to explore some more.

We walked through every inch of it, stepping over the rubble and around the holes, talking about which room would be ours, which would be Joe's. We stopped in one room to admire the eight-sided terra-cotta tiles, or *tommettes*, on the floor, and we stroked the wood beams in the walls. We opened a skinny hallway cupboard and found old books and jars. My heart started beating. Maybe we would find treasures in this house.

After we reached the first floor we walked up another short staircase to a landing from which two other staircases departed, one around the corner to the left, and one immediately to the right. After exploring the two rooms on the landing, which were in truly lamentable shape—the walls and ceilings were covered with graffiti, rubble was strewn on the floor from a fireplace that had been ripped out, everything was filthy—we went up the narrow stairway to the right.

What greeted us was even worse. We had seen it all of course, but now that it was ours we really took it in. There were two rooms that were complete shells, the ceilings rotted out so we could see the roof. The windows were either broken or hanging ajar, lath showed through the walls, and a fine black soot covered everything. Amidst all of this what struck me was an odd little window in the wall between the rooms. We tried to figure out what it was for. I guessed one room was a kitchen, the other a dining room, but it wasn't large enough to pass a plate through. Then I thought maybe it was for confessions, but that didn't really make sense—there was no screen in the window to hide the priest from the parishioner. To this day we haven't figured it out, and as yet no one has been able to tell us what it was.

What Michael first noticed was the brand-new waste pipe that had been installed in the landing. "That will make putting in a bathroom easy," he said with a laugh.

In all there were fifteen rooms in the house, though the two dilapidated ones were not in the architect's drawing that the owner had given us. Evidently if the rooms didn't appear on the architect's drawings then they wouldn't be included in the tax assessment.

With all the rooms, closets, and landings there were, it seemed, hundreds of doors in the house. They were gorgeous and some of them, as the owner had explained to us, were very old and valuable. I remember her pointing to one and saying it dated to 1750. Many had tiny metal plaques with the letters N.D. on them, which I was sure stood for Notre Dame, our lady. All had large, old-fashioned keys in the locks, and I knew that one of my first jobs would be to label them. I could just see Joe, who was almost three, having a field day taking out the keys and mixing them up.

Michael was eager to get to work. Before he could, however, the place needed to be cleaned out, for there was a great deal of junk and rubble in it. "The realtor offered to bring a dump truck over and clean out the house," I said. "I think we should have him do it."

Michael looked at me as if I were crazy. "There's got to be something of value here or he would never have offered," he said. "That statue, for instance." We rushed around to the back of the house where we'd seen a plaster statue of an angel holding a child by the hand. She was still there. We hastily moved her inside. Then we walked down the stone steps into the *cave*, and turned on a powerful flashlight. The dusty bottles we'd noticed were all there. We brought several upstairs into the light. Each was a different hue, from celadon green to a wispy blue, and all were hand-blown. "These are what he wanted," Michael said. "These bottles will put Joe through college."

The following day we moved ourselves into the tiny house in Le Vaudreuil. It was ideal. Florence and her husband, Edouard, with their two children, Marine, a girl of about eight, and Quentin, a boy of about twelve, were the perfect landlords. Florence insisted that Joe use the swing set and sandbox in her garden, as well as the toy room that took up an entire floor in her house and which Marine used only very occasionally. She seemed delighted to have us living in her back garden. The only cloud was her dog, Diva, a golden Labrador with a vicious temperament. Florence kept her in the house, but if she ever forgot and left her outside, the minute we showed ourselves in the garden she hurled herself in our direction, hackles up, teeth bared.

The dog aside, those first months were idyllic. Michael went to Louviers each day to work on the house. I stayed in Le Vaudreuil and worked on my book. We had arranged for our favorite baby-sitter from Maine to join us for several months and she amused Joe, taking him on walks and bicycle rides. Michael was excited and full of plans for the house. I reveled in the beginning stages of my book, and I loved living in Le Vaudreuil, seeing Edith all the time, being part of village life on a daily basis.

Le Vaudreuil is a charming, well-to-do village of 5,000 people. The River Eure runs through it, and its main street ends in a small square with a café on each side, a pharmacy and a *boulangerie*, a tiny *épicerie* with basic supplies and fresh vegetables, and two small restaurants offering simple country fare, from *steack frites* to various preparations *"à la crème,"* in true Norman fashion. Tiny streets lined with quaint stone houses wind away from the square, and there is a church on either end of town, with parishioners staunchly devoted to one or the other.

Louviers, which is about five kilometers and a ten-minute drive from Le Vaudreuil by a small country road, was once an important textile town and still has one textile factory to show for it, as well as a series of canals diverted from the River Eure, which were used in the textile industry. It is known for its extremes of government. When we first arrived, the mayor was a woman known for her conservative and rather bungling ways. Shortly after we arrived elections resulted in an administration that leans increasingly far left and has a permanent overdraft in its bank accounts, primarily because it has as one of its mandates to provide the citizenry with regular music and theater performances, which it offers free of charge.

Louviers also offers many services. There are dozens of banks, real-estate offices, insurance companies, travel agencies, and a small, gracious hospital. The main church—our "cathedral"—is in the center of town, with another Catholic church tucked into a neighborhood less than a half mile away. Cafés line its streets, and restaurants and pizzerias are dotted throughout the main part of town. There is a small, country supermarket in the center of town, and two huge modern supermarkets on its periphery. One can live very easily in Louviers without needing to go anywhere else.

Before Joseph was born, when I visited Edith and Bernard in Le Vaudreuil, friends and villagers who greeted me looked at my stomach before looking in my eyes. "Not pregnant yet?" they would ask. To them it was unthinkable that a married woman would wait so long to have a child.

Like most Americans, Michael and I worked around the clock. We wanted children, but felt we had time, though I did occasionally fear I would be like the woman in the cartoon who, at about age forty, exclaims, "Oh no! I forgot to have children." I used to look at my French friends, most of whom had at least three children and were my age or a few years older, and marvel at them. Through them I realized what a different culture we lived in. To them, having children was what one did—there was no weighing of advantages or disadvantages, no sense as in America that they needed to develop a career first, no hesitation about how a child would fit into their life. Instead they simply had them, one after the other, and managed their personal and professional lives around them.

Admittedly, France is set up for small children. Working mothers are given a lot of time off to have children, and a good deal of financial support from the state as well. There are many options for their babies when they do go back to work—either a state-run *crèche*, which is like a day care center but more personal and set up for tiny babies and very young children, or a *nounou*, a baby-sitter, who generally works at her home and takes in no more than three children at a time.

At age three, children start school, and they can stay there from 8:30 A.M. to 4:30 P.M. each day if parents desire, as lunch, snacks, and nap time are provided.

When I finally, at age 35, had Joe the news was greeted with great joy by our friends in France. When I first brought him to visit, at eight months, Edith's brother Christian, the architect, who has four children, said, "Now that you've started you have to continue."

When we moved to France in 1993 Joe immediately became the *chouchou*, or pet, of every gathering we attended, since our friends all had much older children. With his headful of curly red hair and his round apple cheeks, he was a novelty.

As we settled into living in Le Vaudreuil I realized how different our child-rearing was from that of our French friends. No one could understand why we didn't immediately put Joe in day care, a thought that never crossed our minds. How could we? He didn't understand a word of French, for one thing. For another, we'd just moved and he was unsure of everything.

Edith couldn't believe how much time we spent with him. "Why do you do that?" she would ask. "It's not good for him. He's going to get too used to having you around. Put him in day care. Of course he'll cry, but crying is necessary. It will make him stronger." I looked at her. I looked at Joe. We did spend a lot of time with him, and he was upset right now, which meant we spent even more time with him. He occasionally woke at night crying inconsolably, and during the day his face would suddenly fall as he asked, bewildered, "Where is my house with all my coats?" He didn't like being the center of attention wherever we went. He didn't like the French custom of kissing. He was happy at home with us or with the baby-sitter, and he liked going to Edith's, but he became shy and worried whenever we went to a new place. All those friends back home who had said that as long as we were happy he'd be happy were, I realized, talking through their hats.

I walked into his room one day and he was babbling to himself.

"What are you saying?" I asked him. He looked at me, startled. "I'm speakin' French," he responded. That was when I understood. Much of what he heard was senseless babble, so of course he felt confused. We realized he needed to learn the language, then he could relax. Maybe Edith had a point.

I went to the local public nursery school in Le Vaudreuil, which had a very good reputation, to see about getting him in. I met with the principal, Annie Grodent, a lively young woman who listened to my story then agreed to take Joe, even though he wasn't *propre*, or potty trained. He had been, but moving to France had made him revert to his baby ways. It was highly irregular to take a child who wasn't potty trained, but she didn't care as long as we understood that no one would change his diaper. They weren't set up for that.

We agreed to bring Joe for an hour a day. Michael and I walked him to school the first day and handed him over. He burst into tears. Annie, who as well as being the principal was also the teacher in his class, waved us away. I sat on the edge of a chair at home for an hour, then went to retrieve him. He was still crying—he hadn't stopped. We repeated the exercise that week and the next, two of the worst weeks of Michael's and my life. By the end of the second week he wasn't crying, but he wasn't letting go of Annie, either. She was wonderfully patient. She was surprisingly

HOUSE HUNTING

loving (for a French teacher). She held him, sang to him, took care of him, all the while conducting her class.

By month's end, Joe was comfortable enough to play with the children, and we left him for two hours at a time, then three. By the end of three months he told us he had a friend, though he wasn't sure of her name. One Sunday we went to a children's program at the village *salle des fêtes*, or town hall, and his eyes lit up. "Mama, there she is, my friend," he said, pointing to a gorgeous little bright-eyed girl. I went to meet her and her parents, overcome with gratitude. They said they knew all about Joe. Annie had told me how their daughter, Lydia, though only three years old herself, had taken Joe under her wing and how they had become fast friends. Thanks to Lydia, Joe looked forward to going to school, and after another three months he was speaking French like a native.

Once Joe was comfortable about staying the whole morning at school, we could pay attention to what he was actually doing there. It was remarkable; Annie had the kids doing craft projects, music, theater, gymnastics. She welcomed songs in English, which she tried to teach to the other children. They went on field trips and had circus performers come to teach them juggling and balancing. It was wonderful, and Joe ended up loving it. We regretted that first month had been so hard on him, but it was such a relief to see him happy at last. His night awakenings stopped, and he visibly relaxed.

Héloïse Tuyéras, now in her early seventies, once had provided day care in her home and took care of Joe for us from time to time. She lives in Le Vaudreuil, and her house is the depot for the local

Catholic charity. This means that people with goods to give away simply drop them outside her front door, and she spends her time sorting, mending, cleaning, and ironing everything that comes her way, then makes sure these things go where they are most needed.

When I stopped in to see her during our first week, she pointed out a stack of things she'd been collecting for us. I was surprised. "Héloïse, we're not needy, we can get these things for ourselves," I said, imagining truly needy people going without.

"Don't be silly, Suzanne," she said. "I get so many things, and you need so many things." She convinced me not to rest on my pride and handed me a large bag of Legos for Joe and an ironing board. That began a stream of goods which came our way from Héloïse. One day while we were still in the little house by the river, which Joe referred to as France, she called to see if Michael could pick up a four-burner stove that was almost like new. "You can have it if you want it," she said. "It belongs to a woman who wants to get rid of it, doesn't want to sell it, doesn't need the money." This was a gift from heaven. I was cooking on the two burners that were in the house when we moved in, managing, but I couldn't do any serious cooking or recipe testing. We had been putting off buying a stove, however, for even the simplest are very expensive. Michael returned that afternoon with the stove, which was a modern, dark brown Rosières, a well-known brand. It had three gas burners and one electric burner, a curious but common quirk in French stoves. The electric burner was like an emergency burner should the gas be cut, a design apparently created after World War II when gas often was cut off. Michael made room for it in our little corner kitchen—with Florence's blessing—allowing me to cook real meals again.

We now refer to Héloïse as our guardian angel, for during that year she watched over us, continuing to supply us with things we needed, even before we realized we needed them. She lived just a few houses away and would stop by with toys, books, and clothes for Joe, and would call to tell us about furniture that was available. One day she brought over a laundry rack, the next day a small chair for Joe, or a beautiful cotton sheet . . . small things that made life easier for us. She also invited us over for memorable meals, which always included at least one dish guaranteed to please a child as well as adults, like her famed squash purée with apples.

As the months progressed toward winter, rain and bone-chilling days set in. Michael set off early every morning for the house in Louviers, while I got Joe off to school, then worked in my office. Michael would return at noon to pick up Joe, then he worked on plans for the house while Joe napped and played with him and I worked. We'd been in the little house by the river for two months by then, about the amount of time we thought we would have to stay there. But work on the house in Louviers was going slowly, and it was impossible for us to move in yet. Everything was taking much longer than we expected, since it was all so different from anything Michael had ever done, from the electrical system to the plumbing. I checked in with Florence, who reassured us that her little house was ours as long as we wanted it, so we settled in even more.

When the baby-sitter's tenure was over, we saw her off one gray day. Life began to take on a rhythm. I needed to travel for my research, so at least once a month I left on a Monday and would be gone most of the week, making sure to return in time for the weekend. Then, we went to the Messy House, as Joe called the house in Louviers, which was paradise for him. He could build sand castles in the dining room where Michael stored his pile of sand, or bang nails into boards while Michael built and I cleaned and tried to bring about order.

Our first weekend there was cold, so we were bundled up. We hauled and scrubbed as Joe ran around trying to help. Mid-morning Michael and I both had a longing for coffee, so we all went to the café across the street to take a break and warm up. The owner seemed to know who we were. "Next time if you'd like to take the coffee back to your house you may," she said in a friendly way. We accepted her offer. On days when we were all in the house, Joe and I would go to the café and I would order two *grand crèmes* and a *chocolat chaud*, which the owner would put on a tray. Holding Joe's hand and the tray, I would navigate my way across the busy street feeling like a native. We would all sit in whatever room in the house had a ray of sunshine coming into it or, if it was a particularly nice day, we would sit outside in the garden to sip our coffees and chocolate.

Once Michael got a good electrical line installed I was eager to make coffee in the house. I bought an electric coffee maker and some coffee, brought cups from home, and went to our favorite local bakery, J. Gosselin, to buy *sablés*, Normandy's traditional butter cookies. At morning break time I made coffee in the room upstairs where the owner had lived and where Michael had installed an outlet. This coffee would be the first thing I would prepare in the house, and its making was a momentous occasion. My hands trembled as I fit the paper filter into the machine and measured the coffee into it. I'll never forget the eerie feeling I had smelling that first tempting, warm, human aroma in the house. Michael and I looked at each other. I could tell he felt the same way. How many people throughout the ages had made coffee, or the equivalent hot, comforting drink, in this house?

59

That was the first of many pots of coffee brewed in the upstairs room, where we often lunched on one-portion quiches, or
small tomato pizzas, or *baguette* sandwiches stuffed with ham or
cheese or hard-cooked eggs and vegetables from the bakery.

Progress on the house was steady, but slow. Every time Michael
would start on a room, expecting to be able to proceed easily from
point A to point B, he'd find something that needed fixing first—a rot-
ten beam that needed replacing, for instance. Before he could replace
it, however, he'd have to move a wall, or shore up the floor, or go in
some other direction before he could actually get back to point A. He
desperately needed a helper, not just for the physical help but to assist
him in interpreting the language and the systems of buying materials,
but that was out of the question. With the price of Sheetrock alone
triple what it was in the United States we needed every centime we had
to pay for materials. So Michael worked on alone, slowly developing
systems. He would often come home after a materials-buying trip so
frustrated he could hardly speak. "People here just don't want to give
out information," he would fume. "In the States if you have a question you go in a store and ask the people working there and they fall
all over you trying to answer it because they want your business. Here,
there are a bunch of know-nothing Napoleons working in the stores
and they hear my accent and act like they can't understand a word I'm
saying even if they did know the answer."

Over time Michael learned to avoid the large stores and head
for the smaller ones where the prices were somewhat higher but
the chance of someone knowing something was far greater.

Within a few months of his starting work on the house the
plumbing was functioning, the electricity installed. After we decided
which room would be my office Michael cleaned it up and installed

enough electrical outlets for all my machines. Edith and I painted it white one afternoon and sanded and varnished the floor the next day, then the following day I moved in. What a relief it was to move my office out of our bedroom in that tiny little house on the river. Now, we wouldn't be awakened by those late-night faxes from the States.

I had two phone lines installed, arranged my file cabinets, and Michael painted a wood panel my favorite color, turquoise, and laid it atop them as a temporary desk. He built bookcases and put strips of wood on the wall next to the desk. I pounded tiny nails into the strips and hung a bulldog clip on each one, so that I could hang up current projects to keep track of them. Once all the machines, from fax to answering machine to computer and printer, were installed I settled in to work.

From then on, the minute I dropped Joe off at school I went to work in my office. There was no heat in the house but if I got really uncomfortable I simply plugged in a powerful little space heater and aimed it at my feet.

I loved working in that clean room amidst the mayhem, with its window overlooking the garden, the street, and the side of the church. I would shut the door and revel in the clean white walls and the desk and get to work, stopping occasionally to look out the window. The church bells, which ring on the hour, quickly became a beloved sound. I came to distinguish the funeral dirges from the regular bells and whenever one began I would look at the scene spreading out before me, as the hearse arrived along with the florists and their massive bouquets. The funerals became a familiar element in our lives, right along with the weddings, which are a nearly daily event in the month of June.

I am a lapsed Catholic, but I enjoy going to Mass from time to time. I expected to go once in a while, since it occurred within fifty yards of our front door, but somehow, hearing the hymns and organ music and occasionally the congregation praying was enough.

I do delight in watching weddings, though, and the wedding tradition in France calls for a civil ceremony at the town hall, which is up the street from us. Once that has been done, the wedding party makes a procession to the church, stopping at the side door, directly across from my office window. When the entire party is assembled it proceeds inside. For large weddings a set of double doors is opened, which affords me a view of the interior all the way to the altar. I can see the glint of candles and the silhouettes of everyone inside.

Joyfully ringing bells signal the end of the ceremony, and moments later the bride and groom come out the front door onto the *parvis*, or square in front of the church, followed by the crowd and a storm of tissue paper hearts, many of which float on the wind into our front yard. When Joe was small he loved to chase them all over the garden, carefully hoarding his handfuls. The wedding parties gather outside to await the gaily decorated cars that come to pick them up and whisk them away to what will be hours of eating, dancing, and eating again. Some days there are two or three weddings in a row. If I'm in my office I see the priest finally emerge from the church at the end of the day and lock the door with a satisfied flourish before going on his way.

After my office, the next room to be finished was Joe's room, then our room, then the bathroom, and finally a temporary kitchen, which meant the house now had a working fireplace. All of this took a full year, during which time we stayed in our little cottage on the river. We continued to love it, often taking long walks along the river during summer evenings when it is light until 11 P.M. I worked steadily on the book, traveling at least one week a month and sometimes more.

That first year I drove the winding wine routes of Alsace, knocked side-view mirrors with another car in the Pyrenees as I went to visit a cheese maker, shivered in the cold waters off the coast in Brittany during a visit to oyster beds, and had the thrill of harvesting mussels right outside of Bordeaux. After each trip I would return laden with specialities—bottles of fruity Alsatian Riesling and an assortment of sausages, an entire Ardi Gasna (Basque sheep's milk cheese) weighing just over two pounds, *cannellés* (custardy little pastries) from Bordeaux. We tasted these as I recounted my adventures, making them real for everyone.

EDITH'S ENDIVES ROLLED IN HAM
LES ENDIVES AU JAMBON D'EDITH

Every time I talk with Edith (who is no longer a vegetarian) in winter, it seems she has just made and served this typical Norman dish. "Tout le monde aime ça!" "Everyone loves it!" she exclaims each time amazed, I think, that she's hit upon a dish her four nearly grown children like as much as she and her husband, Bernard, do. Joe and Michael ate it once at Edith's when I was out of town and both told me how much they liked it, so I've included it in my repertoire. Not only is it delicious, but it is easy to make. Serve these with a simple red Bordeaux.

2 pounds/1kg Belgian endives
2½ cups/625ml whole milk

2 dried, imported bay leaves
4 tablespoons/60g unsalted butter
4 tablespoons/32g all-purpose flour
Sea salt and freshly ground black pepper
10 ounces/300g thinly sliced ham, cut in 1½-inch-wide strips
2 ounces/60g Gruyère or Comté cheese, grated

1. Place 3 inches (7.5cm) of water in the bottom of a steamer and bring to a boil. Steam the endives until they are tender and have turned a flat blue-green, about 20 minutes. Remove from the steamer and let drain for several hours.

2. Preheat the oven to 450° F/230° C/gas 9.

3. Scald the milk with the bay leaves in a heavy-bottomed pan over medium heat. Remove from the heat, cover, and let sit for at least 10 minutes. Remove and discard the bay leaves.

4. Melt the butter in a medium-size, heavy-bottomed pan and when it is foaming whisk in the flour. Let the mixture foam and cook for at least 2 minutes. Whisk in the milk and keep cooking, whisking constantly, until the mixture thickens enough to coat the back of a metal spoon, 8 to 10 minutes. Season with salt and pepper and remove from the heat.

5. Lightly salt the endives. Lay the strips of ham out on a work surface and roll one endive up in each ham slice. Lay the endive and ham in a baking sheet with the end of the ham underneath, so it doesn't unroll. When all of the endives are rolled in ham and

placed in the baking dish, pour the béchamel sauce over all, making sure it evenly covers all the endives. Sprinkle with the grated cheese and bake in the center of the oven until the cheese is golden and the dish is hot, about 30 minutes. Remove from the oven and serve immediately, being careful not to burn yourself.

4 TO 6 SERVINGS

HÉLOÏSE'S APPLES AND SQUASH
LES POMMES ET POTIMARRON D'HÉLOÏSE

Héloïse Tuyéras, our friend and a frequent source of toys, household objects, and clothes for the children, makes this recipe often in winter when apples and squash are both at their best. It is sweet, rich, and irresistible. When there are leftovers they get eaten, slightly warmed, for breakfast!

Héloïse prefers to steam the squash as do I, but it can be roasted as well, which gives another dimension to its flavor.

3 kuri or acorn or other small, dense-fleshed squash
(about 3½ pounds/1kg750g total), trimmed, peeled,
seeds removed, and cut into 2-inch pieces
1 tablespoon/15g unsalted butter
1¾ pounds/875g tart cooking apples, cored, peeled, and
cut in eighths

FOR THE BÉCHAMEL:
1½ cups/375ml whole milk
2 dried, imported bay leaves

65

3 tablespoons/45g unsalted butter
2 tablespoons all-purpose flour
Sea salt and freshly ground black pepper
Freshly ground nutmeg

1. Preheat the oven to 425°F/220° C/gas 8. Butter a
9 × 13 × 2-inch/22.5 × 35 × 5-cm baking dish.

2. Bring 3 cups/750ml water to a boil in the bottom half of a
steamer. Place the squash over the steamer and steam until it is tender,
about 12 minutes. Remove from the heat and transfer the squash to
the bowl of a food processor. Purée the squash and reserve. If the
squash is at all liquid, transfer it to a fine-mesh sieve and let it drain
for 30 minutes. Transfer the squash purée to a medium-size bowl.

3. Melt 1 tablespoon (15g) of butter in a heavy-bottomed skillet
over medium heat and add the apples. Cook them, shaking the pan
and tossing them frequently, until they are golden and turning tender, about 15 minutes. Transfer the apples to the buttered baking
dish.

4. To make the béchamel, scald the milk with the bay leaves
over medium heat. Remove from the heat and infuse for 10 minutes. Melt 2 tablespoons/30g of the butter in a small, heavy-
bottomed saucepan over medium heat. Whisk in the flour and
cook the mixture until the butter has bubbled and formed a pale
yellow foam, at least 2 minutes. Pour in the hot milk, straining
out the bay leaf, whisking as you add it to the butter and flour.

Cook, stirring constantly, until the béchamel has thickened to the consistency of very heavy cream. Season to taste with salt and pepper.

5. Whisk the béchamel into the squash purée and taste it for seasoning. The mixture should be quite highly seasoned.

6. Pour the squash béchamel over the apples, dot it with the remaining tablespoon (15g) of butter, and season it with freshly ground nutmeg. Bake in the center of the oven until the béchamel is slightly golden at the edges and the apples are tender, about 25 minutes. Remove from the oven and let cool for about 10 minutes before serving.

6 TO 8 SERVINGS

THREE

Brushes with the Law

ABOUT SIX MONTHS after we'd arrived, a friend of Bernard's who was a reporter for the local paper, *Paris-Normandie*, called. "Suzanne, I want to interview you," he said rather breathlessly. Bernard had warned me he was going to call, that he considered our story something of a scoop. We made a date and I invited him up to my office for the interview. He tiptoed over the building materials, hammers, nails, and rubble in the entryway and gingerly walked up the stairs carefully avoiding the bits of plaster that had fallen on it. My office, by contrast, was a haven of calm and tidiness, though still very basic. He interviewed me all about my book project and the house and wrote a very nice story from it all, which appeared the following week. About a month afterward we received a summons from the *gendarmerie*, or local police station, by mail. The letter stated simply that we were to appear at the police station at a certain time, for questioning. We asked Bernard about it and he had no idea what to say, except that we should show up on time.

We walked to the police station, five minutes from the house, carrying our passports and our *cartes de séjour,* which showed us as legal residents, and any other legal documents we thought might be necessary, including the deed to the house. We were ushered to a drab upstairs office that held a metal desk, where we waited for a good fifteen minutes. Then a gentleman in a suit arrived, and two other men stationed themselves in an adjacent office. The gentleman began to question us, asking us virtually all the questions that had been on the form we'd filled out to obtain our visas. He seemed primarily concerned with where our money came from, and what we were actually doing in Louviers. I explained how I was paid in U.S. dollars, showed him contracts and tax forms, then showed him copies of my previous books. Meantime, the two men in the adjacent office maintained a silent but obvious presence there, sometimes pacing back and forth. I felt like we were in a spy movie, and though I knew we were perfectly legal I started to feel a bit uncomfortable, like I'd done something wrong.

Questions continued. "How many children do you have?" "Where does he go to school?" "Do you know anyone here?" "How long will you stay?" "Why did you choose Louviers?" "What do you drive?"

About an hour and a half after the interrogation had begun it ended; the man shook our hands and told us we could go. We were shaken. We realized that someone in the police department must have read the newspaper article about us and not believed it— cookbook writing is not, after all, a typical French profession. Someone must have obtained our visa application as well, for they followed the questions almost verbatim, except for the few about Joe and school.

We never heard any more from the police. Louviers is a pretty clean little town but it has its dark elements—mostly minor drug dealing. We live near Rouen and Le Havre, however, both major spots for the drug trade, so perhaps they thought we might be involved. Or maybe our foreignness aroused suspicion. Whatever the reason, being called in for questioning was an unpleasant experience, one we hadn't been prepared for, and one that surprised even our French friends. It was one of the moments that made us acutely aware that we were outsiders.

Added to this experience was the behavior of our landlady, Florence. Instead of her usual friendly greetings we were met with cold *bonjours*, and she kept her distance. I was concerned we'd done something that displeased her, but when I asked her she assured me all was well. She is a good friend of Edith's so I asked Edith, who said that Florence hadn't told her anything. We decided perhaps we'd outstayed our welcome, though Florence had continued to insist we stay as long as we like. In any case, the Messy House was nearly ready for us, so Michael speeded up his work and in September, just about a year from the day we moved into the cottage, we moved out. I bought a huge bouquet of flowers and left it for Florence, who was gone when we actually moved, and resolved to stop by at a later date to say good-bye personally. We hadn't figured out what the cause of her behavior change was and had decided we would just ignore it.

Our first dinner guests at the Messy House were Bernard and Edith. We set up a table in our chilly little dining room, right in front of the window that looked out at the church. A few well-placed candelabra, a white linen tablecloth, and the view made for a very dramatic setting.

We began our meal with champagne and a savory baked apple I'd dreamed up after a visit to the market that was filled with peppered fresh goat cheese and sautéed leeks. None of us are big meat eaters and we all love seafood, so I'd decided to simply sauté three different kinds of fish in butter and lemon, and serve them with a salad of baby greens grown in the garden. I had found baby sole, *rascasse* (scorpion fish), and *daurade* (sea bream), each of which has its own distinctive flavor and texture. Following that was a selection of three different qualities of Roquefort cheese because Edith has a particular fondness for this cheese. Dessert was a tart of paper-thin pastry filled with apples and a sprinkling of fresh thyme.

We were eating and marveling at the view when suddenly Bernard said, "I spoke to Florence about you, and she told me what was bothering her." We were all ears. "Apparently she had her family over for a meal and they wanted to know who you were. When she explained that you wrote cookbooks, her brother told her she'd better watch out, that you probably worked for the CIA, since the job of cookbook writer is a famous CIA cover." He was speaking so seriously and with such earnestness that we listened to him, believing every word. When he finished, we both just stared. Then, we burst out laughing. He did, too.

"You're kidding," I said. "I'm not," he said, this time not laughing. "She now thinks you are CIA agents and that you've been spying on them."

Michael and I were flabbergasted. "This can't be true. If we

BRUSHES WITH THE LAW

were CIA agents why would we have been crammed into that tiny little cottage for a year, while Michael worked on this ruin?" I said. "If we were CIA agents wouldn't we be wealthy?"

Bernard shrugged. "I tried to point out to her how ridiculous that was and how we've all known you for so long we would surely know if you worked for the CIA, but she wouldn't hear it," he said. Bernard assured us that her husband didn't share her fear and that, within a few years, she'd forget all about it. Despite this disturbing bit of paranoia, we went on to enjoy our evening in the Messy House, with our friends who had helped make our new life in France possible.

The Subaru station wagon we had shipped from the States arrived safely in Le Havre amidst a *temps de cochon*, or "pig weather," when it was raining so hard you couldn't see the lines on the road. The company who shipped the car had warned us to make sure it was completely empty, for they assured us that anything left in it would be stolen. As I looked at the mounds of things we wanted to send to France, mostly children's toys and books, I thought that a terrible waste of space, but wasn't about to risk packing the car full.

We worried a bit that the radio might be gone but when we picked up the car it was intact. We signed the appropriate papers and got in the car to drive off into the downpour. When Michael, who was driving, turned on the windshield wipers we realized they were gone. We told the director of the office, who looked at us as if he could not understand what we were saying. *"Monsieur, 'dame,"* he said slowly, enunciating. "Many of these cars arrive with headlights broken and radios ripped out. Your problem is nothing, nothing at all."

How were we to see as we drove out of the terminal which fed right onto the *autoroute* and its traffic that whizzed by at more than 100 miles per hour? "This is not our problem," the director said. "You will simply have to buy new windshield wipers. Any garage will have them." What he failed to explain is that there were no garages within a reasonable distance.

We had no choice but to proceed, gingerly. Michael drove with his head craned outside so he could see, sort of. It was hair raising but we managed to get to the first exit where there was a garage. The windshield wipers they had didn't fit the car but they worked well enough so that Michael could see the road and we were soon on our way.

What had been a good car in the ice and snow of Maine proved to be just as good on the slick roads of Normandy, and the U.S. license plates—adorned with a red lobster—kept the local police at bay. They weren't about to meddle with drivers who might not speak French.

The customs police in their imposing skin-tight black pants, knee-high black boots, square-shouldered and silver-buttoned short jackets, and white cross-the-chest holsters were a different story. I always had the feeling their mouths watered when they saw us coming, for they often stopped us. I suppose they were looking for drugs, and cars with foreign license plates must be highly suspect.

I remember getting stopped one day in particular. We had been in France just a few months, so our American driver's licenses were still legal, as was everything about the car, although this would change after a year when we would have to get French driver's licenses and bring the car up (or down) to French standards. We dreaded both of those, since getting a driver's license in France

BRUSHES WITH THE LAW

costs a fortune and takes forever, and because bringing the car within French standards involves changing just about everything about it except the steering wheel. As it was I had nothing to fear.

On that particular day I was driving to the supermarket with Joe, whom I had just gotten up from his nap. He was safely strapped into his car seat in the back and we were singing when I turned onto the main road, a bit too quickly I admit. I was flagged over by the police. I swore inwardly thinking it was my speed until I recognized the uniforms of the customs police. The local police remind me of Dupont and Dupond in the *Tintin* stories, rather fumbling, dim, and harmless. The customs guys are something else. They look down on everyone with hauteur, they don't smile, and with their stark uniforms they look mean. They make me nervous.

I pulled over and stayed in the car as the two officers examined my papers, pulling out my Maine driver's license and checking it on both sides, then examining my *carte de séjour*, which proved I was a legal resident of France. They kept looking over at me and discussing something in a low voice.

I busied myself by looking around at the interior of our car. It was a mess. There were magazines on the front seat, books stacked in the back, and a varied collection of small child detritus like pieces of cracker and ends of *baguettes* and books and toys. I was embarrassed. Normally our car is relatively tidy, but since moving to France it had become something of a third home as we shuttled between our little house on the river and the Messy House in Louviers.

The officers strode back over and one bent down to speak to me. *"Madame, je vous en prie,"* he began, then Joe started to cry. He had just realized, I think, that he was no longer in his cozy bed but was strapped into the car, not his favorite place. *"Madame, nous voulons examiner votre voiture."*

They wanted to search the car. Oh geez. I looked at him, about to cry myself. I'd been carting boxes all week in between trying to work, the house we were renting was chaotic, and the Messy House was a cold, chilly wreck. I wasn't sure my spirit could withstand a howling child and a car search at the hands of these snooty, tight-lipped officers.

"I have nothing in here of interest," I said, agitated. "My child, some books, and a lot of junky paper." Joe was crying louder and beginning to wiggle with frustration. There is something about a strapped-down child crying in the back of the car, just out of reach, which causes my nerves to bunch up—I can't stand the thought that anyone might be uncomfortable, particularly when there is nothing I can do about it.

Despite my inner turmoil I didn't want to defy the customs police, who do not enjoy a humanitarian reputation. I unbuckled my seatbelt and made motions to open the car door. The officers were conferring again in hushed, serious voices. The spokesman returned to me and leaned over. *"Madame, nous avons décidé de vous laisser passer."*

They were letting me go. Whew. What a relief. I had nothing to hide and I still felt like I'd been saved from purgatory. What about all the people who get stopped and do have something to hide?

It was only later as we were on our way home after an uneventful visit to the supermarket that I thought of the contents of my glove compartment. For some reason I was keeping a collection of powdered sourdough starters in there, each in its individual white envelope. Perspiration popped out on my forehead. Oh Lord, what if they had searched the car and found those envelopes? I could just see myself trying to explain what was in them.

75

"Oh yes, officer," I would have said as I watched one or the other of them sift out the fine white powder. "It's just dried *levain*."

Why, they would surely want to know, would someone travel with dried sourdough starter in the glove compartment of their car? That was a question even I couldn't answer.

I nearly started shaking as I thought of what a close call I'd had. Then I burst out laughing. "What's so funny, Mama?" Joe asked from the backseat. I started to say something but I was laughing too hard to reply. I explained it to him, when I finally caught my breath, though the story was not as funny to him as seeing me nearly bent double.

It took us about two years to get used to the *tuyau* system in France. This is an undocumented system that pervades every element of French society and is vaguely comparable to the notion of bypassing the authorities. In its most extreme form it is nothing less than cheating.

We hadn't been at all aware of it before we moved to France, but once here it kept seeping into our consciousness, baffling as well as intriguing us. One of the first places we saw it at work was with Edith and Bernard, who received shipments of wine regularly throughout the year which they bought through a *tuyau*, in this case a friend who knew the vintner. It simply meant they got the wine for a good price because their friend who knew the vintner grouped all his friends together to buy a large quantity of the wine. This was harmless, legal, and to everyone's advantage. In fact, once we found out about it we asked to take advantage of this particular *tuyau*, too.

Michael had parked his old truck on the church square in a paying parking spot and forgotten to move it when he and Joe flew to Italy, where I was researching a project, to meet me for a week's vacation. When he returned his windshield was papered with parking tickets amounting to several hundred francs. Frustrated with his own carelessness he mentioned it to a friend who takes care of our vehicles. Our friend put his hand on Michael's shoulder and said, "Don't worry, I am going to help you." He helped Michael write a letter to an official explaining what had happened, then went to the official to see him in person. According to Michael, he then stopped by the house and said the tickets had all been forgiven. Michael thanked our friend profusely and tried to give him a bottle of wine. "You owe me nothing," he said. "But the official is an *amateur* of whiskey." Within a couple of days we'd sent him a bottle of the finest.

Michael, in the course of talking with a *bricoleur* friend who does a lot of work on his own house, found out that he could buy electrical equipment at cost if he went through this friend who had a friend who worked at an electrical supply house. It involved the minor complication of knowing exactly the type and quantity of material he would need well in advance. For a savings of nearly fifty percent, it was worth it. Michael would write out his orders, our friend would order the equipment under the name of his company, and the discount would be ours.

We have a friend who has a restaurant and when he realized the extent of my recipe testing he told me he could take me to a wholesale supply store where I would be able to buy everything from unsalted butter to stainless steel mixing bowls at just above cost. "No one but registered food professionals are supposed to go, but I'll just take you with me and pay for your things and you can pay me, no problem," he said. The first time I accompanied him I was nervous and hoped it didn't show. My friend assured me there was no problem. "Everyone does this, they just don't say anything," he said.

The *tuyau* system has developed to circumvent the killing taxes placed on every aspect of French life, but it is also an ingrained part of the French, who love to *glisser*, or slip through these kinds of loopholes without being noticed or caught. All of these quasi-illegal exploits are much discussed afterward, usually with pride. A friend who claimed her car was damaged in a parking lot when she was the one who caused the damage told everyone she talked with about it, laughing gleefully to think she'd gotten away with it. Another friend claims he buys televisions for people he knows because he paid his television tax when he bought his own television and he now has the right to buy as many as he wants without paying any more tax, whereas first-time purchasers must pay a hefty sum.

Michael and I used to be aghast at the minor cheating and trickery that fueled dinner party conversation, always bringing much laughter and satisfaction, but now we're used to it and we laugh right along with everyone. It's simply a part of living here.

APPLES STUFFED WITH GOAT CHEESE AND LEEKS
POMMES FARCIES AU FROMAGE DE CHÈVRE ET AUX POIREAUX

I made this simple, satisfying appetizer one evening after finding all the ingredients at the Louviers farmer's market. It is a happy combination, savory and delicious, simple to prepare, and dramatic to serve.

78

Be sure to remove a strip of skin from the circumference of the apple so the apple doesn't burst during baking. Serve these with a red Sancerre.

4 large (about 8 ounces/250g each) apples, cored, one
    strip of skin removed from the circumference of each
    apple
1 cup/250ml white wine such as Sauvignon Blanc
1 dried, imported bay leaf
Fine sea salt
2 tablespoons/30g unsalted butter
2 large leeks (about 9 ounces/300g) total, white part only,
    well rinsed, and diced
2 tablespoons to ¼ cup/60ml bottled water
7 ounces/210g goat cheese
2 tablespoons *crème fraîche* or heavy cream
Freshly ground black pepper
Flat-leaf parsley for garnish

1. Preheat the oven to 400° F/200° C/gas 6.

2. Place the apples in a baking dish and pour the wine around them. Add the bay leaf to the wine. Lightly salt the interior of each apple.

3. Place 1 tablespoon (15g) of the butter and the leeks in a large, heavy saucepan and cook, stirring and shaking the pan, until the leeks begin to turn transparent. Add 1 tablespoon of the water, stir, and cover the pan. Continue cooking until the leeks

are tender, about 10 minutes, adding additional water if necessary to prevent the leeks from sticking to the pan.

4. When the leeks are cooked, transfer them to a mixing bowl. Add the goat cheese and *crème fraîche* and stir until all the ingredients are thoroughly mixed. Season to taste with salt and pepper.

5. Gently stuff each apple with an equal amount of the goat cheese and leek mixture, pressing it into the cavity and mounding it on top. Top each apple with one-fourth (1 scant teaspoon) of the remaining tablespoon of butter.

6. Bake in the center of the oven until the apples are tender and the goat cheese is dark golden on top, about 45 minutes. Remove from the oven and transfer one apple to each of four warmed plates. Garnish the plate with sweet cicely or the parsley and serve immediately.

4 SERVINGS

APPLE AND THYME TART
TARTE AUX POMMES PARFUMÉE AU THYM

One morning I picked reines de reinettes and Cox's Orange Pippin apples from our trees and snipped a handful of thyme branches—which were in flower—from the plants along the courtyard wall and combined them in this wonderful, heady tart. It was simple and sublime!

FOR THE PASTRY:

1½ cups/200g unbleached, all-purpose flour

Large pinch of sea salt

7 tablespoons/3½ ounces/105g unsalted butter, chilled
    and cut in small pieces

5 to 6 tablespoons/75 to 95ml chilled water

1 small egg

FOR THE FILLING:

6 large tart apples, cored, peeled, and cut in ¼-inch-thick
    slices

½ cup/100g vanilla sugar

1 tablespoon fresh thyme leaves

1. To make the pastry, place the flour and salt in a food processor, and process to mix. Add the butter and process until the mixture
resembles coarse cornmeal. With the food processor running, slowly
add the water and process just until combined and crumbly. Turn the
dough out onto a lightly floured surface and gently press it into a
ball. Let the pastry sit, covered, at room temperature for 1 hour.

2. Whisk together the egg and 1 teaspoon of water to make
an egg wash.

3. Preheat the oven to 425° F/220° C/gas 8.

4. Lightly flour a work surface, and roll out the pastry to a
14-inch/35.5-cm circle. Roll the pastry around the rolling pin and
unroll it in a 9½-inch/24-cm, removable-bottom tart tin, with the

edges of the pastry overlapping evenly all around. Gently fit the pastry against the sides of the tart tin and don't trim the edges.

5. Place half the apple slices in the pastry, sprinkle with half the sugar and all the thyme. Top with the remaining apples and the remaining sugar. Bring the edges of the pastry up and over the apples—they won't completely cover the apples, which is fine.

6. Brush the pastry with the egg wash. Place the tart tin on a baking sheet, and bake in the lower third of the oven until the pastry is golden and the apples are softened and juicy, about 50 minutes.

7. Remove from the oven and place the tart tin on an up-turned bowl to remove the sides of the pan. Let the tart cool to lukewarm or room temperature, then serve.

6 TO 8 SERVINGS

FOUR

The Messy House

WHEN WE MOVED into the house on rue Tatin, the outside was fine, gorgeous, in fact, with its beams and plaster walls—called *colombage*—steeply sloping stone roof, and numerous paned windows. The two front doors, both of which have paned windows in them as well, and one that is covered by a stone roof, are just tall enough for us to walk through. The house is shaped like an L, and from what we have found in researching its past, it was once three houses stuck together. The interior of the L was created when one of those houses either crumbled or was pulled down centuries ago. Looking carefully at the large, beamed façade, the one that presents itself to the church and which visitors in town always stop to photograph, the outline of where a door once was becomes obvious, on the second floor.

A friend of ours refers to it as a good witch's house, particularly in spring and summer when it is almost obscured by the old-fashioned roses that climb all over one part of the façade and the small panes of wavy old glass glint in the light.

Inside, all the key rooms were livable. The temporary kitchen was better than most people's permanent kitchens. Michael had built it in the room that we surmised had once been the convent's kitchen, though there was no sink in it, or any other amenity except a lovely old fireplace built into one wall. We asked nuns who live in a neighboring convent and remember when our house was still a convent, and they all agreed that was where three hundred years of simple, sustaining victuals had been prepared. I had a vivid dream one night where I saw a nun in the room standing over a big gas burner stirring soup as she prepared to ladle it out into a bowl and pass it to some hungry soul through a hinged pane in the window. There actually was such a hinged pane in the window that looked out into the backyard, no doubt a catalyst for the dream.

The back wall of the large room, which was lath and plaster and painted a very pale blue, was angled so it looked off-kilter, as was the ten-foot-high ceiling. Two large windows were in the wall on the left, a wall that had clearly been the exterior of the house, and which separated the kitchen from another large room, which Michael surmised was an addition to the main house done some two hundred years ago. The corrugated plastic that covered part of the ceiling only added to its feeling of being an add-on.

Just outside the kitchen at the back of the house was a heavy wooden door. Inside it was a steep stairway and down at the bottom was another heavy door that looked like some giant had gnawed at the top; it had once fit snugly into the carved doorway but time had worn it away. Through that second doorway was one of the prizes of the house, the *cave*, or wine cellar. It had once been enormous, for it had encompassed the *cave* of the house that abuts ours as well. Some time long ago, though, the *caves* had been separated and our house was left with one long rectangular vaulted room off of which there is a tunnel that goes for a certain distance then is blocked. When we are down in the *cave*, which maintains a stable temperature ideal for storing wine, we are directly under our neighbors' house. There is a grating in the *cave*'s ceiling that is covered now. Evidently, when our neighbor's children were small they used to drop things down the grating to try to hit the nuns on the head when they were in the *cave*.

In our temporary kitchen Michael built open shelves all along the back wall and nearly up to the ceiling. He lined the corrugated ceiling inside with white insulation that made it clean and bright, and helped capture some heat. We had ignored the muddy brown tiled floor, but Michael's sister, who visited us soon after we moved to France, decided her project would be to wash it. She got down on her hands and knees and started scrubbing. I heard a shriek and rushed downstairs from my office to see what had happened.

Those muddy brown tiles turned out to be lovely terra-cotta swirled with beautiful ochre and blue. We all stood there with our mouths open. They were gorgeous and very ancient, perhaps dating as far back as the twelfth century as I subsequently learned when visiting a tile collector in a nearby town and seeing the very same tiles in that town's twelfth-century church.

Michael installed a double sink in the kitchen and poured concrete countertops, which he stained pale turquoise and ochre, to see how they would hold up and which one we would like the best. He hooked up the plumbing, so we had running water, though only cold. We had a small refrigerator that fit at one end of the counter, and two used, but superbly functioning, four-burner gas stoves.

I was delighted. I was finally in a kitchen I could move around in, with enough space to store my equipment. I hung my copper pots above the stove, and my strainers, whisks, and various other lightweight equipment on the big window, so the light filtered into the kitchen through them, and I put all my dishes on the open shelves, so I could get at everything easily. I had plenty of counter space so that after a year of working in cramped conditions I could finally cook and test recipes in comfort.

The kitchen soon felt like home. We bought a graceful old round wood table, which Michael painted bright blue, and we set that at the end of one of the counters, near the fireplace, which held a small blue Mirus, the brand name on an outmoded but charming little square woodstove from the twenties that would be our source of heat. When our friends spied it as they entered the kitchen they would always exclaim over it. "My grandparents had one just like that!" they would say, or "We started out with one like that, too. We got it from our parents."

We'd gotten the stove from our friend Edith, who had gotten it from her parents, and we loved its efficiency and the warmth it gave to the kitchen, which was also our living room, since none of the other ground-floor rooms were livable yet. We couldn't build a real fire in the fireplace because it smoked too badly. How, we wondered, had the nuns kept warm—had they simply offered up the smokiness to God?

Joe's bedroom was finished. Once a tiny chapel, we think, it has three small, paned windows set into the thick walls, looking out at the church. Michael transformed it into a sweet, cozy place, working on it for months, literally sculpting it back to life. He vaulted the window casings and created an arch in plaster above the center window, so that the windows echo the three arched doors on the church across the street. The ceiling was so low we could hardly stand up straight in it, so he worked on the angles and embedded lights in it to give it height, and he lengthened the small door so that he and I could walk in without bending double. The floors looked abominable and we had decided to simply buy carpeting and cover them up—until we priced carpeting. Michael sanded them and to our delight those filthy, scuffed wood floors were pine, and they turned a warm, buttery color. It wasn't the last time a tight budget turned out to be a blessing.

Joe was very excited about sleeping in his new room. We had painted the walls bright white and found a pretty wrought iron bed in the attic to tuck in one corner. I bought him a fluffy *duvet* with a soft rust and blue cover and we topped it with his considerable collection of stuffed animals. We added a table and chair, shelves for his books and clothes, and we put familiar posters and pictures on his wall. I remade curtains from those in his bedroom in Maine and did whatever else I could to make the room familiar and reassuring.

Our room, adjacent to Joe's, was nearly finished. Michael had painstakingly replaced all the crumbling plaster between the wall timbers adding electrical wiring and outlets as he went. He reset the good-size window that looked out on the grass and the small brick building behind the house, which belongs to the church; he built in a small closet where a fireplace had once stood; and he completely replastered the ceiling.

The floor was paved with dusty eight-sided terra-cotta tiles called *tommettes*, and my job was to clean them. They needed little

THE MESSY HOUSE

more than a thorough washing and waxing, which I expected to be very quick. The washing was, but finding the right wax for these precious old tiles was another story. Edith swept in and said we should use a sticky mixture of linseed oil and beeswax, as she and her grandmother had. "It's hard to apply and you have to re-apply it every year but it's the best thing for them," she said emphatically. I listened to her, but with one ear. I wanted to use something that would enhance the *tommettes*, but a painful process that needed to be done once a year didn't interest me. I went to the local *quincaillerie*, or hardware store, to ask what I should use. They recommended at least three different products and said it depended on many things. We then went into Paris to the Saint Ouen flea market and a store there that specializes in the restoration of furniture, where we got the definitive answer in the form of two waxes, which needed blending and could then be applied in three coats. The salesman assured us they would give the finish we wanted. "They are used by artisans who restore the ancient monuments of France," he said. "They give a nice shine, not too much, just like silk."

Once home I carefully mixed up the waxes and applied them as instructed on the back of the tins. I repeated the procedure twice more. It was very easy as the salesman had said, but for the life of me I couldn't see any shine on the *tommettes*. They looked just the same as before, perhaps a shade darker. I knelt down and put my cheek to the floor to see if I could see anything. I thought I saw a whisper of a shine.

With the floor waxed all that remained to do in our room was to paint the walls, which seemed simple enough. But first we had to decide upon and find a color. Michael and I both love light, and we both love tradition. In general, our house calls for cool pale blues, grays, and celadon to blue-green, all of which go with the matchless sky out-side the windows. The traditional color in Normandy for the plaster between timbers is deep gold, which was too dark, so we decided on a pale version of that, which would be perfect with the wood and the tiles. We had never seen the exact color we wanted anywhere, so we decided the only way to get it was to mix it ourselves.

Michael and I usually end up wanting the same things, we just have different ways of getting there, which is particularly true with colors. In this case we had a vague notion of our goal, a big vat of white paint and tubes of yellow, ochre, white, red, and black pigment before us. Michael insisted we shouldn't add red, and I felt we had to. We both agreed we should use ochre. As we discussed what we were after we squirted bits of color into the vat of paint as Michael patiently stirred.

"No, that isn't it yet," I said.

"You're right, it needs more ochre," he said, squirting.

"And some more red, and maybe some yellow," I countered, squirting.

"Now more ochre," Michael said, and I agreed. Squirt. He stirred and we squirted until the paint got close to a color we thought was all right. In any case, if we kept squirting we'd soon have black, so we stopped. We looked at each other. "I think I'll put some on the wall and see how it looks," I said. Satisfied, Michael left to do something else.

The paint looked delicious, like *café au lait* without the foam. But I was dismayed. It didn't look like anything I wanted on my bedroom walls. *Zut.* We had overdone it, and we had nothing more in the budget for another vat of paint. Not only that but we wanted to move in the following day, so time was running short.

89

There was nothing left to do but start painting. My heart sank as I brushed the first paint on the walls. It looked dark and institutional, like something the army would issue to paint a barracks. I kept painting. Maybe it will improve when it dries, I thought, without much conviction.

Michael looked in and shrugged. "Oh, keep going. We'll let it dry and see," he said.

I got into the job, its rhythm and sameness. Pretty soon I was paying more attention to the technique than the color, carefully painting alongside each uneven beam, trying not to get any paint where it shouldn't be, wiping it off quickly if I did. Before I knew it, one coat was applied on all the plaster and the ceiling. By then I was starving. I cast a glance at the room as I walked out to wash the brushes.

Outside it was a fine autumn day. I bought *crudité* sandwiches—*baguettes* stuffed with hard-cooked egg, lettuce, tomatoes, and gallons of delicious mayonnaise—and Oranginas from the closest bakery, along with *sablés*, buttery cookies that are a Normandy specialty. I loved these particular *sablés*, for they have chocolate dough swirled in them and look like chocolate and vanilla pinwheels. I put a cloth on our metal table outside and we sat down to eat. The apple tree was loaded with fist-sized green apples, the pear tree looked like it might fall under the weight of the tiny pears, which looked like the Seckel pears on the tree back in Michael's and my first house, in Seattle. As I looked at them I imagined many tarts and *clafoutis* for the winter.

I forgot about the paint and the whole inside of the house as we sat there enjoying the autumn sun, the silence, the gothic curls on the church. I marveled at the talent of the craftsmen who had created them—how was it possible to carve such lacy stonework?

Who served as models for the bishops and saints who stood guard on the front of the church? What inspired the horrific gargoyles who stuck out their snouts on all the corners?

When we entered the bedroom an hour later, the effect was astonishing. The paint had dried into a warm, soft, luscious ivory. We looked at each other and laughed with relief.

I went about cleaning the bathroom adjacent to our bedroom, polishing the sink, washing the floor, scrubbing the seventeenth-century carved closet doors there. I loved opening them, for inside they are painted a rich velvety blue, certainly applied decades ago by a nun sprucing things up. We could never replicate the color, so we decided to leave it there. Pasted on the inside of one of the doors is a very old paper decal of the sacred heart, its once lurid colors faded to soft red and gold, its edges pinked to give it a three-dimensional air. Around the heart are the words "Jesus, your heart is here! Let its reign begin." Tiny lettering at the bottom of the decal gives the value of the phrase at 100 days indulgence. Under that is the name Pope Pie, or Pius, and the date July 1877. I imagined the nuns opening the door to get their towels, much as we do, and repeating that phrase as they did to gain more time in heaven.

I'm not much of a seamstress, so I was happy that our bedroom window looked out on little-used church property behind us, allowing me to put off making curtains for a while. A tiny skylight in the roof on the other side of the room looks into the heavens, so that will never pose a problem.

It was late before we stopped for dinner. We washed up, and Michael got a fire going in the Mirus. I set a kettle on top so we would have warm water for dishes, and went about making a family favorite, a big green salad with apples, walnuts, and Roquefort

THE MESSY HOUSE

cheese, our favorite bacon and chive omelette, and a winter fruit compote. Joe was busy coloring on the Sheetrock wall by the sink, which we had decided should be his canvas to decorate as he liked.

I put a candle on the table and set it with cloth napkins and some antique china a friend had given us. We brought the food out and Michael opened a bottle of smooth red wine from Sablet, a small village in Provence. The stove was blazing and we were incredibly warm and cozy. We ate slowly and told stories to Joe, talking about how fun it was to be camping in our house.

Once upstairs Joe wasn't so sure. He was intimidated by the new surroundings. Tucked in bed, though, under his fluffy *duvet* and completely engulfed by his stuffed animals, he fell asleep and we didn't hear a word from him all night long.

Neither of us slept much, however, as we listened to the unfamiliar moans and creaks of the house. I thought about the nuns who had occupied it for so long, and the various others who might have slept there. I noticed the way street lights came in the windows and listened to the night traffic. I heard clanking and soft voices around 6 A.M., which I learned later were the florists across the street preparing for their workday. It was all new and strange.

Michael got up early to light a fire in the woodstove downstairs and went out for *croissants* and *pains au chocolat*. Joe crawled in bed with me and we snuggled under the thick *duvet* until Michael called us to come down for breakfast. The windows had a light layer of frost on the inside and when my feet hit that cold tile floor I almost screamed. Joe and I dashed through our morning ablutions and rushed into the warmth and smell of coffee and fresh pastries downstairs. We sat at our bright blue table near the stove and breakfasted amid the ruins.

We settled into a routine. Joe was still going to school in Le

Vaudreuil, so I drove him the ten minutes there each morning. Héloïse Tuyéras picked him up and fed him lunch and Michael went to get him in the evenings. During the day, Michael bashed and built and I worked in my office, making slow but steady progress on my book about French farmhouse cooking. My deadline for turning in half the manuscript was looming and I had to grab every second I could to work on the book. We ate lunch together each day, which was sometimes a recipe test, other times leftovers from the night before. We would talk about our various projects, both of us completely lost in what we were doing.

I loved being in our own home. It was rustic and cold, but it was gorgeous. The entryway had a dirt floor, which we covered with sheets of plywood so that Joe had a place to play. Naturally warm-blooded, he has an extreme resistance to cold. Bundled up, he never seemed to notice the temperature. Now that same entryway is covered with golden, brushed concrete and heated from underneath. It couldn't be further from what it was, nor more comfortable.

Michael installed an instant hot water heater upstairs in the bathroom so we could bathe, but there was no hot water downstairs. What I couldn't heat on the stove I would haul from the bathroom in a big black bucket, feeling like Laura in *Little House on the Prairie*.

We had decided to hire a local plumbing company to install our furnace, because Michael didn't feel confident that he could do a perfect job. After soliciting opinions from everyone we know we hired the best company in town and established a date when they would begin. It came and went and we never saw anyone. I called, they apologized, and we set a new date. It came and went. This went on for six weeks. We were entering into what would be one of the coldest winters on record since the turn of the century, and we were really concerned.

THE MESSY HOUSE

Finally, when yet another date had gone by with no plumbers I took Joe and went to the plumber's office, which is also an appliance store, and made a little scene, shaming them for putting off the work when we had a small child to keep warm. It worked, of course. Making scenes is often the only way to get action in France. Everyone gets excited and raises his voice, says regrettable things he forgets later, and whatever is at issue is resolved with no hard feelings. It's not a bad way to live, actually. Violent crimes of a personal nature are relatively rare in France, and I think one of the reasons is that the French way of life involves arguing on a daily basis. Emotions are vented, not suppressed.

After my scene the workers showed up at the house within the week and wasted no time. I've noticed the very few times we've called in anyone to work on the house it's always the same. Getting them here is the hard part. Once here, they work with record speed and efficiency. Two men arrived that first day at 8 A.M., shook hands all around, unpacked their tools, and went to work. Michael followed them around because he wanted to learn how they installed radiators and hooked up pipes, figuring correctly that it was a skill he would need one day.

They broke for coffee at around ten, smoked a cigarette, then returned to work. The church bells chimed noon and they were gone, tipping their hats. An hour and a half later they returned, usually just as we were finishing lunch. If I had baked dessert I would give them some, and they always had coffee with us, then I wouldn't hear anything from them until about four, when the aroma of coffee drifted into my office from the kitchen below, where Michael was brewing a pot for them. By 7 P.M. they were gone.

This went on for two weeks and the two workers became part

of the family as they rushed in and out of the bathroom, the bed-rooms, the office, laying their pipe and placing the radiators. Once the work was finished they were gone, and we were warmer and could expand into other rooms with comfort. Not only that, but we had a steady supply of hot water upstairs, though it would be a year before Michael routed it down to the kitchen. I didn't mind. Having hot water in the kitchen, even if I had to carry it there in a black bucket, was one of life's pleasures.

APPLE, ROQUEFORT, AND WALNUT SALAD
SALADE DE POMMES, ROQUEFORT, ET NOIX

This simple salad is a favorite in our home, and I make it often as a main course for lunch or as a first course for dinner. I use a mix of lettuce or fresh young spinach, Papillon Roquefort, one of the best qualities available, walnuts from our friend Danie Dubois's farm, and apples from our own trees. Serve this with a Languedoc red.

FOR THE VINAIGRETTE:
    1 teaspoon sherry vinegar
    2 teaspoons Dijon-style mustard
    Fine sea salt and freshly ground black pepper
    ¼ cup/60ml extra-virgin olive oil

FOR THE SALAD:
    10 cups (about 8 ounces/250g) mixed salad greens such
        as curly endive, romaine, and arugula, torn into bite-
        size pieces

1 large (8-ounce/250-g) tart apple, cored, peeled, and cut
    in ½-inch cubes
½ cup/60g walnuts, lightly toasted
3 ounces/90g Roquefort cheese

1. Place the vinegar and the mustard in a large bowl, add a
pinch of salt and pepper, and whisk together. Whisk in the olive
oil slowly until the mixture emulsifies. Adjust the seasoning.

2. Add the salad greens, apple, and walnuts and toss until
they are all coated with the dressing. Crumble the Roquefort
over the salad, toss well, and season to taste. Serve immediately.

4 SERVINGS

BACON AND CHIVE OMELETTE
OMELETTE AUX LARDONS ET AUX CIBOULETTES

*Omelettes are the salvation of a busy day, and a gastronomic treat
when made with fresh farm eggs. I take delight in being able to whisk
together eggs that come from a nearby farm and season them with fresh
chives from the garden. I always have bacon in the refrigerator, which
makes this practically an instant meal served with salad and fresh
bread. French omelettes are slightly runny in the interior. If you prefer
omelettes cooked through, simply cook it longer than specified.*

*Slab bacon in France is very lean and requires a bit of oil when
it cooks. American bacon is so fatty that the olive oil will most
likely be unnecessary. In fact, if the bacon gives off too much fat*

simply drain all but 1 tablespoon from the pan before making the omelette. Serve this with a simple red wine, such as one from the Languedoc.

6 large eggs
Fine sea salt and freshly ground black pepper
1 bunch/5g fresh chives
5 ounces/150g slab bacon, rind removed, cut in thin slices
    then cut crosswise in thin strips
1 tablespoon olive oil, optional

1. Place the eggs in a medium-size bowl and whisk just until they are broken. Season with salt and pepper and whisk again just enough to mix in the spices.

2. Mince the chives and stir them into the eggs.

3. Place the bacon and the oil (if necessary) in a large omelette pan over medium-high heat and sauté until just beginning to turn golden, 4 to 5 minutes. Add the eggs to the pan and let them sit for about 30 seconds, then bring the edges gradually toward the center, tilting the pan so the uncooked egg in the center runs to the edges of the pan. When the omelette is set but still slightly runny on top let it cook for an additional minute then slip it out of the pan, folding it as you do so, onto a warmed serving platter. Serve immediately.

4 SERVINGS

FIVE

Transformations

I AM ALWAYS amazed at what I don't notice. Living on rue Tatin with the cathedral floating gracefully in front of us all day long as though it had wings, I have become, perhaps, inured to architectural details, since I have such a surfeit in front of my eyes at all times.

But there are other things I do notice. A day never goes by that I don't stroke the rosemary hedge that shields us from traffic on rue Tatin. I try to run my hands through the scrubby thyme plants that grow in our front courtyard daily, too, for thyme loves company. My hope is that daily contact will make them as lush as I think they should be. I want them to know how much I love their presence— to look at, to smell, and to add to soups, salads, and even apple tarts.

I admire daily the deep blue gate that Michael made several years ago, with its fanciful top, and when I work in the garden, kneeling to pull weeds from among the lettuce and ruby chard plants, I always turn to look at the "holy stone" with the cross carved in it at the end of our house. About two and a half feet high and eighteen inches across, it sits embedded in concrete right in front of the window on the L of the house, surrounded by *hortensias*, or hydrangeas, and *muguets*, or lilies of the valley. Joe often opens the window wide and climbs out onto the stone and stands on it, like a statue. I always ask myself the same questions about it—where did it come from, how old is it, who put it there? I haven't found the answers, but it doesn't really matter. I know the stone is old, and it's almost more fun to dream that it is truly ancient than to know it was hewn perhaps just a few hundred years ago.

I also notice, when I walk inside our house, if it is cool or warm. Usually, it is cool when it needs to be, during the height of summer, warmish when necessary, from Christmastime into February. I notice if the house is clean and our on-and-off housekeeper, Colette, has been and gone.

I met Colette when I was looking for someone to help me part-time in my office. She had some training in office work, and she was happy to get the job as she had been unemployed for some time, but it became obvious quite early on that office work wasn't her cup of *exprès*. She didn't like being confined to a desk, the mere sight of English—which she doesn't understand at all—threw her into a panic, and as she typed and filed I could feel the tension in her build. I would give her jobs that got her out of the office—going to the post office, running various errands in town, emptying wastebaskets—until finally she was cleaning the house and doing a variety of other odd jobs for both me and Michael. She is what I call a *femme à tout faire*, a woman who knows how to do everything from ironing to refinishing wood surfaces, and I've never met anyone who works harder or better. While I missed the help in the office, I was delighted with her help around the house.

Small and wiry, she is aged beyond her years no doubt from the two packs of no-filter Gauloises she smokes daily. *"Oui, je sais, ce n'est pas bon,"* she says when I tease her about her habit. "I know, I know, it's not good for me." Then she offers a cigarette to Michael, a very irregular smoker, and they go off and smoke together outside.

Colette has three grown children and her husband passed away many years ago so she lives alone with her dog, Max. She has many curious little habits, which she brings with her when she comes to work. One is smoking, though she is respectful enough to do it outside and only when she sorts through papers to put recyclables where they belong.

Another is her penchant for bleach, which she uses to wash everything, so that the house smells strongly after she's gone. I've asked her not to use so much bleach but she just doesn't feel like she's doing her job without it, so it always creeps back into her wash water.

The other thing is the fact that she works in the dark. I first noticed it when she was tucked in one of the rooms upstairs ironing. I walked up there to ask her something and though it was daytime, very little light came into the room and she was literally working in the dark.

Colette is an artist with an iron. Clothes, napkins, and even underwear are so beautifully ironed and folded that I'm tempted to photograph her work, and it always pains me to destroy the careful folds she's made. When I walked into that room with no light I was sure there was something wrong. There was no way she could get such perfect results without light. I flipped the light switch. Colette jumped, looked up ruefully, and said, *"Merci, Madame Loomis."* (I've tried to get her to call me Suzanne but she won't.)

After that I observed Colette when she came to work, and I realized she cleaned in the dark as well, never seeming to think about putting on the light. There is never a speck of dust to be found after she has passed through a room so it isn't like I need to insist she turn on the lights. She misses cobwebs but that's only because she's so intent on what she's doing she forgets to look up.

I've seen her sewing on buttons in the dark, refinishing banisters, painting, scraping, organizing, cleaning. I ask her why she works in the dark. *"Je ne sais pas, Madame Loomis,"* she says with a smile, "I don't know why, Madame Loomis," and continues on her way.

I think I know why. I've met lots of older people in France who do much the same thing. I think it dates to before and during World War II when electricity was scarce, then very expensive. It is still outrageously expensive. One look at a French electrical bill and anyone would be tempted to spend their lives in the dark. We've almost gotten used to the price we pay for electricity, and I certainly don't want anyone working with us to feel they can't turn on the lights. I think with Colette it is such an ingrained habit that she never even thinks about it.

Working in the dark is one of those French "things" like the national dislike for Jerusalem artichokes (they were the main staple for most people during World War II), the conviction that all ills result from the liver (though we hear less and less reference to *le foie* than we used to), the belief that tailgating is perfectly safe, and the notion that crying is good for babies because it strengthens their lungs. There is no real sense in arguing about any of these things, nor in trying to change anyone's opinion. It's part of the national character and you have to love it or ignore it.

I can usually tell where Joe is simply by following the trail of roller blades, the basket with his shoes and the part of his snack he didn't eat in it, and whatever outer clothes he was wearing. These generally end at the dining room table where he is leaning or sitting, reading something, whether his monthly subscription to *J'aime Lire,* a lively compendium of stories, cartoons, and games, or *Mickey Parade*, a fat comic book starring Mickey, Donald, and Scrooge.

I always check the smell of the house, which ranges from temptingly delicious and herbal to dusty and sometimes mildewed. When it is the former it means I've been cooking and the food aromas have lingered. When the latter, it means Michael has been at hard physical labor, digging into the bowels beneath our house where over the course of the years he has found parts of old stone sinks, chunks of the house's foundation, gravestones, and even animal bones. Or it might mean that he was wrestling with the chimney, which he completely dismantled before rebuilding.

I poke my head into whatever room Michael is working in to say hello, though I don't always see what he is doing. I look, but I don't see—perhaps because I do it on the fly, or maybe because the messes are always so major that I can't stand to really look. This is what happened while he was working in the dining room, the long room on the ground floor of the house whose end window looks right at the church, and outside of which stands the "holy stone."

The room is long and narrow, about twenty-three by twelve feet and set at an L to the rest of the house. It has white stone walls about one-fourth of the way up, then timbered walls the rest of the way. A brick chimney angles up one end of the room to the ceiling, and the floor is ochre concrete with the tracings of a carpet design in it that Michael did, for fun.

Before the concrete floor was poured our entire ground floor was paved in gravel. It was an improvement over the dirt and rubble we had found at first, and our friends had found it chic. One couple rushed home after visiting us to call their architect and see how they, too, could have gravel on the floor of their house.

But I loved it when that hard concrete went in. It was clean, and it allowed us to move into the room and use it. The floor heat took off the chill. It wasn't exactly cozy—the fireplace would help, and so would plugging up the random holes throughout the room—but it was eminently livable.

About a year after the floor was poured Michael was ready to "attack" the room and fix it up. He hung a heavy curtain at the doorway, which connected the room to the rest of the house, and that was the last I saw of it in its cleaned-up state. The next time I walked in it was a work site, as he set about building inner walls that resemble the outer walls so that he could tuck insulation between them. Those first days of work on a previously lived-in room are always a bit discouraging. We seal ourselves off from a certain pattern we've established and crowd into the rooms that are livable. And we get used to the fine old dust that settles on everything no matter how careful Michael is to seal it in.

I tend to stay away from the work sites for several reasons. When Michael works he's a loner, so involved in what he's doing that he doesn't like interruptions. I learned that during the years he sculpted full-time. The atmosphere of his studio was always intensely personal, as if he were encased in transparent steel—untouchable, unreachable. It is much the same in the house though less peaceful, for he can't often control what he's going to be doing. He will uncover one wall intending to do one thing, only to find that its support has been eaten away over the years by wood-loving insects, which requires him to replace all the wood, or reorient his work so that he can avoid a pitfall. Nothing is simple or straightforward, or even straight. The angles are always off, and nothing matches. All of this, while enormously challenging, is also often enormously annoying, one more reason not to disturb him at his work.

But of course it is impossible to stay away. So I peek in and sometimes wander around, looking. I walked into the room one day, braving the dusty turmoil. Michael isn't a full-time smoker, resorting to cigarettes only when confronted with a particularly knotty problem. This day he was smoking, so I doubted he was in a conversational mood, but I was curious about what he was doing. I walked gingerly about. Michael is an extremely orderly worker, but there are still life-threatening traps everywhere for the uninitiated—boards with ugly nails sticking out of them, piles of rubble here and there, gullies where he's had to dig into the concrete to bury something, stacks of pale white local rock he was using to rebuild the lower wall, bags of ochre to dye the plaster, bags of plaster which, if one should somehow fall on a foot or a leg, would crush it.

Then I just stood and looked around; the stone foundation wall that runs around the bottom fourth of the room was taking shape. He was currently tapping on the lovely, local white stone he was using for it, which he had gone to great effort to salvage, using his sculpture techniques to make the pieces the exact size he needed while keeping them natural looking. This work approached sculpture and while it was slow, tedious going, I could sense his satisfaction in it. He'd been working on the room for several months at that time, having completed a stone wall at one end of the room near the fireplace, which previously had been dirty and uneven and now was pristine and lovely, all of the wiring, and now a good part of this small stone wall.

I marveled at what he had already accomplished. I never understand space myself, and I am in awe of his talent. He looks at a rough, dirty, unfinished space and almost immediately figures out how to make it functional and beautiful. When he's in the midst of it, as he was now, his hair white with stone dust, tools everywhere, the two pieces of furniture in the room covered in white cloth looking like misplaced polar bears, his mind is fixed, intent on the challenge before him.

I looked at all he had done—the walls, the floor, the ceiling—and my eyes rested on a face carved into one of the support beams. Hmm, I thought to myself. I don't remember seeing that before. I walked closer, to look at it. It grew organically out of the dark beam, an ancient-looking face with slightly Asiatic features; its eyes seemed both opened and closed. It was calm and quite beautiful. I felt silly for not having seen it before, caught once again in my unobservant state.

"That face is gorgeous," I said to Michael, who had stopped tapping for a minute. "When do you think it was done?" He took off his goggles and asked me to repeat what I'd said, so I did. He laughed.

105

TRANSFORMATIONS

"I did it," he said. "About two months ago. I was so frustrated with the electrical wiring and the beams and the way things wouldn't come together that I just had to do something." I looked up at the face. Most people, in a similar situation, might have run out of the house screaming or strangled the first person who came in the room. The kind of frustration I know Michael experienced wasn't mild. It was the "goddamned frigging stupid little wires and dumb little lights" kind of frustration that, though silent, shakes the windowpanes. His solution was to carve a beautifully restful face in a support beam.

It gave me a shiver. Michael is deeply talented, I know that. But to create something so lovely by making use of frustration takes something more than talent. To me it was an expression of hope, of commitment, of beauty amidst mayhem.

While Michael was working on the electrical wiring for this room I could tell it intrigued as much as maddened him. Each phase of this house is the same as he tussles his way through it, finding the appropriate materials and figuring out how to use them. For this room, he had discovered an inexpensive source for spotlights, each of which required rewiring before he could use it, which he did in his painstaking fashion. Then he decided to embed them right into the old, thick, wavy beams in the ceiling, which took forever, and everyone who sees them is amazed. While we have to get approval from the office of historic monuments for any changes we make to the outside of our house, we are free to do as we like on the inside, so Michael works unfettered.

It took Michael a year to finish the room as he built walls, plugged up holes, mixed up pale ochre-colored plaster to fill in between the timbers, pointed the brick chimney, rebuilt the fireplace box, and made the room an elegant work of art. When visitors walk in they are astounded by its beauty. Then, to really wow them, Michael turns on the lights, a hallmark of his work. He doesn't just install an electrical system, he installs the most complex and efficient electrical system he can, and since he's not an electrician, and particularly not a French electrician, he's learning as he goes.

There are twelve switches that control the spots, so the mood can be somber, elegant, or brightly lit. Delighted with the result, Michael loves to give a light show.

Guests inevitably notice the face in the beam. I often catch them looking at it. They assume that it is ancient, considering it one more marvel of this marvelous house. When they find out it is Michael's work, they realize how much he has made this house his own.

NORMANDY MUSSELS
MOULES À LA NORMANDE

The waters off the coast of Normandy are filled with sweet mussels and we eat them often. I like this preparation with its local hallmark of cider vinegar, which sets off perfectly the sweetness of the mussels. Serve these in Norman fashion, with plenty of fresh bread and sweet butter and hard cider.

6 pounds/3kg mussels
1 cup (about 10g) firmly packed flat-leaf parsley
2 small shallots, sliced in half then cut in paper-thin slices
4 dried, imported bay leaves
¼ cup/60ml cider vinegar
Sea salt and freshly ground black pepper

107

1. Just before cooking the mussels de-beard them. (To de-beard mussels, gently but firmly pull out the byssus, or group of fine threads that hang from their shells.) Rinse them well in cool fresh water and place them in a large stockpot. Coarsely chop the parsley and add it, along with the shallots, bay leaves, and cider vinegar. Shake the pot so that all the ingredients are blended, and bring the liquid to a boil over high heat. When it is boiling reduce the heat to medium-high and cover the pot. Cook the mussels until they just open, shaking the pan from time to time so the mussels cook evenly. Once the mussels are open, continue to cook for an additional minute, checking the mussels frequently and removing those that are wide open so they don't overcook. If, after 2 to 3 minutes there are mussels that refuse to open, discard them as they are either dead or empty.

2. Transfer the cooked mussels to a large serving bowl, or simply return all of the mussels to the stockpot. Season them generously with salt and pepper and serve.

6 TO 8 SERVINGS

THE FISH MERCHANT'S STUFFED CABBAGE LEAVES
CHOUX FARCIS À LA POISSONIÈRE

This is a winter specialty from Aline Aubé, owner with her husband, Olivier, of the Poissonerie du Centre in Louviers, on rue Général de

Gaulle. Each day Aline makes a half dozen different dishes to tempt her customers, using whatever fish is abundant and in season. One day she offered these tempting little packets, which customers were buying so fast I decided I'd better try them, too. Mme Aubé carefully placed the last two in a container for me, then scooped up the remaining cream sauce intended to bathe them. She looked at them, decided there wasn't quite enough cream, and added a generous dollop more from a bowl that sits in ice on her fish counter.

I reheated the dish gently at home and we all loved its delicate flavor, such a departure from the traditional hearty meat-filled stuffed cabbage. I asked Mme Aubé what gave her the idea for this unusual dish.

"When you work with fish all day long and love it the way I do, you naturally think about using it everywhere," she said modestly. "This dish simply made sense to me, and our customers love it."

Though Mme Aubé bathes the fish-stuffed cabbage leaves with cream for her customers, when she makes them for her family she drizzles them simply with lemon juice. I like a combination of both, first drizzling the little packets with lemon juice, then with a bit of cream. I have adapted Mme Aubé's recipe by adding a touch of lemon zest to the filling.

Serve this with a lightly chilled Sauvignon Blanc.

1½ pounds/750g fish fillets, preferably lingcod, flounder,
    cod, or whiting, bones and skin removed
1 shallot, minced
¾ cup/180ml *crème fraîche*
Sea salt and fresh finely ground black pepper
6 large, pale green inner leaves savoy cabbage

Zest of 1 untreated lemon, minced
2 tablespoons/30ml freshly squeezed lemon juice

1. Place the fish, shallot, half the *crème fraîche*, and a generous sprinkling of salt and pepper in the workbowl of a food processor and process until homogeneous and elastic, which will take a minute or two. Cook a teaspoonful of the filling in a small pan over medium heat and taste it for seasoning. Adjust if necessary.

2. Prepare a large bowl of ice water. Bring a large pot of salted water to a boil over high heat. Add the cabbage leaves and cook them just until they lose their crispness, but not until they become limp, 2 to 3 minutes. Carefully remove the leaves from the water and transfer them to the ice water. Leave them in the ice water just long enough for them to completely cool off. Carefully transfer them from the water to a surface covered with a tea towel, and pat off any excess water.

3. Gently smooth out the cabbage leaves on a work surface. Trim away the thickest part of their stems. Divide the lemon zest in thirds. Reserve two-thirds for the packets, and stir the other one-third into the remaining *crème fraîche*.

4. Divide the fish filling into 6 equal-size portions. Place one portion of the filling in the center of a cabbage leaf. Sprinkle some of the reserved lemon zest over the fish filling, then fold the cabbage leaf over it to completely enclose it. If the leaves threaten to come apart, keep them closed with a skewer. Repeat with the remaining fish filling, cabbage leaves, and lemon zest.

5. Bring water to a boil in the bottom of a steamer and place the packets in the steamer, seam side down. Cover and steam until the fish filling has turned completely opaque and is cooked through, about 20 minutes.

6. While the packets are steaming, place the *crème fraîche* with the lemon zest in a small saucepan over very low heat so that it heats just to the steaming point. It should not boil.

7. To serve, place one packet in the center of a warmed dinner plate. Squeeze about 1 teaspoon lemon juice over the packet, then pour on about 1 tablespoon of the hot *crème fraîche*. Sprinkle with sea salt and serve immediately.

6 FIRST-COURSE SERVINGS

HEARTY LAMB STEW
CIVET D'AGNEAU

This recipe comes from my butcher, Jean-Louis Richard, and it is an uncommonly delicious treatment for lamb. Monsieur Richard uses what he calls the "lesser pieces" of lamb like the collar and the shank for this dish, which are ideal for long, slow cooking because they are fattier and more flavorful than standard cuts like the shoulder or the leg. You can use shoulder or leg, however, but be sure to check the dish frequently and add water as it cooks so it doesn't dry out. Serve a lush Bordeaux with this dish.

3 pounds/1.5kg lamb, shank and/or collar, cut into
    2-inch/5-cm pieces
1 bottle/750ml hearty red wine, such as a Minervois from
    the Languedoc
2 dried, imported bay leaves
20 sprigs fresh thyme
20 black peppercorns (preferably Tellicherry)
3 tablespoons/45g unsalted butter
2 medium carrots, peeled, trimmed, and cut in very thin
    rounds
1 large onion, cut in paper-thin slices
3 tablespoons/25g all-purpose flour
Fine sea salt and freshly ground black pepper
½ cup/5g loosely packed flat-leaf parsley, for garnish

1. Place the lamb in a shallow, nonreactive baking dish, and
pour the wine over it—it should be about ½ inch/.75cm deep in
the dish. Add the herbs and the peppercorns, stir, cover, and
marinate for 48 hours in the refrigerator, stirring occasionally so
the pieces marinate evenly. Remove the lamb from the refrigerator at least 1 hour before you plan to bake it.

2. Preheat the oven to 425° F/220° C/gas 8.

3. Remove the lamb from the marinade and pat it dry.
In a large skillet, melt the butter over medium heat and
lightly brown the lamb on all sides. Remove the lamb
from the pan and add the carrots and onion and cook,

stirring, until they are slightly golden and beginning to soften, about 5 minutes.

4. Remove the vegetables from the pan and stir in the flour. Cook, stirring, until the flour is bubbling and golden, at least 2 minutes. Pour the marinade and herbs into the pan and cook, stirring, just until the mixture thickens slightly.

5. Place the lamb (with any juices it has given up) and the carrots and onions in the same baking dish that the lamb marinated in, arranging them in an even layer. Season with salt and pepper and pour the thickened marinade over it. Bake, covered, until the lamb is very tender and can just about be cut with a spoon, 1 hour to 1 hour and 15 minutes.

6. Remove from the oven and let cool for 5 minutes.

7. Mince the parsley and sprinkle over the lamb just before serving.

6 SERVINGS

MAMIE JACQUELINE'S CHOCOLATE CAKE
GÂTEAU AU CHOCOLAT DE MAMIE JACQUELINE

One of Joe's friends, Florian, accompanies us on vacation from time to time and his grandmother often sends along a little treat for us all. This cake was an offering once and we tucked into it the minute we arrived at our destination. It was tender and delicious. When we returned, I asked Mamy Jacqueline for her recipe and she scoffed, "Oh, that simple little cake?" When I pressed she rattled off the ingredients by heart. A surefire success whenever I make it, you need only serve it simply sprinkled with confectioners' sugar.

¾ cup/100g cake flour
Sea salt
7 ounces/200g bitter chocolate,
    such as Lindt 70%
8 tablespoons/125g unsalted butter, softened
1 cup/200g sugar
4 large eggs, separated
Confectioners' sugar

1. Butter and flour a 9½-inch/24-cm round cake pan. Preheat the oven to 375° F/190° C/gas 5.

2. Sift the flour and a generous pinch of salt onto a piece of parchment paper.

3. Melt the chocolate in the top of a double boiler over medium-high heat. Transfer the chocolate to a medium-size bowl and whisk in the butter until the mixture is smooth. Vigorously whisk in all but 1 tablespoon of the sugar, then add the egg yolks and whisk until the mixture is smooth. Using a

wooden spoon, stir in the flour mixture 1 tablespoon at a time until combined.

4. In a large bowl whisk the egg whites with a pinch of salt until they are foamy and begin to thicken. Add the remaining tablespoon of sugar and continue whisking until they form soft peaks. Fold the egg whites into the chocolate mixture, then turn it into the prepared baking pan and bake in the center of the oven until the cake springs back, 20 to 25 minutes.

5. Remove the cake from the oven and let it cool to lukewarm in the pan, then turn it out onto a rack to cool thoroughly. To serve, sprinkle it with confectioners' sugar.

6 TO 8 SERVINGS

SIX

Mornings in Louviers

LOUVIERS IS MAGIC in the mornings. In winter when I wake up and walk downstairs I look outside at the church, which is a mass of shadows and shapes against the dark blue sky. Our little garden is snug in front of the house, the apple trees snaky forms against the dramatic backdrop. A few early risers drive by on their way to work. Part of the magic is that the house is warm inside, something I never take for granted having lived here before the furnace was installed.

Our stairways are wood except the very last step, which is made of local white stone. I love walking barefoot down the cool wood stairs, hitting the cold stone stair, then putting my foot on the brushed concrete floor, which is warmed from underneath by coils of hot water. The contrast feels luxurious.

We all breakfast together in the dining room. If it's very cold, either Michael or I build a fire and its flames flicker on the beamed walls as though we were eating by candlelight. Michael buys a fresh *baguette* every morning and we eat it slathered with Breton butter that is crunchy with sea salt, and either fresh lavender honey or homemade jelly or jam. Many mornings Michael makes hot cereal with a wonderful blend of grains called Mixepi, and we usually have a bowl of *café crème* or tea, and Joe has Banania, a French powdered drink made of chocolate and bananas that is mixed with hot milk. We linger over breakfast until finally it is time for Joe to put on his socks and shoes—we all walk barefoot on our heated floor—and by 8:15 we are usually out the door.

Light is just beginning to brush the winter sky as we walk through the center of town, past Alà Page, the bookstore where the owner, Monsieur Fontaine, and his staff can aways recommend the right book. Down the *rue piétonne*, or pedestrian street, past Le Petit Restaurant, a tiny affair where I read the menu posted outside every day to see if there are any changes. Parents and children are approaching the school from all directions either by car or on foot. The traffic is terrifying as cars swing in and park this way and that, disgorging their charges. I'm always amazed that everyone makes it through the morning alive.

In the springtime after I've dropped off Joe I like to walk home through the Place des Halles, the square in the center of the commercial district just down from Monsieur Richard the butcher, for it is planted with ornamental cherry trees that turn it into a fluffy bower. My favorite pharmacy on the square is just opening and if I need anything I go in then, before it becomes crowded with customers.

Pharmacies in France do a land-office business, as French doctors have a penchant for prescribing large quantities of medicines for the slightest ailment. Our family doctor, a homeopath, is in Paris so we visit him just twice a year for checkups. The rest of the year I call him for advice and treatments, which are always reasonable. For the little incidents of daily life we consult a local doctor who is both a homeopath and a conventional medical doctor, and when Joe is sick in the middle of the night we rely on the doctor on call who comes to the house.

I take any prescription into the pharmacy to discuss it with the pharmacist, whom I've come to know quite well since I see her around town and at school where she drops off and picks up her children. She and her staff are exceptionally warm and friendly and they smile when they see me come in with a prescription, knowing I'll choose not to take most of what is written on it, and often agreeing with me. Sometimes I arrive when they are having coffee and they never fail to offer me a cup.

If I have time in the mornings I love to *lécher la vitrine*, which literally means to "lick the window," or window-shop, at the *parfumerie*, or perfume shop, a boutique with slick, colorful wares. From the minute its doors open it is busy as customers buy their soaps, perfumes, the multiple skin treatments that help French skin look so lovely.

Applying a unique scent is an innate French skill, shared by men and women. I never fail to be fascinated when, for instance, a plasterer friend comes to help Michael work on the house and I catch a whiff of his perfume as we exchange our obligatory four kisses—two on each cheek. Parents as they walk their children to school leave a sweet scent behind them, as do baby-sitters and truck drivers, café owners, and the mayor.

Next to the *parfumerie* is a *graineterie*, a throwback to another era. Half of the quaint old store is filled with animal cages where hamsters and guinea pigs (and sometimes mice) scratch and snuffle or birds chirp, and aquariums where languid fish swim to and fro. The other half is filled with beautiful packages of flower and vegetable seeds, which hang from Peg-Boards. I go in each spring to buy seeds and generally emerge with enough to fill a small farm, my eyes bigger than our garden. Depending on the season, the *graineterie* has tiny lettuce plants outside, or cabbages, or spinach, peppers, or tomatoes alongside flower bulbs and flowering plants, garden tools, pet accessories. We don't have a dog, but if we did we would probably go to the *graineterie* to buy its collar, rawhide or plastic bones, leash, or a tiny plaid coat with four little sleeves for its limbs. Dogs are royalty in France and nothing, but nothing, is too good for them. In fact, Louviers has two grooming salons for dogs and a third in the planning stages, and they administer everything from nail clippings to haircuts.

On Wednesdays when school is out and our regular bakery, Aux Délices de Louviers, is closed, we go to the bakery kitty-corner from the *graineterie* and buy their *pain passion*, a heavy, sturdy crisp-crusted *baguette* that costs a fortune, for it is sold by weight, but which we love. The bakery is so busy it has lines of hungry people outside in the mornings and just before mealtimes as people buy their breads, *quiches*, sandwiches, tarts, and flaky pastries. Some Wednesdays we go to yet another bakery whose *baguette* is also delicious, behind the church on the rue du Quai. The pastries there are tempting and occasionally I buy *chouquettes*, tiny cream puffs with sugar crystals embedded in them, which are a national favorite for a four o'clock *goûter*, or snack. When Joe comes with me he chooses a *beignet* filled with raspberry jelly; a *pépite*, or

119

croissant dough filled with custard and tiny chocolate chips; or a *patte d'ours*, a puff pastry bear claw filled with apples tossed in butter.

When I need organic food, or grains, or naturally scented beauty products, I go across the main square, past the convent of the Sisters of Providence right behind our house, and through the Place des Pompiers (formally known as the Place de la République but since the fire station is there, too, everyone calls it Fireman's Place) to the Maison des Simples, an *herboristerie*, or herb store.

I love opening the old wood and glass door there for it causes a tiny bell to tinkle into the hushed atmosphere, which smells like thyme, lavender, and rosemary. Perhaps it's the effect of the intense herbal aroma in the shop, but everyone inside the Maison des Simples is exceptionally calm.

La Maison des Simples, which means the House of Healing Herbs, isn't easy to describe. It has been at this site for several generations and is a combination of a health food store, a church, a doctor's office, and a place to visit with friends. Many people come in with ailments that they describe to the owner Babette Dewaele or her colleague Marie Thuliez, both trained herbalists, who go right to the old, deep wooden drawers that line an entire wall and begin selecting the dried herbs within. They mix these in a large bowl, which sits on an old-fashioned brass scale, then carefully tip them into plain brown paper sacks. As they explain how to use them to make a tea or a tincture, they write the methodology and dosage on the sack and the client walks away happy and relieved. Nearly half the store is devoted to organically produced food, from baby cereal to fresh vegetables to smoked tofu, and another corner offers organic beauty products with luscious aromas.

When I go to the Maison des Simples I love talking with Babette, who is passionate about food. She and her husband, Jean-Lou, are both remarkable cooks. They are primarily vegetarians, and their delicate and refined food gives vegetarianism a good name. I am particularly enamored with Jean-Lou's vegetable *nems* (spring rolls) and Babette's savory *galettes* and citrus marmalade.

Babette and Marie are both friendly, and their warmth as well as their expertise in healing herbs encourages confidences. I often hear customers confiding in them about health and family troubles and I am constantly amazed at the patience with which both women listen. I once asked Babette if it didn't drive her crazy that so many people poured out their physical and emotional troubles to her. She looked at me and shrugged lightly. "Sometimes it is hard to listen to people's troubles, but it's not just the herbs that heal. People often just need to talk." It doesn't matter what the ailment is, whether a diaper rash or a sore throat, Babette or Marie can offer a treatment or advice.

Monsieur and Mme Fichot at the café across from our house run a thriving, smoke- and coffee-fueled business. A well-dressed and prosperous-looking couple, they spend their days behind the counter of their neo-classic bar pulling *café exprès* or draughts of beer, making deliciously rich hot chocolate, and selling stamps, candies, and pack after pack of cigarettes. Cars are constantly shrieking to an illegal halt in front as driver or passenger jumps out, runs in, and emerges with a pack of Gauloises or Camels. I often see children run in and come out with cigarettes for their parents, and whenever I go in I am immediately surrounded by a warm swirl of choking smoke. The clientele is varied: *habitués* who languidly play pool at one end of the café, businesspeople who stop in for a quick *exprès*, groups of teenagers who nurse Oranginas or *cafés crèmes*.

I go over there when we run out of coffee and are desperate for a cup, or to buy the occasional stamp. We have a friendly relationship with the Fichots and Madame is forever asking me for recipes or giving me one of hers. Her background is Portuguese, which is noticeable in her jet black hair, beautiful white skin, and stately proportions, and in her food, which is fresh, lively, and unusual. We often talk with each other through the gate as she passes our house on her way to run errands or take a breath of fresh air. She doesn't like the smoke-filled atmosphere of the bar but shrugs and says if she wants customers she has to let them smoke.

Across the street and next to the florist is a boutique so tiny it's easy to miss except for the tumble of baskets on the sidewalk that almost obscures the front door. To walk up its two steps and inside the door is to step into a wonderland of *cadeaux*, everything from fine and fragile porcelain de Rouen with its lacy gold and deep blue designs, to stuffed goslings and doll house miniatures. The owner, Brigitte Tois, a cheerful, pretty woman of about fifty who grew up in the store and has literally worked there all her life, has become a good friend. She is always outside in the morning arranging baskets on the sidewalk and when I walk by she carefully removes her glasses and we exchange *bisous* then discuss the weather, the neighborhood, what she will cook for herself and her husband, Alain Pitette, that day.

The shop is called Laure Boutique and it is crammed from floor to ceiling with merchandise. I always find something to buy when I go there—I've purchased glass-topped gilt boxes for graduation gifts, plaster Easter bunnies, chickens and eggs for baskets, Christmas decorations, postcards, gorgeous cut-glass vases from Czechoslovakia, New Year's crackers from Britain, and first-Communion cards. Brigitte has literally everything, and finding it in the shop is never too much trouble. Sometimes she has to pull out a ladder and climb halfway up to the very high ceiling to pull down a tiny little box, or make her way back into her firetrap of a storeroom where she will emerge with the perfect basket, the ideal apron, a wonderfully ridiculous child's toy. Brigitte is the unofficial tourist bureau for Louviers and dispenses free maps of the city as well as plenty of advice on where to go for a picnic, get your hair trimmed, buy a box of matches or a phone card. Once I was looking for an American flag and after twenty minutes of searching she pulled out an old one from a drawer underneath the cash register. "I remembered I had this somewhere," she said as she handed it to me. It was yellowed and delicate with age. When I asked the price she said, "No, I don't want any money. I must have been saving it for you."

Because our house is located in the center of town we often have unexpected visitors, friends who are doing their shopping and have a few moments to spare or want to check on Michael's progress with the house. I hear them crunch over the gravel as they cross the courtyard to knock on the wooden front door. Michael, who is usually downstairs working, answers the door and if I have time I run down to see who it is and say hello. If it's a relaxed day we usually take time for a coffee, sitting outside if the weather is fine, or standing around the kitchen if it isn't. In this way we keep in touch with friends and get to know our neighbors or the local merchants.

We have a varied and eclectic group of friends and acquaintances. Patrick, our neighbor, works for the French phone company and he walks by every day with his tiny dog, Lola, usually on his way to buy cigarettes at the café or a chop at the butcher's. If we're outside he says hello and stays to have a glass of wine. Nadine, who is married to our friend Christian, an architect, and is a very close friend, comes by after the market on Saturday, usually with one or the other of her four gorgeous and now grown children. Babette, the small, rail-thin, and very pretty owner of the *herboristerie* in Louviers, comes over on her way from the bank and usually stays long enough for a cup of coffee and a conversation about recipes.

Annie Grodent, a small blonde fireball of energy, and Joe's very first teacher at the *maternelle,* flies in once in a while for a quick visit, and Soeur Françoise, the keeper of the keys of the church who lives in the convent down the street from us, always greets us through the fence and our rosemary hedge. It took her years to accept an invitation to come into the courtyard, but we finally got her there, and once she even came for Joseph's birthday.

Joseph-Claude Miquel, whose family was one of the wealthiest in Louviers before World War II and the city's textile industry crash, divides his time between painting and giving tours of the church and the town, wearing a deep blue cape and hat in winter, and a cream-colored silk suit in summer. He makes a very distinguished figure as he walks through town, stopping to greet absolutely everyone with a joke or a racy comment, and he invariably opens the door to our courtyard and leans in to wish us well. Old Monsieur Bruhot, who lives in the house adjacent to ours, was born on rue Tatin in 1913, and his bright blue eyes dance when he talks about Louviers and its past, or the five years he spent in a Russian prisoner of war camp during the war (which was a painful experience for him, rife with bravery and bad food, and one he loves to talk about). The food in the camp turned him off onions permanently—amongst other things—and whenever I cook them he lets me know later how much he hates their aroma.

Our cast of characters also includes Lena, a friend from Sweden who has very American—and familiar—attitudes about raising children, and her husband, Bruno, a professional chef; Martine, her brother Jean-Pierre, and her husband, Patrick, who own a farm and just three years ago turned one of its outbuildings into an instantly successful restaurant serving delicious food. Edith's father, Michel, or her Aunt Miche stop by occasionally to check on things as well.

Usually we see these people individually, when they stop by or come for dinner, or when we are invited to their homes. But once or twice a year we assemble everyone for a fête.

The first fête we had included Bernard—who has always been involved in local politics and was the senator from our district for many years—and Edith, Christian and Nadine, a handful of teachers (who seem to come in twos since they meet and marry while still in teacher's school), and a prison guard and his lovely, fun wife. We had a great time, all of us, and Edith called me the following day to thank me.

"You know, normally you would never invite a politician and schoolteachers to the same dinner," she said. I was dumbfounded.

"Why not?" I asked. She explained that politicians, particularly centrists like Bernard, and schoolteachers, who are generally left of the left, don't usually mix.

"But you don't have to worry," she said. "Bernard had a great time and was surprised at how much he liked everyone."

When I spoke with one of the teacher friends later he admitted that he'd been uncomfortable at first—not so much just to be with Bernard, but to be with people whom he considered bourgeois—

but that he'd also been pleasantly surprised. I was shocked, but now that we've lived here for so long and I understand politics a bit better, I wouldn't think of repeating the experience!

We also see a lot of people we know while we work in the garden on Saturday afternoons and Sundays or early summer evenings. We're usually all out there, with Joe jumping on the wooden bridge Michael built him, which has as much play in it as a trampoline, climbing the small apple tree, bouncing his basketball on the postage stamp–size brick entryway. When we first moved in people often stopped to comment on the garden, the flower boxes, the minor changes in the exterior of the house. It was particularly the older generation who noticed, and they would thank us for undertaking the improvements.

As soon as the weather is fine we eat all of our meals out front, and as people walk by and spy us through the fence and the hedge they invariably wave and say *"Bon appétit!"* whether or not we know them. Juliano, our Italian hairdresser from down the street, booms out a *"Ciao!"* as he walks by. Line, who with her husband, Gilles, owns the real estate agency across the street, waves a cheerful hello and often stops in to talk. We see pharmacists, schoolteachers, the mayor, and city council members as they walk by on their way to this meeting or that, or to and from the *épicerie* or bakery. We love the rhythms of the city, the calm of Mondays when shops are mostly closed, the activity of Sunday morning when the bells ring for 11 A.M. mass and people stream in and out of the church, the bustle of the rest of the week as people do their shopping and run their errands.

In many ways Louviers is a dream town for me. Its vibrant streets are lined with clothing boutiques, hardware stores, food shops, pet stores, jewelry shops, florists, a perfume boutique, a handful of makeup/day spa shops, and more coiffeurs than I've ever seen in one place. As a neighbor—whose husband is a coiffeur—told me, the ideal number of coiffeurs is one per thousand inhabitants. Louviers excels with at least twenty-five coiffeurs, and they all seem busy all the time.

Everything I need is within walking or bicycling distance, from the freshest of produce, cheeses, and wines at the *épicerie* next door, to freshly roasted coffee, to dozens of varieties of crisp-crusted, chewy loaves of bread, flaky, buttery pastries, and luscious fruit tarts. An old-fashioned toy store run by a dynamic mother-son team, who seem as enthralled with what they sell as are their customers, has aisles so tiny two people can't pass in them. It satisfies Joe's needs, which are those of most eight-to-ten-year-old boys. He loves *châteaux* and knights and theatrical battles with *épées*, or swords, trading marbles, and a game called *jojos* based on the ancient game of *osselets*, or knucklebones, and all the accoutrements can be had at the toy store, and lots of dreams besides. The town boasts a few stores whose windows look as though they haven't changed since the twenties. Inside one of them I find treasures like old-fashioned cheesecloth, which is so pretty I want to hang it at the window, bolts of ticking once used for pillows but which would make ideal slipcovers (if I only had the time to sew!), old-fashioned, flint-driven stove lighters that I swear by. The owners are a very discreet couple who greet customers at the door and follow them until they've made their choice, acting miffed if no choice is made.

I love the *merceries*, or button and yarn stores, in Louviers, where flat wooden drawers hold treasure troves of embroidery thread in vivid colors, buttons of every shape and size, spools of silken thread, bolts of ribbon, ancient embroidery patterns. The particular store I'm thinking of also carries designer handbags for women and girls, scarves, and an echo of the accessories worn by the well-dressed owner who sits behind a wooden counter, her tan skin glowing, a portable telephone often clamped to her ear as she converses with her husband, gives orders to her children, answers questions from a distant customer.

I also particularly enjoy going into one of the several lingerie shops in Louviers, where the owner, a slender, attractive woman, is always doing five things at once, from helping a customer try on her wares to helping another find what she wants, to advising a man on what to buy for his wife—whom she knows—to hailing a friend walking outside. The lingerie is lovely, the show entertaining!

It takes me five minutes to walk from our house to the butcher, where I get the most flavorful tender lamb and dozens of different cuts of pork, full-flavored chickens, beef, ducks, and guinea fowl, all with incomparable flavor and texture. I've never seen raw meat look as appetizing as it does in this shop. The butcher is usually good for a cooking or butchering lesson, which I get while I'm waiting in line, craning my neck to look past the *pâtés*, the head cheese, and the lasagna that his wife makes.

From watching the tidy, dapper Monsieur Richard, who always wears a carefully knotted tie under his impeccable white apron, I have learned how to trim the fat on a lamb chop so it rests in an attractive curl once cooked. I now know how to tie a loin of pork so it not only holds abundant stuffing but looks graceful on a platter. Through his influence I have come to accept turkey as something more than a bird that is stuffed and roasted; its tender, tasty meat can be braised, stewed with herbs and vegetables, breaded and sautéed. He has taught me to cook young shoulder of lamb longer than a mature shoulder so it is perfectly tender, and whenever I wonder what cut of meat is best he is there to supply the answer and the goods.

One day I was in his shop musing over what to buy for lunch. I often choose his skinny, herb-flecked pork sausages, but that day I wanted something different. He suggested *tripes à la mode de Caen* (tripe cooked in apple cider) and I wrinkled my nose. At his perplexed look I explained that I've never been able to get over the aroma of tripe. He cut a thick slab which he wrapped and gave to me, throwing down a gauntlet. "If you don't like MY *tripes à la mode de Caen*, I'm no butcher," he said, then instructed me on just how to heat and serve it. I accepted the challenge, followed his directions, and both Michael and I, to our immense surprise, were converted.

My latest epiphany at Monsieur Richard's involves chicken. He sells only farm-raised poultry, and when I asked him for one he chose a particularly plump specimen for me, with its head and feet intact. While it is common for the head to be left on, I was surprised to see the feet. "It's true, most people don't eat them anymore, but I refuse to cut them off," he said. "They're delicious. My brothers and sisters and I fought over them when we were kids."

I expected him to simply weigh and wrap up the bird and hand it to me with the bill, but no. First he had some work to do. He carefully burned away the invisible (to me) pinfeathers and proceeded to sear the feet with a tiny propane flame. "Makes them

129

more tender," he explained as he scraped and trimmed them. He turned the bird this way and that, inspecting it minutely, trimming it, patting it, arranging it so that, once trussed, it would make a compact oval. When he was finished with the bird it looked as though it had spent two hours at a spa. I was entranced. Monsieur Richard carefully wrapped it in his signature red and white waxed paper and handed it to me so I could tuck it in my basket. I went home to roast it and it not only looked gorgeous but was exceptionally flavorful and delicious.

Across from the butcher is the *poissonerie*, a chilly, blue-tiled, mirrored-ceilinged shrine to the sea. Depending on the season there are sweet triangular skate wings with their slimy spotted skin; pearly white fillets of cod; *julienne*, a cod-like fish; regal, nutty-flavored little sea bass with their deep blue side stripe; and always a fillet or pile of salmon steaks, usually from the fjords of Norway and generally bland as water. More exciting are the tiny little squid or the miniature monkfish tails. When I spy these I get them, for they are too rare to pass up. At least to an American. Baby monkfish tails are limited to a very short season and their meat is so tender yet firm, so white, and so lightly sweet that I can never resist them. I love them prepared as simply as possible, usually rolled in flour and sautéed in butter. The tiny squid I either sauté or deep-fry in olive oil and serve with a piquant vinaigrette. What delicacies! There is always a table out front of the *poissonerie* with rustic baskets filled with at least three different sizes of oysters, two different varieties of blue-black mussels, and tiny, plump, wavy-shelled clams. Shellfish is my *péché mignon*, or downfall, and I often succumb to a couple dozen oysters or a liter or two of clams and mussels.

The *poissonier*'s wife makes a handful of dishes that sit proudly on the sidelines inside the shop, near the live lobster tank. They change every day, depending on what is fresh or what needs to be cooked. In the winter there is always a scallop dish, usually drowned in cream and garnished with golden bread crumbs. There is almost always a seafood *quiche*, often a marinated shellfish salad, and sometimes little puff pastry *bouchées* or cups filled with either white fish or crabmeat or chunks of lobster. Each dish is available by the serving and they all look delicious. I'm sure they are since by late afternoon not a spoonful of any of them is left.

There are *charcuteries*—the French version of a take-out, which specialize in pork creations, from *pâtés* and sausages to stuffed roast pork—about every hundred yards it seems. It may be that they hold a constant competition for the most appetizing window display for they seem to outdo each other. There are the cone-shaped, bread crumb–dusted *jambonneau*, a braised pork hock that has been rolled in bread crumbs and is intended to be eaten cold and thinly sliced. There is head cheese enclosed in gelatin, *pâtés* with strips of bacon and bay leaves on top, tripe stewed with carrots and herbs, near-black coils of blood sausage, fat white sausages flecked with wild mushrooms or truffles, and air-dried *saucissons*, *quiches*, or tiny little tomato pizzas with puff pastry crust. Then there are all the other tempting dishes like seafood terrines and freshly made salads . . . the offerings go on and on. On days when I'm not in the mood for cooking I go to one or the other of the *charcuteries* and buy a pizza, a slab of *coulibiac* (salmon in a crust), some *boudin blanc* sausage, or a huge square of *gratin de pomme de terre* so rich with cream that a little goes a long way. We could eat from the *charcuteries* every day for months and never try the same thing, for the dishes change with the seasons.

At one of the *charcuteries* on the way to school, individual pizzas baked with an egg right in the center look tempting in the morning, as do the *crêpes* filled with creamed spinach, and the little puff pastry *chaussons* that bulge with aromatic sausage meat. And this particular *charcutier* must have a love affair with gelatin for he makes dozens of fanciful creations where gelatin is a main ingredient. Joe and I often stop to look at them, marveling at the tall, skinny cones with green peas floating in slightly golden gelatin above a bed of rich pink salmon and under half a hard-cooked egg. With their mayonnaise decorations, these appetizers look like they are dressed for the prom. There are brick-shaped ones, too, with slices of sausage and swirls of spinach and almost always, it seems, at least part of a hard-cooked egg. They are more amazing than appetizing. When my older brother, Jeff, visited us, he couldn't get over these fantastic creations with their jewel-like appeal. For his last meal with us I bought four cone-shaped treasures to serve as an appetizer. "Wow," Jeff said. "This is so French." It's true, I thought, where else would anyone take so much time to create something so elaborate as a single appetizer? They weren't the best things we had ever eaten, but they were dramatic.

Perhaps the best part of Louviers, and indeed of living in France, is the Saturday morning farmer's market. Then, the town center turns into a rural fair, a festival of colors, aromas, and sounds as the market unfurls.

Joe and I walk through the market on our way to school, weaving through the boxes of produce stacked in the middle of the street as farmers and vendors prepare their stands. The Portuguese olive vendor gives us a shy smile while Jean-Claude and Monique Martin, my favorite farmers, wave vigorously. Others, if they notice us at all amidst the hubbub, call out a cheerful *bonjour*.

I roll my wicker basket along with me, which causes Joe to die a thousand deaths. "Mama, only old ladies have baskets like that," he says to me under his breath as we go along. I explain to him how I must bring it because I would lose too much time if I went back home to get it, how important it is for me to get my marketing done before the crowds arrive and the lines lengthen, but he doesn't care. "Mama, I'm so embarrassed," he says, cringing.

He leaves me at the door to the schoolyard with a certain relief and I wheel myself back into the fray of the market, eager to assess the produce. I always go directly to the Martins, who have their crates organized before anyone else and are already doing a brisk business. Everyone in Louviers knows their produce is among the best to be had. I join the line of customers, enjoying the tableau before me as Jean-Claude jokes and flirts as he weighs out zucchini blossoms or bunches of mauve-splashed turnips, cuts into a fat pumpkin, or grabs a handful of shallots. Monique is more serious about her work, though she laughs and rolls her eyes a good part of the morning at his charmingly corny humor.

When Jean-Claude spies me his greeting is always the same. "Ah, Susanna! How is America?" Then he leans over for the traditional exchange of *bisous*, a kiss on each cheek.

The Martins' daughter, Myriam, helps as well, and though shy and demure, she can joke right along with her parents if there aren't too many people to serve. She hasn't yet learned the subtle art of comedy and salesmanship, though she's got two of the world's best teachers to guide her along. I leave the Martins, my

MORNINGS IN LOUVIERS

basket bulging with celery root, leeks, carrots so sweet and flavorful I can't wait to grate them for salad, raw beets, which are such a rarity in France where most beets are cooked in the farmer's field and sold ready-to-eat, and heads of *feuille de chêne* lettuce so gorgeous they look like giant reddish-brown roses.

I remain loyal to the Martins because I like them and the quality of their produce is irreproachable, but beyond that I am free-wheeling, without particular allegiances. One cannot afford to become too attached to a vendor because the tableau of produce changes constantly, and while one farmer might be an artist at cultivating radishes, for instance, his curly endive might be less than perfect. I want to be free to buy what is best.

After the Martins, I head directly for the only organic produce stand in the market to inspect what they have. The produce comes from a farm owned by the state and run by indigents who are trained there for re-entry into the workforce, and though the variety is limited, it is of excellent quality. I buy what I can there, then move on. There has been a recent influx of young farmers at the market and one of them, a chubby and cheerful young man who is always shaking his impossibly corkscrew-curly hair from his eyes, cultivates Belgian endive the old-fashioned way, in the soil rather than hydroponically. The fat, ivory torpedo-shaped endives are sweet and bitter and I buy at least two pounds each week while they are in season in winter. He also has luscious potatoes with names like poetry—the amandine, the Mona Lisa, which are smooth and silky as though they had cream in them, and the vitelotte, which are knobby and purple and have the flavor of chestnuts.

There are many chicken vendors, but I always go to a young woman whose plump birds are consistently flavorful. She also has an array of dark-meated *pintades*, or guinea hens, small, succulent rabbits, and an assortment of turkey parts, all equally delicious. Farther along the street is a dynamic young woman whose specialty is *foie gras* and all its offshoots. For a real treat I buy her *magret de canard*, which have the flavor of nutty butter and the texture of a tender, toothsome steak. She advises simple cooking for *magret*. Following her advice I simply sear it over high heat, cook it just until it is rare in the center, then deglaze the pan with cider or balsamic vinegar. It is exquisitely satisfying.

After trying every egg in the market, I've settled on hers as the freshest, for the yolks sit right up when I break them into the pan and they have an incomparably rich flavor. The cream she brings in big buckets drips like fresh paint from her ladle as she transfers it into glass jars and I buy some each week to add to vegetables or soup, include in a pasta sauce, or stir into a dessert.

A goat cheese maker off on a side street is one of the most popular vendors at the market. He dispenses jokes and opinions along with his pure, fresh cheeses, some of which are flavored with shallots, parsley, garlic, or paprika and are at varying stages of maturity. "Hey," he always says to me, bringing a laugh from everyone around. "When is it that you're going to change the laws in America so I can export my cheeses?" We prefer his tender, fresh cheeses, which are perfect for spreading on fresh bread and topping with jam in the mornings.

Another butcher specializing in pork, on the corner across from the Portuguese olive vendor, dresses in a clean white smock and offers gorgeous, hand-cut pork chops, meaty, lightly smoked bacon, and pig's heads—perfect for making head cheese and for causing small children to say *"beurk,"* which is French for "disgusting."

A north African butcher in the center of the market offers nothing but lamb, whose small carcasses swing from the roof of his stall, which is actually the side of his truck that flips up to reveal his "shop" and work counter inside. He will cut whatever piece of lamb you want, to order.

Occasionally I am tempted by the blood sausage at *charcuterie* Guy-Guy, an impressive concern offering everything from home-dried ham to burnished chunks of smoked pork belly called *rillons*, to massive *pâtés* and jellied *pieds de porc*, or pigs' feet. The aroma from his steaming vat of *choucroute* (sauerkraut) vies with that from farm-raised rabbits roasting on spits across the way, and I usually cave in to one or the other for a sumptuous Saturday lunch.

I stop by the cheese stand for runny Camembert and fragrant Livarot, a slab of fruity Comté or Beaufort, or a box of pine-bark-wrapped Vacherin Mont d'Or, a seductively creamy cheese from the mountains, which is only in season for a few short months in winter.

Every third week the olive and almond oil soap man comes and I stock up, and about once a month a shy farmer sets up a card table on a corner and sells fresh and flinty lentils and tender green *flageolets*. They are of such quality that I buy them each time I see them.

When I don't have a week of heavy recipe testing before me I let my desires of the moment dictate my purchases. I often buy *nem*, Vietnamese spring rolls, from a young Asian couple or gorgeous creamy feta cheese and rich-tasting olives from the Turkish vendor in the center of the market.

"*Bonjour, madame,*" he says shyly, extending his hand, now that I'm a regular customer along with all of the Turkish women who are swathed from head to foot, except their faces, as their religion dictates. The north African vendors offer vegetables I can't find anywhere else such as cardoons, skinny Italian peppers, chayote squash, and prickly pears. Sprinkled throughout the market sit elderly women on their hard chairs with an array of chickens, eggs, milk, a rabbit or two, bouquets of rhubarb or Swiss chard, or flowers spread at their feet, there as much for the socializing, it seems, as for the commerce.

As spring arrives one of the corners of the market comes alive with wildflower bouquets sold by a white-haired woman who reminds me of a benevolent children's book character. I'm certain her garden is inhabited by good fairies who make her flowers more beautiful than anyone else's.

The *quiche* truck is a favorite stop at the market. The cheerful woman who runs it, Madeline, is Monique Martin's cousin and the individual *quiches* her husband, Jean-Claude, bakes in the small oven at the back of the truck are tender, custardy, and delicious. They also make apple pound cake and turnovers, raisin flan, and a variety of other simple, homey pastries. We invariably stop there on the way home from school to buy a *quiche* for Joe, which Madeline makes sure is warm but not too hot so he can eat it as we thread our way through the market to home. "How is the young man doing?" she asks if he doesn't happen to be with us, in a conspiratorial air. "Are his grades good? Does he work hard?"

The market is an anchoring aspect of life in Louviers, a true and authentic moment of give-and-take with producers. If ever I grow discouraged at the way "progress" is fanning through France bringing with it supermarkets and fast-food restaurants, vegetables wrapped in plastic, and soft, flabby chickens, I have only to go to the market to feel restored. The farmer's market is the best of France. It is unimaginable that the country and the culture could survive without it.

Whenever we want a break from the city sounds and traffic we all get on our bicycles and race through town and out rue François Camus into the countryside. Within five minutes we're bicycling through wheat and rape fields, past farms and gardens. I often think, as I glide along the road, how lucky we are. Michael and I have lived in Paris, Seattle, and New York, and we love the movement and hum of the city. But right now we couldn't be happier than we are in Louviers, where everything we need is at our fingertips or, at most, an hour's train ride away. And where, when the notion takes us, we can get on a bicycle and leave the world behind.

———————

MARIA'S CHICKPEA SOUP
LA SOUPE AUX POIS CHICHES

Maria Fichot, who, with her husband, Philippe, is the proprietor of Le Progrès, the bustling café across the street from us, loves to cook. Whenever I bump into her or go to the café for stamps or the occasional cup of café exprès *(espresso) we talk food, and her recipes always sound delicious. She mentioned this soup as a family favorite, and it turns out to be one we love, too, for it is simple yet richly flavored. Try a simple Côtes du Rhône with this soup.*

    1 pound/500g chickpeas, rinsed
    1 large onion, cut in quarters

4 whole cloves

5 tablespoons/75ml extra-virgin olive oil, plus additional
   for garnish, optional

3 to 4 quarts/3 to 4 liters filtered water, heated just to the
   boiling point

1 *bouquet garni*
   (4 dried, imported bay leaves, 3 sprigs parsley, several
   sprigs thyme, and 2 green leek leaves, if you have
   them, all tied together with kitchen string)

Fine sea salt

1 head butter lettuce

Freshly ground black pepper

1. Place the chickpeas in a large, heavy-bottomed pan and cover them by 2 inches (5cm) with water. Bring to a boil, remove from the heat, cover, and let sit for 1 hour. Drain, discarding the soaking water.

2. Reserve one quarter of the onion and pierce it with the cloves. Mince the remaining onion and place it, with 1 tablespoon of the oil, in a large, heavy-bottomed saucepan over medium heat. Cook, stirring occasionally, until the onion is translucent, about 15 minutes. Add the chickpeas and stir so they are coated with the oil, then cook them for 1 minute. Add 3 quarts (3 liters) of the water, the *bouquet garni*, and the onion quarter pierced with cloves, stir, cover, and bring to a simmer. Simmer the chickpeas for 1 hour, stirring them occasionally. Season them lightly with salt and continue cooking them until they are tender, for about another hour, adding additional water if necessary to keep them moist.

139

3. While the chickpeas are cooking remove the outer green leaves from the butter lettuce, leaving just the heart intact. Reserve the heart for another use, such as drizzled with vinaigrette and eaten as salad. Rinse and pat dry the outer leaves and tear them gently into large, bite-size pieces.

4. When the chickpeas are tender, remove and discard the *bouquet garni* and pass them through a food mill to remove the skins and reduce them to a rough purée. Return the purée to the saucepan and bring it to a simmer over low heat. Whisk in the remaining 4 tablespoons (60ml–¼ cup) olive oil with salt and pepper and season to taste. Just before serving, add the lettuce leaves to the soup, stirring as they wilt, which should take a minute or two—no longer as the ribs of the leaves should still retain a crunch. Serve the soup immediately, with additional olive oil for those who wish to add it to the soup.

6 SERVINGS

BRAISED CHICKEN IN WHITE WINE AND MUSTARD
POULET BRAISÉ AU VIN BLANC ET À LA MOUTARDE

Monsieur Richard, my butcher in Louviers, is nimble with his knife and cleaver, a joy to observe. He dispenses advice and his wife dispenses recipes.

In this recipe the chicken emerges from the oven perfectly crisp on the outside and moist inside; the mustard and wine give it a rich tang, and the onions balance with their sweetness.

The Richards make this dish at home on Sunday nights, and they assure me it is one of their family's favorites. It has become one of ours as well, the ideal kind of dish that is quick to assemble yet emerges tasting as though hours of work went into its preparation.

Serve this with a luscious red Burgundy.

1 cup/250ml light, perfumed white wine such as a
 Sauvignon Blanc
3 tablespoons/45ml Dijon mustard
2 tablespoons extra-virgin olive oil
One 3½- to 4-pound/1.5- to 2-kg chicken with giblets,
 cut in serving pieces
2 medium onions, cut in paper-thin slices
Sea salt and freshly ground black pepper
Flat-leaf parsley, for garnish

1. Preheat the oven to 475° F/245° C/gas 9.

2. In a small bowl, whisk together the wine and the mustard. Reserve.

3. Heat the olive oil in a large, flameproof baking pan or skillet over medium heat and brown the chicken on all sides, 6 to 8 minutes. Remove each piece of chicken from the pan as it browns. Add the onions to the pan, stir, and cook until they are tender and turning slightly golden at the edges, 4 to 5 minutes. Return the chicken to the pan along with the giblets, and season it and the onions with salt and pepper.

141

4. Pour the wine mixture over the chicken and place the pan in the center of the oven. Bake until the chicken is golden on top, about 25 minutes, turn each piece, then continue baking until the chicken is baked through, an additional 20 to 25 minutes.

5. Transfer the chicken to a serving platter. Place the pan over low heat, and, using a wooden spatula, stir the cooking juices in the pan, scraping up any browned bits that have stuck to the bottom. Taste the sauce for seasoning, then pour it evenly over the chicken. Garnish the platter with the parsley and serve.

6 SERVINGS

DUCK BREAST WITH CIDER
MAGRET DE CANARD AU CIDRE

I buy fattened duck breasts at the market quite often and prepare them in a variety of ways. This recipe, suggested to me by the young woman who raises and sells duck at the Louviers market, is one of my favorite ways to prepare it. The hard cider adds both a tang and a sweetness to the duck, which emerges so tender you can almost cut it with your fork.

If you can't get fattened duck breast try this with regular duck breast, or with your favorite cut of steak. (If using steak, moisten the pan with about 2 teaspoons unsalted butter before placing the steak in the pan, and judge the cooking time by the way you like your steak. Steak will cook more quickly than the duck breasts.) Serve this with asparagus and steamed new potatoes, or with young greens dressed in olive oil and lemon juice.

A full-bodied red, such as a St-Joseph from the Côtes du Rhône, is the perfect accompaniment.

NOTE: Duck breast toughens if overcooked, so do not cook it beyond rare.

Two 13-ounce/390-g fattened duck breasts
Fleur de sel or fine sea salt and freshly ground black pepper
1 cup/250ml hard cider

1. Heat a heavy skillet over medium heat. When it is hot but not smoking, place the duck breasts in it, skin-side down. Cover and cook them until the skins are deep golden, about 8 minutes. Turn the duck breasts and cook them for 2 to 3 minutes on the flesh side, then remove them from the pan. Drain off all of the fat and return the duck breasts to the pan, skin-side down. Continue cooking them, covered, just until the meat is done on the outside, but is still very rare inside, 5 to 6 additional minutes. Remove the duck breasts from the pan and season them with fleur de sel and pepper. Add the cider to the pan, scrape up any browned bits from the bottom, and reduce the cider by about half, until it is slightly syrupy, 4 to 5 minutes.

2. To serve the duck breasts, cut them crosswise on the bias into thin slices and arrange these either on a warmed platter or four warmed plates. Drizzle the slices with the cider sauce and serve immediately.

4 SERVINGS

TINY BAKED POTATOES WITH CREAM
POMMES DE TERRE EN ROBES DE CHAMPS

It was a chilly, post-Christmas morning at the Louviers market, and I was in the mood for potatoes. Standing at Jean-Claude and Monique Martin's stand I surveyed the varieties they offered. When I saw the small charlottes (similar to Yukon Gold) that were about the size of a fat thumb I knew they would be my choice.

Jean-Claude carefully chose a kilo all about the same size when I told him I planned to bake them. A woman waiting in line next to me made an appreciative sound at my idea and offered me a recipe. "I precook the potatoes, then open and stuff them with crème fraîche *and chives," she said.*

I decided to leave out the precooking step. I simply scrubbed the potatoes and baked them in a hot oven until their skins were golden and they were tender, then followed her instructions. Now I prepare these fabulous morsels at the same time I am baking Braised Chicken in White Wine and Mustard (page 140). I place the chicken in the oven and after 15 minutes I place the potatoes on the floor of the oven and bake them right along with the chicken. The timing is usually just perfect, but if the potatoes take a bit longer than the chicken it doesn't matter—the chicken simply needs to be kept warm as they finish.

NOTE: You can make a slightly lighter version of these with butter and parsley.

1½ pounds/750g small (about 2 ounces/60g each) baking
potatoes, such as Yukon Gold or Yellow Finns, scrubbed

1 bunch chives (about 10g) or a mixture of herbs
    such as fennel fronds, garlic chives, chives, and
    chervil
Fine sea salt and freshly ground black pepper
$^1/_4$ cup/60ml *crème fraîche*

1. Preheat the oven to 475° F/245° C/gas 9.

2. Place the potatoes on a baking sheet leaving room between
them, and bake them in the center of the oven until their skins
are golden and they are completely tender through, 45 minutes to
an hour (the baking time will depend on the freshness and variety of the potatoes).

3. Just before removing the potatoes from the oven,
mince the herbs (you should have about $^1/_3$ cup minced
herbs).

4. Remove the potatoes from the oven and transfer them to a
warmed serving platter. Quickly cut a deep slit down the length
of each. Working as quickly as possible, squeeze the ends of
each potato toward the center, to open it up. Season the potatoes
lightly with salt and pepper, then place a generous teaspoon of
crème fraîche in each potato. Sprinkle the potatoes with the herbs.
Serve immediately.

6 TO 8 SERVINGS

GOAT CHEESE WITH RASPBERRY VINEGAR AND LAVENDER HONEY
FROMAGE DE CHÈVRE AU VINAIGRE DE FRAMBOISES ET AU MIEL DE LAVANDE

Jean-Lou Dewaele, a friend whose wife, Babette, owns a popular herb and organic food boutique in Louviers, created this lovely combination of flavors using goat cheese from the market in Louviers and his homemade raspberry vinegar. He served it to us one night as part of the cheese course. I often follow his lead now, for it is a fresh surprise on a cheese platter. It is so tasty that sometimes, when it is just family, I serve it as dessert. We all love it.

2 medium-size fresh goat cheeses (about 11 ounces/330g total)
2¹/₂ teaspoons raspberry vinegar
1 tablespoon/15ml lavender honey

1. Place the goat cheese in a medium-size bowl and, using a fork or a sturdy whisk, mix in the raspberry vinegar. Pack the cheese into molds that have been rinsed in water first (so the cheese is easily removed from the mold), or simply into a small dish, and refrigerate for several hours or overnight.

2. At least 30 minutes before serving, remove the cheese from the refrigerator and remove it from the mold if you have used one. Just before serving, heat the honey just enough so that it liquefies (if it has solidified), and pour it over the goat cheese.

Alternatively, you may want to make quenelles of the goat cheese by forming it into ovals using 2 soup spoons, arranging 2 to 3 ovals on each of 6 serving plates, then drizzling each serving with an equal amount of honey.

6 SMALL SERVINGS

SEVEN

Chez Clet

IT NEVER FAILS that as I get ready to cook in the evening I discover I'm missing an essential ingredient. It shouldn't really matter—improvisation is the mother of fabulous dishes. But I'm usually testing recipes and adhering to a schedule, and I need what I need right away. Luckily I can solve the problem by walking out the courtyard, turning the corner, and walking in the door of Chez Clet.

Chez Clet is the neighborhood *épicerie*, or grocery store, one of the two in the center of town. It opens early and stays open until 8 P.M., perfect for emergencies. The glass-fronted façade opens up, and crates of fruits and vegetables are stacked on the sidewalk and sometimes in the street when there is a particular abundance, providing a tempting and aromatic panorama of fruits and vegetables.

Monsieur Clet, the owner, often finds a bumper crop of something at the wholesale market when he goes there on Tuesday mornings and it will then become part of the seasonal displays. It might be rosy-hued, furry-skinned apricots in the summer, intended for jam. In winter it might be *pot au feu* vegetables—fat bunches of leeks, purple-tinged turnips, crates of yellow onions, occasionally even rutabagas, a rarity here.

Protocol is strict at Chez Clet in the old style. It is understood that the customer looks but doesn't touch, and the salespeople are carefully trained to provide the customer with the best there is. To that end, service is relatively slow as each item is carefully examined before being put in a small brown paper sack, weighed, then set carefully in a wooden crate or whatever receptacle is preferred by the customer. I don't mind waiting. I enjoy watching whomever is helping me carefully inspect each peach, push back lettuce leaves to be sure the center of the head is white and fresh, squeeze a cucumber to be sure it is firm. It is a pleasure to know that when I get home and open my bag I'll find only the best.

François Clet, the owner of Chez Clet, is a moody, energetic young man who rushes about the store, a pencil in his ear and a furrow on his brow. His assistant, Alain, a short man with puffy, curly hair, is the store's jokester, often saying things to himself that are funny and which often earn him a laugh from the customers. The glint of a gold side tooth adds an extra sparkle to his smile and he has an infectious laugh.

Another manager, Isabelle, is an attractive woman with a tough style. She answers curtly and goes about her work with the look of a drill sergeant—which in a sense she is. For the rest of the staff at Chez Clet is made up of *stagiaires*, or apprentices, who work there for a period of time—generally from one to three years—as part of their education at a local technical school, and it falls mostly to Isabelle to ride herd on them. And no one, but no one, messes with Isabelle. I have the inside scoop on her, though, because our sons are playmates and I know her to be kind.

The *stagiaires* are one of the best things about Chez Clet. All young women, they are always eager, perfectly dressed, and shyly polite at first. As the year progresses and they become familiar with the store, the customers, and the humors of Monsieur Clet they relax. I often go into the shop in mid-afternoon, a slow time, and find them shouting jokes or playful insults to each other across the store. When they see me they instantly sober up and become the picture of professionalism. *"Oui, madame, qu'est-ce que vous voulez, madame?"*

Quarters in the store, which is very long and narrow and sandwiched between two other businesses, are very close. Monsieur Clet and Alain tend to bump into each other while they work, with arms and repartee flying. Isabelle and the rest of the staff try to stay out of their way. The situation is complicated by the fact that the *stagiaires* aren't allowed to ring up purchases when they first begin working at Chez Clet. They can only serve, then a customer must wait until one of the permanent staff, or one of the more senior *stagiaires*, is available to handle the checkout. This creates a logjam at the registers as a *stagiaire* hangs back with her carefully chosen produce, waiting for just the right moment to grab someone who can ring it up for her. The minute she hands over that responsibility she's back into the fray with a new customer, fielding questions, gently prodding fruit and vegetables, fetching liters of milk, pounds of butter, weighing out chunks of cheese, or ladling thick fresh cream into containers. When the goods are rung up the *stagiaire* has to stop what she is doing and return, hand over the produce to the customer, help the person out of the store if necessary, and politely and at great length say good-bye. During all of this time, the customer who was being assisted by the *stagiaire* waits. Most of the customers are regulars and accept the elaborate dance that is shopping at Chez Clet. Only once have I seen a customer react negatively. He must have been from out of town—I had never seen him before. Handsome and well dressed, he had a clutch of items in his hand as he waited for someone to help him. Everyone at Chez Clet was deeply into their usual routine of stepping forward, then stepping back, waiting, joking, laughing, and teasing when finally the man boomed, "You all may have all day but I'd like to get waited on."

A silence fell over the store. Without looking at the man, Alain said out of the corner of his mouth, loud enough for everyone to hear, "Well, some people certainly are impatient."

The man replied, without looking at Alain, "That's right I'm impatient and I want to buy some mushrooms."

"Well, some people just don't know how to wait," replied Alain, to no one in particular.

"I don't have time to wait, and you shouldn't be making me wait," the man replied, to no one in particular.

This went on for several more minutes, with each man addressing the air. Finally, a trembling *stagiaire* stepped in, helped the man, and got his things rung up. He fumed out the door, head down.

CHEZ CLET

"These Parisians shouldn't even come here," Alain said. "They don't any of them know anything about how to live."

Whether or not the man was a Parisian I will never know, but Alain's remark caused many indulgent smiles throughout the store.

Watching other shoppers is almost as entertaining as watching the staff. There are those without budgetary concerns who stand and point at this and that, call Monsieur Clet "François" in syrupy tones, and often have a tiny, furry dog at the end of a leash. Then there are the many men who shop at Chez Clet, a category unto themselves. I'm always curious about them—do they do the cooking? Do they simply come with lists written out by their wives? They are gourmands one and all, this I can vouch for after seven years of observing them. Listening to the men as they request ingredients is often a lesson in seasonal cooking, as they are even more punctilious than their female counterparts.

When Monsieur Clet isn't to be found on the ground floor or in his small office upstairs, he is downstairs in the chilly, gravel-floored wine cellar, his pride and joy. He adores taking a customer there to show it off, to give his advice, to share his excitement over a new find, or a rare bottle. His shelves are heavily stocked with Bordeaux, what I call the wine of Normandy. Normandy doesn't actually produce wine—the locally produced beverage is hard apple cider. But since Normandy was a stop on the historic trade route between Bordeaux and London, Bordeaux is the wine most Normans know and drink. Michael and I have a preference for Côtes du Rhône and Burgundy, but we welcome the chance to learn about Bordeaux, so when we are in the mood for something new and different, I go talk with Monsieur Clet.

I'm not only a regular at Chez Clet, but some days I go in there three or four times as I develop a menu. Occasionally I've forgotten my purse at home or don't have quite enough change. This is not a problem. My debts are written in a leather-bound accounting book under the name *L'Américaine*, or The American Woman. It took at least three years for it to dawn on anyone at Chez Clet that I had a name. When they finally asked me what it was and I told them, I was Madame Loomis for two years after that. Finally, I became Suzanne, though for purposes of tallying debts, I remain *L'Américaine*. I always apologize for my lack of ready cash. The response is always the same. "It is no problem. If you don't pay, we know where to find you."

Learning shopping habits in a different culture took me some time. Milk is a good example. In America, milk is easy to find. When you want it, you go to the store and get a gallon, never thinking twice about its availability. In France, it's another story.

By milk I mean fresh milk, not the thick sterilized milk that tastes like sweet cardboard and is always available here. We use only fresh milk, and we go through a fair amount of it, with *cafés crèmes* and morning cereal. Fresh milk is sold by the liter, which doesn't go very far. We usually discover we've run out in the morning, before school, so either Michael or I run to Chez Clet, which usually opens at 7:30 A.M., to get more, and often we find the shelf bare. One day I asked Isabelle if they would be getting more milk. She looked at me and said, shortly, "No, there won't be any more this week," as though my question was unreasonable. I asked her why. "Because it's only delivered once a week, and when it's gone it's gone, that's why," she responded tersely.

Since they seemed to be out of milk often, I asked her why they didn't order more.

"*Ah, non!*" she replied vigorously, shaking her head. "*Ah, non!* We can only order it by lots of five liters. Yes, perhaps we would sell seven or eight, but then we would lose two, and this is not acceptable. We would lose too much money. *Non.* It isn't possible to do it any other way. If you want milk, you must tell me and I will put it aside for you."

"Ah!" I thought as I left the store, having ordered two liters for the following week. "Another key to the mystery of French culture and thrift."

There are few American foods that we miss, but corn on the cob is one and until recently it was nearly impossible to find. Now I see it occasionally, wrapped in cellophane and never very appetizing. During our second summer here, Chez Clet had some that was displayed proudly out front. Like all the corn I see wrapped in cellophane, it already looked tough, but it was a thrill to see it nonetheless. I didn't buy it, and no one else did either so that by about the fourth day on display it was looking pretty tired. Monsieur Clet still put it out front every day, leaving it in plain sight as it became more and more dry and wizened. By the end of the week it was embarrassing, a blot on the display. I couldn't figure out why Monsieur Clet wasn't throwing it away. I felt I had a duty to help.

I found Monsieur Clet and pulled him aside. "Monsieur Clet," I said in a hushed tone. "I don't like to say this but those ears of corn you've got out there are really an embarrassment." He raised his thick dark eyebrows. "An embarrassment, why what is wrong with them?" he asked me. I tried to explain. "You see, Monsieur Clet, I wouldn't venture to say this if I didn't completely understand corn. When it looks like that, it is inedible."

"Oh, it's inedible," he echoed. "Why do you say that? I thought it was fine."

For a man who has spent his life among produce Monsieur Clet's ignorance about the shelf-life of corn was surprising. On the other hand, corn on the cob is something exotic in France, where it has only recently become available at all.

I forged ahead, explaining about the kernels, the silk, the fine quality of corn when it is fresh, and the sad state it degenerates into when it isn't. "If you want people to respect your store," I said, "you must get rid of that corn. Anyone who knows corn and walks in here and sees that will walk right out again, I assure you."

Monsieur Clet looked at me, frowning. I already knew enough about him to know that if he thought he could sell something, he wouldn't take it off the shelf. I suspect he was asking himself who I thought I was to try and advise him about corn. I could tell he wasn't convinced. So I pulled out both barrels.

"In America we live on corn in the summer," I said. "It is a traditional food, one we all grow up eating as children. All Americans know corn intimately. I am American, and I know corn. I promise you, that corn shouldn't be in a store as fine as yours."

The cultural angle was persuasive. He smiled in understanding, picked up the corn, and tossed it in the trash. "I thank you, Madame," he said and returned to his work. Monsieur Clet continues to stock cellophane-wrapped corn on the cob, though now, if it gets beyond its prime he is quick to remove it from the shelf.

BAKED EGGPLANT APPETIZER
AUBERGINES AU FOUR

Garden-fresh eggplant is a vegetable apart—sweet, tender, and succulent, unlike the bitter supermarket variety. The owner of the sporting goods store down the street from us grows them in her huge garden in Acquigny, about four miles from Louviers, and every now and then she brings me a basket full of them or I get them garden-fresh from Clet. I rush to cook them as quickly as possible for, like any delicate fruit or vegetable, the sooner they are eaten the purer their flavor.

This is one of my favorite things to do with fresh eggplant. I often serve it as a first course in summer, letting the eggplant cool to room temperature if the ambient temperature is very warm. But the contrast between hot eggplant and room-temperature tomato sauce is also appealing.

Serve additional olive oil on the side as well as a Côtes du Rhône.

NOTE: When eggplant are very fresh it isn't necessary to salt them before cooking as they aren't bitter. On the other hand, the skin of under-ripe eggplant is very bitter, so use mature eggplant.

1½ pounds/750g ripe tomatoes, peeled, cored, seeded, and cut in small dices

Fine sea salt

½ teaspoon sugar

1 tablespoon/15ml balsamic vinegar

2 pounds/1kg fresh eggplant, trimmed and cut lengthwise
   in ½-inch/1.3cm slices

2 to 3 tablespoons/30–45ml extra-virgin olive oil

1 cup/10g loosely packed basil leaves

1. Combine the tomatoes, ½ teaspoon sea salt, the sugar, and vinegar in a medium-size bowl, transfer to a sieve set over a bowl, and let drain for 1 hour.

2. Preheat the oven to 425° F/220° C/gas 8.

3. Brush the eggplant slices generously on both sides with olive oil and arrange them on two heavy baking sheets. Sprinkle the slices with salt, and bake them in the bottom third of the oven until they are golden on one side, about 12 minutes. Turn the slices, sprinkle them with salt, and return to the oven to bake until they are golden on both sides and tender, an additional 8 to 10 minutes.

4. Arrange the eggplant slices on a warmed platter, overlapping them slightly if necessary. Top with the tomato sauce, garnish with the basil leaves, and allow to cool or serve immediately.

4 TO 6 SERVINGS

RUSTIC NECTARINE AND APRICOT TART
TARTE AUX NECTARINES ET ABRICOTS

We are tart fanatics and I make them all the time during summer with whatever seasonal fruits I find at Chez Clet. This style is my favorite, because it is quick and gives a gorgeous result—the pastry is neither chilled nor prebaked.

The oven must be preheated and the pastry rolled out and fitted into the tart tin before the fruit is cut up and combined with the sugar and cornstarch, so you can turn the fruit mixture immediately into the pastry, finish the assembly, and bake it. If the fruit sits, it gives up a great deal of juice, which can prevent the pastry from baking properly.

1 small egg
Pastry for one-crust tart (see Apple and Thyme Tart,
     page 80)
$^{1}/_{3}$ cup/65g sugar
2 tablespoons cornstarch
1 pound/500g apricots, pitted and cut in quarters
About 5 nectarines/$1^{1}/_{4}$ pounds/625g, pitted and cut in
     eighths

1. Preheat the oven to 425° F/220° C/gas 8. In a small bowl, whisk together the egg and 2 teaspoons water to make an egg wash.

2. Roll out the pastry to a 13-inch/$32^{1}/_{2}$-cm circle. Fit it gently into a $10^{1}/_{2}$-inch/26-cm removable-bottom tart tin, leaving

the pastry to hang over the edge of the tin. Brush the bottom of the pastry with the egg glaze.

3. Combine the sugar and the cornstarch in a large bowl. Add the fruit and stir until all the ingredients are combined, then turn it into the prepared pastry. Quickly fold the edges of the pastry over the fruit—they will be somewhat uneven but don't be concerned. Quickly brush the pastry with the egg glaze, place the tart tin on a baking sheet, and bake it in the bottom third of the oven until the fruit and the pastry are golden and cooked through, 35 to 40 minutes.

4. Remove from the oven, place the tart on an upturned bowl, and immediately remove the edge of the tart mold from the tin. Let the tart cool to room temperature, and serve.

6 TO 8 SERVINGS

AUTUMN FIG JAM
LA CONFITURE DE FIGUES D'AUTOMNE

I was first introduced to thick and chunky fig jam many years ago by Danie Dubois and it was a delight. Each year I buy enough figs at the market to make jam, and this is my favorite recipe, a perfect showcase for figs, for it is not too sweet.

NOTE: I partially peel the figs to eliminate some but not all of the skin, which can be tough but adds interesting texture in small doses—it also contributes to the lovely, deep rosy hue of the jam. Ripe figs are ultra-sweet and need very little additional sugar to make a wonderfully rich jam. Because of the low sugar content this jam must be well-sealed to keep. If the seal is questionable keep the jam in a very cool place and eat it as quickly as you can.

4½ pounds/2kg figs, trimmed, partially peeled, and cut in eighths

1½ pounds/750g sugar

½ cup/125ml bottled water

2 lemons, preferably organic or at least untreated after harvest, ends trimmed, cut lengthwise in quarters then very thin triangles, seeds removed

Place the figs, sugar, water, and lemons in a large, heavy-bottomed saucepan, stir so the ingredients are well combined, and bring to a boil over medium heat. When the mixture is boiling cook it until the juices thicken slightly, which will take about 25 minutes. The mixture will still seem thin but will thicken as the jam cools. Remove from the heat and seal according to jar manufacturer's instructions.

ABOUT 8 PINTS/4 LITERS

EIGHT

A Hair in the Soup

ONE OF THE FIRST THINGS I noticed about our house
that September when we came to claim it was the proliferation of
carts and potted plants in the small backyard behind the house.
They belonged to the florists at L'Art Floral across the street who,
decades ago, had claimed the spot as their storage area. Our front
yard had served as the exercise run for the family's German shepherd, though the florists had been thoughtful enough to discon-
tinue that practice before we moved in.

The plants were something of a problem. So were the elderly
women who parked their bicycles at different times throughout the day
near the front door and returned some hours later with full shopping
bags. And then there were the gentlemen who walked casually into the
courtyard looking neither right nor left, headed to an old raised drain
with a faucet over it in the corner outside the entry room window, un-
zipped their trousers, and used the drain as an outdoor toilet.

161

The notary who supervised the sale of the house was aware of this use of our property, and he had told us in no uncertain terms that we should turn out everyone. I mentioned the elderly ladies to him and without skipping a beat he closed his eyes, turned down the corners of his mouth, and made a wide sweep with his hand. "Everyone," he said, coldly. "If you do not get them out now, you will never get them out."

Speaking firmly to the florists and the gentlemen who used our courtyard didn't bother me much. But how to evict the elderly women?

One morning before we had actually moved into the house, I opened the large metal gate that served as the entry into the courtyard and I came face-to-face with a woman who was wheeling out her bike. Well dressed and cheerful, she greeted me with a hearty *bonjour*, which I returned. My stomach was in knots. I couldn't do it, I just couldn't. Then, a vision of the notary flashed through my head and I screwed up my courage. "Madame, I am sorry to have to say this, but my family and I now own this house and we will soon be living here and . . ." I trailed off. She looked at me, expectantly. "I must ask you not to park your bicycle here any more." My face was hot.

"But of course, madame, it couldn't be any other way," she said, graciously. She climbed on her bicycle and with a quick *au revoir*, rode off down the street, never to return. I was relieved, but I still had two more women to go. One responded pleasantly, but the other looked hurt. "I've always parked my bicycle here," she said. "Couldn't I still do so once in a while?" I relented immediately, of course, but she never did. I think she realized that once we had really taken possession of the house, leaving her bike in our courtyard would be a bit like parking in our living room.

I surprised a gentleman at the drain in mid-flow one day when I returned from a quick trip to the store on my bicycle. This was an opportunity I relished. I wheeled in, propped the bicycle against the apple tree, and walked right up to him, my eyes on his. "Monsieur, this is now my home, and you are in my garden. I must ask you to leave." I've never seen anyone zip faster than he did. He hastily nodded his head and hurried off. Neither he nor any of his compatriots ever returned.

The situation with the florists was harder to approach. I knew from observation and from comments dropped by others that they were none too happy to have us as neighbors. A *bonjour* on my part elicited nothing but a cold look and I feared that once they were turned out the invisible cool barrier that ran right down the middle of the street would turn to ice.

It was a shame because we all loved living across from a florist. We could smell the hyacinths and the roses if the breeze blew toward us on a warmish day, and we loved the vividly colored tableau of potted plants and tall bouquets of flowers that spilled out onto the sidewalk creating a sweet, fragrant maze. The shop's picture windows were filled with funny little accessories I had never seen before, from rustic little benches made of birch bark to delicately wrought porcelain flowers intended for gravestones. There was always a panoply of dewy-eyed plaster elves that swung back and forth from fake trees and fawns that mechanically sipped water. I bought bouquets from time to time hoping to thaw the chill but my money was accepted without expression or comment.

A HAIR IN THE SOUP

One day I was in our courtyard when Monsieur Taverne, one of the florists, walked through on his way to the back to get plants. I politely asked him to move his wagons and plants, explaining that we would soon move in. He brushed me off with a *"Oui, oui, oui,"* and continued on his way. I wasn't yet working at the house everyday so I couldn't keep tabs on the situation, but Michael was, and about a week later I asked if there had been any movement. There hadn't. Several days after that I saw Monsieur Taverne again and repeated the request. Again I got the French brush-off.

Time passed. We moved in. November rolled around and with it a huge stock of Christmas trees, all stacked tidily behind our house. "There is a positive side to this," Michael observed. "We can walk out the back door and choose our tree—call it rent on the property."

I tried to think of everything I'd ever read about the French mentality and diplomacy. How to go about elegantly turning these people and their plants from our property? Asking them wasn't enough. What was the turn of phrase that would do it? I became fixated on the situation, dreading it yet knowing there must be a way to proceed that would make them feel good about removing their wares from our garden.

One unseasonably fine day as I was digging out weeds from the garden in preparation for planting spring arugula and *mesclun*, a flavorful blend of lettuces, Monsieur Taverne boldly came through the garden to get his plants. I watched him, impressed with his *culot*, or brio. He obviously felt he had a claim on the property, and he undoubtedly viewed us as a temporary annoyance. After all, he'd been storing his plants and carts and trees there for decades and the previous owner had never said anything.

I watched him return with his wagon full of plants and I was suddenly infuriated. To hell with diplomacy: we needed action here. I put myself right in his path. "Monsieur, I have asked you three times to remove your things from our garden and you have done nothing. I want everything out of here by tomorrow!" I said. Then I turned and went into the house where I fumed for awhile.

We left the house that day as usual at 4 P.M., to pick up Joe from school, and Monsieur Taverne was slouching his way through the yard with an empty wagon. My blood started to boil, but I told myself to forget it, we'd figure out something.

When we returned the following morning to our surprise every plant, leaf, tree, and wagon was off the property. I was impressed. Monsieur Taverne had resisted, but when pushed had erased the habit of thirty years in a mere twenty-four hours. Of course the temperature had dropped a few more degrees when I walked past the shop later that week, but though we didn't like the situation there was no alternative. I would have liked to have walked up to the florists, shaken their hands, and thanked them, but in truth I would have died rather than attempt it. Besides, it would have been useless. Time would, I hoped, ease the situation.

About two weeks later we had friends—Parisian restaurateurs who had just moved to a new country house near us—over for Thanksgiving dinner. They firmly believe in contributing to the communities they live in, and during the meal they regaled us with stories about their community projects in Paris and in the country. I mentioned the elderly ladies and unembarrassable men, and our situation with the florists.

Claude, one of our guests, put a finger to his mouth and looked at us thoughtfully. "You must understand, it's normal," he said. "You've arrived here like a *cheveu dans la soupe*, a hair in the soup. No one asked you to come. And, you're American."

He reflected.

"Forget about the ladies and the men. They are no problem. Here is what you do about the florists," he said. "Tomorrow you take them some of these incredible *petits pains* that you've made and explain about Thanksgiving and tell them this is a family recipe. That will open the door for you."

I was skeptical. "You think they care?" I asked.

"Of course they do," he replied. "They have no idea what you are like, and they only imagine the worst. The food will help."

I wasted no time. The very next day I bundled up a dozen of my grandmother's legendary Thanksgiving rolls, which I had had in the freezer and baked fresh that morning. I grabbed Joe by the hand—for courage—and we walked together across the street. My heart was in my throat. I climbed the steps up into the florist shop and practically ran into the two stern-faced, gray-haired sisters, the owners. Squeezing Joe's hand, I gave them the rolls, told them about Thanksgiving and how I always made them, then offered a suggestion on how best to heat and serve them. I'm sure I spoke in a rush because I was so nervous. Joe, who didn't really know why we were there, was looking around curiously, his little round face beaming. He has what the French call a *bonne bouille*, or darling face, and I hoped it was softening up the florists. We didn't linger, however. Once my speech was done and the rolls accepted, we were gone.

When we got outside the shop Joe looked up at me and asked, "Mama, why were you squeezing my hand so tight?" Poor child. I had probably cut off the blood circulation I was so nervous.

I didn't expect miracles and there were none but the temperature rose slightly, and my *bonjours* were returned by both the women and Monsieur Taverne, who was the husband of one of them. I couldn't tell which, because I couldn't really tell the two women apart and at this point it didn't matter. The important thing was that we had gained some ground. I called Claude to report on the progress, and he cheered me along.

A couple of weeks later Michael began decorating the house for Christmas. He hung cedar boughs over every door and window then wove tiny white lights through them. He lit up our gnarled apple tree and hung multicolored lights in the three tiny paned windows in Joe's room. I made and hung a giant wreath on our gate, festooning it with gold beads and a big red bow and we put candles at all the windows. Since our house is right in the center of town across from the church we felt a certain obligation to decorate sumptuously.

Once the outside of the house was done we put up a tree (which we didn't buy at the florist, because we were too cowardly) and decorated it and the rest of the interior by hanging decorations and boughs from the raw beams, on the ragged brick fireplace, and the not-yet-plastered walls. Our windows have tiny panes in them and most are curtainless, so the golden glow within was easily observed from without, and the house looked like a fairy-tale dwelling, standing out starkly from the shops and apartments around it, which were more modestly decorated. We knew it was appreciated because we saw cars slow down and necks crane, and more than one person came with a camera and stood out front clicking away.

I have always baked a variety of cookies for Christmas and being in France didn't change that, even with the wealth of bakeries at our fingertips. I'm a firm believer in tradition—ours and others'—and I didn't see how it would be Christmas without Christmas cookies. Joe and I took an afternoon to mix, roll, and decorate. Then we filled several gaily decorated cellophane bags and delivered them to the florists, the café owners, the crew at the Chez Clet, Brigitte, the owner of Laure Boutique next to the florist, and the family who ran the real estate agency across the street, along with an explanation of their place in our Christmas tradition. I was taking Claude's suggestion seriously.

Two days before Christmas while I was baking, Michael was working, and Joe was playing in the chilly entryway. Suddenly Joe ran to get me. "Mama, there's someone at the door, those two ladies," he said with his lisp. I went to the door, wiping my hands on my apron. Michael, in his studio, had heard Joe and he emerged as well. It was dark already, and I switched on the outdoor light and opened the door. There, framed by the light in our doorway, were the twin sisters, a huge bouquet in their hands. They didn't say anything and just stood there. I was stunned and unsure of what to do, so we had a standoff for a moment, then they handed me the bouquet. I had tears in my eyes and they did, too. Michael, standing back just a bit, was equally moved. We didn't say anything. Finally, I said *"Merci"* and they said simply *"Bon Noël."* They handed Joe a little gift, shook our hands, and were gone. We stayed in the doorway looking after them.

I looked at Michael, who looked back at me. "The rolls and the cookies. They worked," he said, smiling. We all felt as if a miracle had occurred, a cultural breakthrough that would improve the quality of our daily lives. Our first Christmas on rue Tatin couldn't have offered us more.

That Christmas was a watershed, and none of us have ever looked back. Over the subsequent years we've developed a close relationship with the florists and found them to be warm and loving neighbors. Year-round they bring us bouquets of flowers that they can't sell but that still have many days of life in them. I take them cookies, or cakes, or whatever it is I'm baking when it's something really special. Their grandchildren come over occasionally to play with Joe and I'm even nice to Jonquil, their German shepherd, though in my heart of hearts I'm sure she's going to attack me one day.

Ironically, last Christmas found us urging them to store their Christmas trees in our backyard, as their usual storage area was damaged. It's easier now, of course, since we all know and appreciate each other, but still I had a quiet laugh about it.

MONSIEUR TAVERNE'S EVERYDAY
FISH WITH TOMATOES
LE POISSON DE TOUS LES JOURS

Monsieur Taverne, the florist who lives across the street from us, has described this as one of his favorite dishes during the summer tomato season. This dish is so fast and easy you'll be surprised what an elegant presentation it makes. I suggest cod or halibut because in Normandy they are the obvious choice, due to their abundance. You can use any white fish. Just make sure it is the freshest possible. Of course, you need a really ripe tomato with some acidity and character. As for herbs, use the recipe as a model and choose the herbs you prefer. Capers are also a welcome addition here, tossed over the tomatoes just as you remove the dish from the oven. Serve a delicate, lightly chilled Sauvignon Blanc with this dish.

NOTE: The cooking time will depend on the thickness of the fillet.

1¼ to 1½ pounds/625 to 750g cod, lingcod, halibut, or
    other firm white fish fillets, trimmed, bones removed
1 tablespoon/15g unsalted butter
1¼ pounds/625g tomatoes, cored and cut in 6 wedges
    each
2 tablespoons/30ml freshly squeezed lemon juice
Fine sea salt and freshly ground black pepper
¼ cup/5g loosely packed fresh tarragon leaves or another
    herb of your choice such as basil, dill, chives, or
    parsley

1. Rinse the fillets, pat them dry, and refrigerate until ready to cook. Preheat the oven to 400° F/200° C/gas 6.

2. Butter a large baking dish. Lay the fish in the dish (skin-side down if there is skin on the fillets), and arrange the tomato wedges around the fish. Drizzle the fish and the tomatoes with the lemon juice, then season all with salt and pepper. Sprinkle half the tarragon leaves over the fish and bake in the oven until the fish is opaque and the tomatoes are tender, about 15 minutes.

3. Remove the dish from the oven, scatter the remaining tarragon leaves over the fish, and season with a fine sprinkling of pepper. Serve immediately.

4 SERVINGS

THE ROLLS THAT BROUGHT US TOGETHER
LES PAINS DE RAPPROCHEMENT

These are rolls that break down cultural barriers. Make them and you'll taste why! This recipe was first published in Farmhouse Cookbook, *Workman Publishing Inc., 1991.*

These must be served hot from the oven!

1 cup/250ml milk
8 tablespoons/125g unsalted butter, at room temperature
1 package/$1/4$ ounce/7g active dry yeast
$1/2$ cup/100g sugar
$4^1/2$ cups/650g all-purpose flour
2 large eggs
1 teaspoon fine sea salt

1. Scald the milk over medium-high heat. Pour it into a large bowl or the bowl of an electric mixer and add the butter. Stir until the butter has melted. Set the bowl aside until the mixture is lukewarm.

2. Stir the yeast and sugar into the milk. Add 1 cup/145g of the flour and mix well. Add the eggs, one at a time, beating well

after each addition. Add the salt and 1 more cup/145g of flour, and mix vigorously until the dough is elastic and smooth, at least 6 minutes by hand or 3 minutes on medium speed with an electric mixer.

3. If you are mixing by hand, add the remaining 2½ cups/ 360g flour and mix until the dough is slightly firmer but still very soft and smooth. Turn it out onto a lightly floured surface and knead just until it is smooth, which will take 2 to 3 minutes. If you are using an electric mixer, add the 2½ cups/360g flour and mix just until it is incorporated. Then turn the dough out onto a lightly floured surface, and continue kneading by hand until it is smooth.

4. Place the dough in a bowl, cover it with a kitchen towel, and set aside to rise in a warm spot (68 to 70° F) until it has doubled in size, about 2 hours.

5. Lightly flour 2 baking sheets.

6. Turn the dough out onto a well-floured surface, divide it in half, and roll each half to form a circle that is ⅛ inch/.3cm thick and 16 inches/40cm in diameter. Cut each circle into quarters, and cut each quarter into 4 wedges. Roll the edges up, beginning at the wide end, to form crescents.

7. Place the rolls on the prepared baking sheets, leaving 2 inches/5cm between them and arranging them with the tips rolled underneath, so they won't pop up during rising and bak-

ing. Cover the rolls with a kitchen towel and let them rise in a warm spot (68 to 70° F) until they have nearly doubled in size, at least 4 hours.

8. Preheat the oven to 350° F/175° C/gas 4/5.

9. Bake the rolls in the center of the oven until they are golden, 10 to 12 minutes. Remove, and serve immediately.

32 ROLLS

NINE

The Priest

A FEW DAYS AFTER we'd moved into 1 rue Tatin I heard a knock on the front door. There on our stoop was a timid young couple who asked me when the pre-marriage classes began. I looked blank, and the young woman asked me if this was the *aumônerie*, or parish house. I said no and pointed to where the *aumônerie* was, right behind our house, and thought nothing more about it. The following day two couples stopped by, and by week's end I'd had at least five different young couples knock on the door and ask the same question. Over the ensuing weeks many people knocked at the door or simply barged right in the house looking for the priest, inquiring after a baptism or communion, wondering about other church business.

As the weather warmed, we ate outside often and nine times out of ten people walked through our garden while we were in the midst of a meal. Either it was the priest or one of his assistants or the young couple who volunteered at the church in exchange for lodging in the *aumônerie* behind us. Being well brought up these intruders always said *"Bonjour!"* and shook our hands whether we were eating fried chicken, had our mouths full, or had guests.

It became obvious that much of the parish assumed our house was the parish hall, and that our garden was public property. This was the result of a decades-old mix-up in addresses that had the parish hall listed at 1 rue Tatin, our legal address. At first when people made the mistake and came to our house we directed them kindly and eagerly to the proper address. Even when people walked right in the house we would stop them and explain, then show them the way. After a few months and many disturbances, however, it became tedious.

We tried locking the door but that wasn't practical for Michael, who was constantly in and out with buckets of this and barrels of that. I put a handwritten sign on the door explaining where the *aumônerie* was, but that didn't seem to deter anyone.

One evening I was upstairs in Joe's room reading him a story when I heard a heavy foot on the stairs and a strident *"Allô! Allô!"* I walked out of his room, through our room, and into the bathroom. There stood an imperious elderly woman with a cane. *"Je suis ici pour le curé!"* she said. "I'm here for the priest." I felt the weight of a last straw.

I don't think I even responded but took her by the elbow, steered her back downstairs, and then had the presence of mind to explain that the *curé* didn't live in our house, that it was a private family home, and would she please tell all of her friends. I admit to being annoyed, yet I couldn't blame these individuals.

Once we realized that all these intrusions were a simple matter of a mistaken address I mentioned it to the priest and to his lay helper, asking them to change it. Both brushed me off with a *"Oui, oui."* Nothing changed. I called the city planning office and the gentleman I spoke with was aghast. *"Madame*, this is not your job to ask them to change their address. It is our job. We will write them a letter and all will be well," he gushed.

Nothing changed. After about six months I called the city planning office and they affirmed they had sent the letter. I explained that nothing seemed to have changed and they promised to send another one. I'm sure they did, but there was no sign that any heed was taken.

We had known when we bought the house that the deed specified an easement for the priest, so that he could have easy access to his house (though it also has an entrance on another street). Over the years the easement had been unofficially extended to all the parishioners, who thought nothing of walking through the garden of a basically derelict house to get to the parish hall. The woman we bought the house from had told us few people walked through the yard. Either she had lied or she had simply never spent enough time at the house to really know how much traffic there actually was.

We had tried all the legal means to make people change their ways. We'd told everyone who walked through our garden that there was another entrance and that this was a private home. I had put signs on our front gate and our front door explaining that this wasn't the parish hall and directing people around the corner. In Paris I bought a lovely enameled sign that read *privé* and put that on the door. The French are very respectful of privacy, and I was assured that *privé* would do the trick. But our door continued to open and parishioners continued to wander into our living room.

The true final straw came on a warm Sunday morning. I set our table outside for breakfast, and when Michael returned from the *boulangerie* we all sat down to freshly squeezed orange juice, coffee, croissants, and brioches. The church bells rang out the mass, the sun was warm but not too hot, and we were basking in our good fortune. Joe had gone inside to play and we were outside reading the paper when suddenly I heard him yell "Mama! Mama! What are all those ghosts doing in our yard?" I looked up from the paper to see a line of white-robed children, large wooden crosses hanging around their necks, standing in our garden. They were about to make their first communion and were flushed with devotion, eager and pure. Beyond them a clutch of parents was trampling my herbs and lettuces as they angled to get photos. We were flabbergasted yet charmed at the same time and we sat as if nailed to our chairs.

We weren't about to make a scene for these people on such an important day, so we sipped our coffee and observed the spectacle. These poor kids, I thought, dressed up like friars and sober brides. I was getting a look at my own religion from a new perspective. Joe was hanging on to me, frightened and fascinated. I reassured him that they weren't ghosts, but I'm not sure he believed me.

I spoke to the priest's assistant the following day to ask him to please let us know when there would be another event like communion, so we would be prepared. He looked at me blankly. "We are just doing things the way they have always been done."

We felt that the priest and his entourage had no empathy with

THE PRIEST

what had become to us an unbearable invasion of privacy, and would do nothing to change it. We decided we had to act, and that the best solution would be to offer to build an entryway, at our cost, on church property. That way all the parishioners would have direct access from the parish hall and the priests' house to the church without cutting through our garden. It seemed to us to be a perfect solution.

We had to make our proposal to the priest in charge, and I called around to find out which of the two who resided behind us—who were familiarly referred to as "Sandale" and "Bicyclette," since one always wore sandals, and the other always rode a bicycle—I should contact. I sought out the *"chef"*—Bicyclette—and invited him over for cake and coffee. He accepted.

I was testing *gâteau Breton* recipes at the time and I made one for him, along with what I thought was a rich pot of coffee. I used one of our old-fashioned Helem coffeemakers—a wondrous, bulbous contraption that looks like part of a chemistry set—because that is what we use when there are more than just the two of us. I didn't know it well enough yet to realize that it had to have boiling water put through it several times to remove a sort of reedy taste from the filter.

It was cold that day and our house was chilly, but I made sure it was tidy, and Michael and I dressed up. We were, after all, receiving the town priest. I set the buttery, golden cake on the table and brought out our best, multipatterned coffee cups and cake plates. I was nervous. We were newcomers to town and had the distinct feeling that no one was too thrilled to have us here.

The priest arrived and looked around. He made a few complimentary comments. I went to make the coffee, he stayed and talked with Michael. I relaxed a bit, thinking "This isn't so bad." I poured the coffee, which didn't smell very rich at all, and cut into the cake. To my horror, it was slightly gummy in the center.

"Oh, God," I thought, perhaps appropriately. But I served it, and we dug in. The cake tasted as undercooked as it looked, and to this day I don't know what happened. The coffee was thin. I was dying inside.

But conversation flowed just fine. I got up to make more coffee. When I returned Michael had just explained our idea to the priest and was laying out his plan. I could tell immediately that the atmosphere had changed. The priest's shoulders were hunched up tensely around his ears. His back was stiff. I could feel his displeasure. I offered him coffee and he refused, instead spitting out several questions about our plan, which we answered. He quickly made his excuses and was gone. Michael and I looked at each other. "Uh-oh," we both said. "This will not be easy."

I threw away the cake. Since then I've made dozens—my favorite being one with ground walnuts incorporated into the batter—and they have always been delicious. Perhaps it was divine intervention.

The priest had said he'd get back to us about our idea, and two weeks later he came to talk to Michael, who was outside trimming the rosebushes. I was in my office and could look down on them, their backs to me. As I watched I suddenly saw Michael straighten up. As surely as if smoke were pouring from his ears I could tell he was angry, and not just a little bit angry. I ran outside to intervene.

Flames licked around the eyes of the priest, Michael was opening and closing his fist. The priest didn't waste a moment or a drop of his wrath, turning on me quickly and vehemently, telling me that he thought we were most selfish people. He said he would never allow us to build a new entry, that the situation would never change, that he would never grant his approval. I asked why. *"J'ai mes habitudes."* "I have my habits," he barked, looking me hotly in the eye.

I explained how awkward it was for us, and for those who walked through our garden. I explained how often the gate was left open, and how dangerous that was for our son, for he might run out into the busy street. I described in the most polite way I could how much better the new fence would be, and how we would pay for every bit of it, and how it would be done quickly and efficiently. He glared at me. *"Madame,"* he said, spitting nails. "You talk like an owner."

Normally one calls a priest *père*, or father. The word stuck in my throat. I addressed him as Monsieur, which I knew came close to being an insult, but I wanted him to understand how he impressed me. *"Monsieur,"* I said. "I am an owner, the owner, of this house. And I want you, right now, to get off my property."

I have often been told that when I'm angry my French is perfect. Whether or not my words were perfect or not, my glare said it all and so did Michael's. This man disgusted me, and I didn't try to hide it. He gave each of us an angry look and was gone.

I was shaking. I looked immediately heavenward to see if a

lightning bolt was on its way down to strike me. I don't practice my religion, but once a Catholic always a Catholic. I was sick to my stomach. I had never, ever spoken to a man of the cloth in such a way. In fact, I've never been angry enough to ask someone to get off my property. Michael was gray with fury. From that moment forward, he hated the man in a deep and personal way. This, I feared, was war.

When I cooled down I tried to talk with Michael about it. He had nothing but unprintable things to say about the priest. I called a friend who is actively involved in the church to find out who was above this priest so we could talk with him. I got a name and tried to call, but never got a response. I heard through the grapevine that even as far away as Évreux, the county seat and headquarters of the parish about twenty minutes from Louviers, there was a certain prejudice against us.

The priest came through our garden more often than ever, usually accompanied by several people, for protection I guessed. Michael was often working on walls, or paving, or in the garden outside so he had to face them. While the situation bothered me it became an obsession with him.

We decided to consult a lawyer. We didn't want to go to court, but we did think a letter from a lawyer, outlining what we wanted to do and why and directed to the right person, might help. After all, our idea was sensible—it would hurt no one and help everyone. After hearing our story, the lawyer agreed with us. She knew our property—everyone in Louviers does—and she was incredulous at the priest's position.

She agreed to help us and threw herself into our cause. She

came to the house several times to look at what Michael was proposing. She met with church officials and talked to influential Catholics in Louviers. All we had expected from her was a well-written letter to the parish in Évreux. Instead, we got her full attention.

After a year, during which the traffic continued, she arranged a meeting with the priest and a representative of the bishop in our garden.

We were nervous. We knew this was do or die. If we didn't get an okay from the bishop today we never would. The lawyer was pretty sure of herself, but she was straight with us, too. "It could go either way," she said. "But I'll do my best."

I prepared another cake and coffee—making sure they were delicious—and everyone met in our garden at 9 A.M. on a beautiful morning. The priest avoided our gaze. The bishop's representative gave us each a hearty, warm handshake and the lawyer began a soliloquy about the case, explaining elegantly just what we wanted, and why. Caught up in her speech, she portrayed us as ambassadors of our country, come to France to restore a piece of historic Louviers, doers of good. It was terrific. Michael and I swelled with pride.

We walked the boundary of the property as Michael explained where he would put in the new entry, and how it would work. We talked. It was very congenial, except for the silent presence of the priest.

When the tour was finished we all stood outside the house in the shadow of the cathedral, while the lawyer succinctly described, once again, just what we proposed—to build an esthetic entry, at our cost, so those destined for the parish hall would have direct access and we would have tranquility. When the lawyer was finished, the bishop's representative looked at the priest. "I don't see anything wrong with this plan," he said. "It makes perfect sense." The priest didn't look up.

We'd won. The bishop's representative looked at us. "It's a good idea. You have my permission, and the permission of Évreux. Go ahead," he said.

I was weak with relief and I could tell Michael was, too. The bishop's representative shook our hands and, with the deflated priest, quickly went on his way.

It took a good month for Michael to build the path from the sidewalk to the parish house, and cut a hole in the fence and fashion a gate. I didn't tell anyone else what had happened unless they asked, but when they did I told all. Meanwhile, Michael finished up the new gate, installed a lock, and presented a key to one of the helpers at the parish hall, as required. Then, he cut a large piece of metal to fit across our gate to afford us some privacy.

We planned a gate-locking ceremony and invited a few friends. It was summer and sardines were in season, so I prepared several dozen to grill and Michael built an impromptu brick fireplace in our courtyard, for a barbecue. I made gazpacho with cucumber ice sorbet for a first course, and a simple nectarine tart for dessert. Michael opened a bottle of champagne and, glass in one hand and key in the other, went to lock the gate. Our friends had all been privy to the two years of discomfort this whole process had caused, and they all cheered with us as he turned the key in the lock.

Not twenty minutes later we saw the priest emerge from the

church and head for the gate. We saw the handle turn, then saw the yank, then the priest's red face as it popped above the gate. He looked at us there enjoying our meal, turned on his heel, and stomped away.

For the first time since we moved in we felt at home in the garden. The headaches were over. Michael could breathe more easily, and return back to work on the house. We could look forward to many Sunday breakfasts and evening meals in our garden, undisturbed.

The priest still held and exercised his *droit de passage*, or legal access through our garden, at least once a week, entering through a small wooden door in the wall next to the gate, which we left open at all times. A priest appointed after Michael built the new entry also walked through, but they were the only traffic we saw.

We did many other things to create privacy for ourselves. Not allowed, by the terms of our deed, to build a wall on the property line between our land and the parish hall, we instead planted espaliered apple trees—two Cox's Orange Pippins and two reines de reinettes, both luscious old varieties. Required to leave a passageway through the yard for the priest we planted rosebushes along part of the boundary, leaving just enough room for him to get through. The first time he walked through after they'd been planted he bellowed to Michael about scratching his feet on the thorns. Needless to say, Michael's sympathy was limited.

Many of our French friends hadn't really understood the problem. "Just lock the door and build a wall, don't worry about it," they had advised. "That's what we would do. It's not like anyone would ever make you change anything."

That is where being foreigners makes us different. Having not been brought up in France, we don't inherently understand the elasticity of the law. When we read that we can only let our trees grow to a certain height, we trim them once they get to that height. When a deed indicates we can't lock our gate, we don't lock it. Even our immediate neighbors are astounded at our adherence to the law. "But you must lock your gate," Mme Bruhot, our elderly neighbor, said. "It's unthinkable to leave it unlocked at night." When I mentioned the deed, this upstanding and respected member of the town simply shrugged.

We are learning to be more French about these things. It has been two years since the priest has walked through our garden. It must have ceased to be an amusement to him. We've relaxed a bit, as well. The rosebushes have grown wide and tall—though there is still space to get through if one steps carefully enough—and our apple trees are at just about five feet, higher than specified in our deed. We realize there won't be any repercussions for these minor breaches.

We see the priest often, sailing by on his bicycle. He's active in the parish but now there's another priest we see much more often, closer to the type I recall from my childhood. Albert Dedecker, or simply Albert as everyone calls him, appears to be a *bon vivant*, a cheery soul who has instituted many changes, most of them seemingly for the better. He loves bells, and they ring with abandon all the time. He has begun a prayer service in the parish hall behind our house, so that on certain nights we look into the windows and observe the faithful in a room lit only by candles that surround a large statue of the virgin. It's a beautiful, peaceful sight.

GAZPACHO WITH CUCUMBER SORBET
GAZPACHO AU SORBET DE CONCOMBRE

This delightful chilled soup with its cloud of cucumber sorbet in the center is an inspiration of Parisian three-star chef Alain Passard, who makes the gazpacho in summer when tomatoes are ripe and filled with summer's warmth, cucumbers are crisp and flavorful, and bell peppers are bursting with sweetness. I added the cucumber sorbet as a further way of cooling off when the temperature soars. Serve this with a lightly chilled rosé. Salad burnet has a flat, round, serrated leaf and a fresh cucumber flavor.

6 medium (about 1¼ pounds/600g) ripe tomatoes,
    peeled, seeded, and diced
3 ounces/90g diced red bell pepper
1 large (about 8 ounces/250g) cucumber, peeled and diced
1 small garlic clove
1 small/2½-ounce/75-g onion, quartered
4 ounces/120g fresh fennel, coarsely chopped
½ cup/125ml extra-virgin olive oil
1 tablespoon freshly squeezed lemon juice
Pinch of fine sea salt

FOR THE CUCUMBER SORBET:
2 large cucumbers (about 1 pound/500g each), peeled
    and diced

8 fresh mint leaves
2 tablespoons freshly squeezed lemon juice
$\frac{1}{4}$ teaspoon fine sea salt, or to taste

FOR THE GARNISH:
18 chive tips
Salad burnet leaves, optional

1. To make the soup, place the tomatoes, bell pepper, cucumber, garlic, onion, and fennel in a food processor or blender and process to a coarse purée. Transfer the mixture to a nonreactive fine-mesh sieve placed over a bowl and refrigerate for 2 to 4 hours.

2. Remove the soup from the refrigerator. Transfer what remains in the sieve to a medium-size bowl. Discard the juice in the bowl. Stir in the olive oil and the lemon juice, then season to taste with salt. Return to the refrigerator.

3. To make the sorbet, purée the cucumbers in a food processor, place in a nonreactive fine-mesh sieve placed over a bowl, and refrigerate for at least 2 hours. Just before freezing the sorbet transfer the cucumber pulp to a medium-size bowl. Mince the mint leaves and stir them into the cucumber pulp, along with the lemon juice and the salt. Taste for seasoning, transfer to an ice-cream maker, and freeze according to manufacturer's directions.

4. To serve the soup, divide it among 6 chilled, shallow soup bowls. Using 2 soup spoons, shape the sorbet into an elongated oval (quenelle) and place it in the center of each bowl of soup.

Garnish the soup with the chives and the salad burnet leaves and serve immediately.

6 APPETIZER SERVINGS

ROSEMARY GRILLED SARDINES
LES SARDINES GRILLÉES AU ROMARIN

Summer means eating outside in the courtyard at the foot of Notre Dame. I stuff meaty sardines with rosemary and grill them over a wood fire and serve them with fresh green salad from our garden, or freshly made tomato and pepper salad, and a full-flavored rosé.

About 16 fresh sardines or small mackerel, cleaned
Sea salt and freshly ground black pepper
4 tablespoons/60ml extra-virgin olive oil
16 sprigs fresh rosemary
Fleur de sel, optional

1. Light a small fire in the barbecue.

2. Carefully rinse the sardines and cut down along their backbone from the inside and rinse them again, to remove any blood or impurities inside that might make them taste bitter. Pat them dry and lightly season them inside with salt and pepper. Rub each fish on the outside with olive oil, using about 2 tablespoons

(30ml). Place a sprig of rosemary inside each fish, and set them on a platter in the refrigerator.

3. When the coals are red and dusted with ash, set the grill about 3 inches (7½ cm) above them. When it is hot, carefully lay the fish on the grill. Cook the fish until they are opaque, about 3 minutes per side. If the fire is too hot and starts to flame, simply put a cover on the barbecue, which will result in slightly smokier fish.

4. Carefully transfer the sardines to a platter and drizzle with the remaining 2 tablespoons (30ml) olive oil and sprinkle lightly with fleur de sel, if desired. Serve the sardines either hot or at room temperature.

SERVES 4

WALNUT GÂTEAU BRETON
GÂTEAU BRETON AUX NOIX

This is my variation on a traditional butter cake from Brittany. Its dense, rich, and very buttery flavor is amplified by the lightly toasted walnuts, which give it a whole other dimension. In Brittany this cake is served for an afternoon snack, with coffee, or after a meal. I sometimes put it on the breakfast table as well.

½ cup/60g walnuts, lightly toasted
1¼ cups/250g sugar

7 large egg yolks

16 tablespoons/250g salted butter, melted

2 cups/265g unbleached, all-purpose flour

1. Preheat the oven to 300° F/150° C/gas 3/4. Butter and lightly flour a 9-inch/23-cm cake pan.

2. Place the walnuts and 2 tablespoons (30g) of the sugar in the bowl of a food processor and grind so that most of the walnuts are finely ground but not anywhere near a paste.

3. In a large bowl, whisk together 6 of the egg yolks and the remaining sugar until the mixture is blended, just a few minutes; there is no need to use an electric mixer here. It will be thick and yellow but shouldn't form a ribbon. Slowly whisk in the walnuts and sugar, then the butter. Sift the flour over the mixture and whisk it in just until the mixture is homogeneous. Don't overmix the batter or the cake will be tough.

4. Whisk together the remaining egg yolk and 2 teaspoons water to make an egg glaze.

5. Turn the batter, which will be quite stiff, into the prepared pan and smooth it out. Lightly but thoroughly paint it with the egg glaze. Using the back of the tines of a fork, deeply mark a crisscross pattern in the top of the cake, going three times across it in one direction, then three in another. (The marks in the cake will fade, leaving just their trace on the top of the cake.)

6. Bake in the center of the oven until the cake is deep golden on the top and springs back slowly but surely when it is touched, about 1 hour and 15 minutes. Using a knife or cake tester isn't recommended as it always comes out looking slightly damp because of the amount of butter in the recipe.

7. Remove from the oven, transfer the cake to a wire rack, and let it cool for about 10 minutes before turning out of the cake pan. Let it cool thoroughly before serving.

8 SERVINGS

TEN

The Rug Salesman

I ANSWERED A KNOCK on the door one spring day and found a short, robust, balding man standing outside rubbing his hands together and staring at the church across the street. He turned his head slowly and introduced himself. "*Bonjour*. My name is Monsieur Richard Lafertin and I have a selection of rugs I would like to show to you," he said in careful French. "I asked around the neighborhood and everyone told me to come to this house and see the Americans."

I must have stared at him, for he repeated himself. He looked perfectly respectable, so I invited him into the entry, which at that time was still a dingy mess of plywood sheets placed over a dirt floor, stained plaster walls, and very dim lighting. His face revealed nothing as he looked around, though the sight must have been disconcerting to someone with rugs to sell. Michael emerged from upstairs where he was installing more electricity and came down to meet Monsieur Lafertin, who explained once again who he was and what he was doing. Michael laughed. "Well, you can see we're not quite at the rug stage," he said. Monsieur Lafertin shook his head. "This does not matter. Let me tell you about myself and my rugs," he said, and proceeded to talk to us about the generations his family had been in the rug business, how they handled very select merchandise, how he traveled throughout Europe to get it, and was often called in by families as they divided up inheritances to evaluate and buy their rugs. We were fascinated, not only by the story, which he told seriously and with dignity, but also by the fact that he was spending his time doing so when it was obvious we weren't going to buy rugs, since we didn't yet have any decent flooring.

Michael and I told him we were delighted to meet him, which was true. He was absolutely charming and at another moment we might have wanted to see his rugs, since we both have a weak spot for them. But we assured him now was not the time. "It doesn't matter," he said. "It's just that everyone said 'Go see the Americans,' and of course I had to do so!"

We laughed. None of our neighbors knew us or what we were doing, and we had already suspected that they viewed us as the "rich Americans." How could they not think that? We'd bought one of the oldest, most showy houses in town and were fixing it up. Neither one of us seemed to work. The only times anyone saw me I was leaving the house with an empty basket and returning with it full of groceries. The only time they saw Michael he was driving off in an empty truck or returning with it stacked with sheets of plywood or Sheetrock or squares of marble or loads of gravel. Of course they sent the rug salesman to us.

We looked at Monsieur Lafertin and he laughed right along with us. "One day we'll need rugs," I explained, shrugging. "But not right away."

"No problem, I'm delighted to have met you and here is my card," Monsieur Lafertin said, then with a gracious smile excused himself and left.

What a charming man, Michael and I agreed, then returned to our respective tasks and forgot him.

A year later, I answered a knock on the door. There stood a young, dark-haired, robust man who introduced himself as Monsieur Lafertin, a *marchand de tapis*. I stared, reaching back in my memory. "Oh yes," I said, remembering the other Monsieur Lafertin.

"My father came to see you a year ago," this young man said. I invited him in. He was charming, smooth, polished, and well-dressed, the way any good rug salesman should be. He looked around at the entry. It was much improved in a year's time—the floors were now covered with clean gravel, the walls had been plastered and painted, a long wood table sat in it off to the side and the stairway had been dusted and polished so the house looked, to a casual observer, lived in and chic.

"I've got some beautiful rugs out in my van I'd like to show to you," Monsieur Lafertin said in a jovial, sincere way. We explained that we still weren't in the market for rugs. "I know, I know, my father told me all about you," he said kindly. "But he also told me that you have an interest in rugs and I'd like to show you a couple of things that I have, for you'll never see any like them anywhere."

We knew we couldn't buy any rugs and we knew we shouldn't look at them so I explained once again, telling the young Monsieur Lafertin that I didn't want him to work for nothing.

"No problem," he said. "Let me bring them in anyway. It will be a pleasure for me."

We looked at each other. We shrugged. Monsieur Lafertin left to get his rugs.

Within minutes he was back, humping an impossible number of rugs over his shoulder. He eased in through the narrow front door and set them down gently, like eggs, on the floor. I glanced above him at Michael. What were we in for, I wondered.

He proceeded with the polish of a ringmaster to unroll his treasures, talking all the while about their origins, their beauty, their quality, and how we would never see anything like them anywhere. He smoothed and caressed each rug.

And the rugs were gorgeous. Mostly from Iran, they were all sizes, from two by three feet to large area rugs, to hall runners. The colors, all natural according to Monsieur Lafertin, were spectacular, the designs unusual, intriguing. Monsieur Lafertin treated each rug gently, turning over a corner to show us the tight, artful weave, the quality, the expert workmanship, stroking the fringes, pinching the tight pile. He spoke moderately and thoughtfully, pausing now and then after whispering, "Can you imagine the work this involved," or "These were made by a family and they were meant to be hung in a mosque," or "This, this is from a mountain tribe and was used to cover the floor of a tent," or "This, you see, this rug with the double signature means it was made by two families."

We were impressed, and not just by the rugs. This young man's performance was masterful, award-winning. He had the right mix of confidence, charm, and humor.

There was one rug in particular that kept calling to me. Smallish, it was an alluring deep rose with touches of turquoise and salmon. Its wide border was filled with subtle and complex designs and its center was a green-gray geometric pattern. I could tell Michael was intrigued by it, too. We said nothing, but such was the skill of Monsieur Lafertin that he kept placing that rug on top of the others, showing it to us in one light then another, in one direction then another. "You see how it changes color depending on which way you set it on the floor," he said. "It is magnificent."

Finally we ran out of things to say and I asked him about prices. He looked at the one we both preferred. "This is the one you like the best, is it not?" he asked. When we agreed he looked at it, long and thoughtfully.

"I know you don't have much money, but I know how much you love rugs, and particularly this one," he said, then mentioned a figure. "Because I understand what you are doing and because you are new clients."

The sum he mentioned was between expensive and astronomical. I already knew we didn't have the means to buy any rugs—we were still weighing the cost of flooring, paint, electrical wires, and Sheetrock—but I had been sorely tempted by the beautiful rug at my feet and urged on by Monsieur Lafertin's epic performance. However, his price made it easy. I refused him, then he looked at Michael, who refused him, too. Then he looked back at me and cut the price in half. I was shocked. That made the rug a decent deal. As we looked at the rug and struggled with our decision (which we knew we really shouldn't have been considering at all), Monsieur Lafertin explained further about the tribe who had made it, how he'd obtained it, and how, though he was making an extreme sacrifice, he was happy to do it so we would be the owners of the fine rug.

It's not that we believed he was making a sacrifice for us. It really wasn't that which made us cave in. It was the fact that the rug would be exquisite in our bedroom.

Monsieur Lafertin was naturally delighted, promising us we would be forever happy with the rug, that it was such a good investment we'd never be sorry. He offered us whatever terms we wanted and when we decided on postdated checks he pocketed them, rolled up all his rugs except the treasure he'd sold us, and beamed at us.

"I will be on my way. Do not worry, if there is any problem you just call me, I will return your checks and take back the rug, I promise you," he said. "And if ever you decide to sell this rug you call me and no one else. I must be the one to buy it back from you."

With that last, artful assurance he was gone. And we were left with an absolutely beautiful rug that we couldn't afford but would cherish, I was certain. Not only that but we felt positively wonderful for having acquired it.

Since that first visit Monsieur Lafertin has stopped by our house regularly three or four times a year, always with new stories about his hunt for merchandise, and always with different rugs. As

THE RUG SALESMAN

each new room in our house is completed we adorn it with a rug or two from Monsieur Lafertin's seemingly endless supply. He appears to live in a whirlpool of rugs as he buys, sells, buys back, and sometimes resells rugs to the families who have sold them to him in the first place.

While our relationship with Monsieur Lafertin is clearly one of buyer and seller, we've grown very fond of him. We don't always buy from him but we always drool at his selection, and he remains accommodating in every way. Once we bought a very expensive rug, then realized, almost as soon as he'd walked out the door, that we might crash into bankruptcy if we actually tried to meet the payments we'd set up. I called and told him we had changed our minds. Within a few weeks he was back with our uncanceled checks and no rancor.

Monsieur Lafertin often seems to stop by on a Wednesday, when Joe is home from school. Since he has three young children of his own he knows how to talk to kids, and he has won over Joe, too, who gets down on his hands and knees to look at the warp and weft and the knots in the rugs, and to peer at the colors. He always wants all of them and often comes up to me, his back to Monsieur Lafertin, and mouths, "Mama, we HAVE TO KEEP THIS ONE!"

One day when Joe was home from school to participate in the affair we decided on two rugs. At the conclusion of the deal Monsieur Lafertin looked at Joe. "I have something for you," he said, and went out to his van. He returned with a lovely, vividly colored rug. "This rug was made to use in a tent; here is the color turquoise, which represents the city it was made in, and it is made of goat hair," he said, turning it over so Joe could see the weave and having him feel the tufts of goat hair that bordered either end of it. "It is a beautiful rug and it is yours, *jeune homme*," he said.

Joe has that rug at the door of his bedroom and beware anyone who tries to move it elsewhere.

Monsieur Lafertin is also an incorrigible gourmand who loves to talk about food. We always know he's going to launch into a food story when he pats his considerable bulk, looks down at his highly polished and very expensive shoes, and shakes his head mournfully. "You know," he says each time, "I love to eat and my wife, my wife, she is a wonderful cook."

One day he eyed a crusty loaf of bread that Michael had just brought from the oven. He didn't say anything but his eyes were drawn to it repeatedly, hungrily. I offered him a piece and to my surprise he accepted, for he has never eaten or drunk anything at our home. But that piece of bread broke down a barrier. He left that day—after selling us a rug—with half the loaf of bread in a bag, as happy as if we'd given him gold bricks.

Monsieur Lafertin loves to hunt, too, and many of his gastronomic stories involve hunting with his band of friends. Frenchmen always hunt in bands and there are never, at least that I know of, any women involved, neither in the hunting nor in the subsequent feasts that follow, which sound opulent. While I have a hard time relating to the actual hunt, the food these men prepare and eat afterward is the stuff of medieval banquets, as haunches, shoulders, and ribs are all served and duly sauced and spiced, and the wine flows like a river.

I love watching Monsieur Lafertin as he talks about food; his brow develops a sheen and he uses enthusiastic and forceful hand gestures. After one particularly lively description he stopped suddenly and said, "I will bring you something from my next hunt, yes, this is what I will do."

While we like Monsieur Lafertin very much, we suffer no illusions. He is a terrific salesman, the best we've experienced. We know the rugs he has are valuable, but we also know we are paying good prices for them. We are not always sure that when he tells us they are unique they truly are, but we don't care. What we care about is their quality and that we love them. The rest of his performance we simply enjoy, so when he promised to bring us some fresh game I didn't think much about it, just chalking it up to a good sales technique and the fervor of the moment.

I underestimated Monsieur Lafertin, for not a month later he came by, a small package in his hand. "I promised you I would bring you something from the hunt and I have; I've brought you some *côtes de biche*, or deer chops," he said. I opened the package to find a delicate little rib roast which, as Monsieur Lafertin advised, would be wonderful roasted whole and even better grilled over the coals.

"Oh, and I've got some beautiful rugs, too. Just let me show you one or two; I know you're not in the market to buy any," he said, hurrying out the door to get them.

He brought the rugs in and, as usual, they were stunning. We resisted, however, and he left, reminding me as he walked out the door how to cook the deer.

That night I cut apart the chops and quickly grilled them over the coals in Michael's newly rebuilt fireplace in the dining room, with just a bit of salt and pepper. Tiny, delicate little things, they cooked in minutes and emerged crisp and lightly smoked, delightfully tender and juicy. Along with a green salad from the garden, a simple chocolate cake, and a bottle of Burgundy they made an elegant meal. It was the first time I'd cooked in the fireplace, after dreaming of doing so throughout the year it was under construction, which added to the meat's exquisite flavor.

Another time Monsieur Lafertin brought a haunch of very small wild boar. "I had a good week," he said, then proceeded to tell me exactly how to cook it. I've noticed that when I receive a gift of food in France, whether it be a piece of wild animal or a half dozen eggs, it is never given without a litany of directions on how to care for and cook it. I sort of followed his recipe—he likes a lot more cream than we do—and it was delicate and delicious.

His most recent visit—which involved the purchase of yet two more rugs, one of them from Chechnya that is filled with such joy and spirit in both its color and its design that we immediately felt our house and our lives would be less without it—was notable for the discussion about wine. Monsieur Lafertin is, naturally, a connoisseur. "I have many clients in the wine business," he said. And he went on to cite the names of their wines, which are among the best France has to offer.

Monsieur Lafertin has become a fixture in our lives, and we are somewhat astonished at the good fortune that first brought him our way. We are also somewhat astonished at our willingness to entertain him, for what is more of a cliché than a traveling rug salesman? But when he arrives we enjoy ourselves, knowing all the while that we are participating in one of the oldest sorts of commerce, and that we are being taken for a very entertaining ride.

ROASTED LEG OF WILD BOAR
RÔTI DE CUISSE DE SANGLIER

Wild boar isn't an everyday meat, though since we've lived in Louviers we've had a regular supply. Once October dawns and the hunting season begins, Jean-Pierre Dubosc, our friend, farmer, and restaurateur, takes to the woods with his rifle, his camouflage clothing, and his band of camarades *and spends the day leisurely tracking* sanglier, *usually in his own woods that surround his farm. Whoever gets an animal shares it with the group. If they get two they have more than they can eat and they share the excess with friends, which is where we enter the picture.*

The boar here range in woods and fields and feed on acorns and whatever they can steal, and their meat is lean and flavorful. (They are anathema to farmers, which is one reason Jean-Pierre takes delight in hunting them.) If you don't have a ready supply of wild boar, try this with a pork shoulder or haunch. Serve it with an elegant Burgundy.

One 6-pound/3-kg leg of wild boar
¼ cup/50g coarse sea salt
¼ cup/30g coarsely ground black pepper
1 bottle/1 liter hearty red wine
4 dried, imported bay leaves
80 sprigs fresh thyme, rinsed

40 black peppercorns

12 cloves

1 medium carrot, trimmed, peeled, and cut in
     ¼-inch/.7cm chunks

1 medium onion, cut in eighths

¼ cup/60ml best-quality red wine vinegar

TO ROAST THE WILD BOAR:

20 whole cloves

2 to 3 tablespoons/30–45ml olive oil

FOR THE SAUCE:

2 cups/500ml chicken or veal stock

3 tablespoons/45g red currant jelly

Flat-leaf parsley, for garnish

1. Rub the leg of wild boar all over with the salt and the pepper. Place it in a shallow dish, cover it loosely, and refrigerate it for 36 hours.

2. Bring the wine, half of the herbs and the spices, and the vegetables to a boil in a medium-size saucepan over medium-high heat and cook for about 3 minutes. Remove from the heat and let cool to room temperature. Strain and whisk in the vinegar. Discard the herbs, spices, and vegetables.

3. Quickly rinse the salt and pepper from the boar to remove most but not all of it. Pat it dry and place it in a shallow dish. Stir the remaining herbs and spices into the cooled marinade and

pour it over the boar. Return it to the refrigerator, loosely covered, and let it marinate for 36 hours, turning it at least four times.

4. Preheat the oven to 450° F/230° C/gas 9.

5. Remove the leg of wild boar from the marinade and pat it dry. Make 20 tiny slits in it all over, and insert a clove into each slit. Transfer the boar to a baking dish, drizzle the oil over it, and pour one-fourth of the marinade over it. Roast in the center of the oven until the boar is golden on the outside, and when you cut into it is a very faint pink, but not in the least red, which will take about 2 hours (about 155° F/68° C on a meat thermometer). Check it occasionally and as the marinade cooks away replenish it with the remaining marinade.

6. When the boar is roasted, remove it from the oven, and set it on a platter in a warm spot, loosely covered, to sit for at least 20 minutes so the juices have a chance to retreat back into the meat. To prepare the sauce, heat the pan with the cooking juices in it over medium heat, scraping up any browned bits from the bottom of the pan. Transfer to a medium-size saucepan. Whisk in the stock and bring to a boil over medium-high heat. Reduce by about one-fourth, then stir in the red currant jelly. Continue cooking and whisking until the sauce is smooth and satiny, 8 to 10 minutes. Remove from the heat.

7. Before slicing the boar remove as many of the cloves as possible. Thinly slice the wild boar and arrange it on a platter.

Garnish with flat-leaf parsley. Either pour the sauce over the meat or serve it on the side.

8 TO 10 SERVINGS

MELTING APPLE CUSTARD
FONDANT AUX POMMES VANILLÉES

Our neighbor across the street, Line Roussel, saw me come home from the market one day with a basket full of apples and ran over with this recipe, which she claimed was the best apple dessert she had ever made. Rich and cream-filled, it is now one of my favorites. It is best made with tart baking apples—I use Cox's Orange Pippins or Boskoop. If you can't find these varieties, use Empire, any Spy apple, or Jonathan.

3 pounds/1.5kg tart cooking apples, peeled and cored
7 tablespoons/100g unsalted butter
1 cup/200g sugar
6 tablespoons/95ml Calvados, optional
1 whole vanilla bean, split down the middle
3 large eggs
2 large egg yolks
1¼ cups/300ml heavy cream, not ultra-pasteurized

1. Preheat the oven to 425° F/220° C/gas 8.

2. Cut the apples in quarters. Heat the butter in a skillet over medium-high heat. When the butter is hot and foamy add the ap-

THE RUG SALESMAN

ples and sauté them until they are golden all over, about 10 minutes. Add $^1/_2$ cup (100g) of the sugar and cook until the sugar has caramelized, shaking the pan so the apples and sugar are moving across it and the sugar doesn't burn. If using the Calvados, pour it into the pan and swirl it around. Then, standing back from the pan so you don't get burned, light a match over it and flame away the alcohol in the pan, gently shaking and swirling the pan until the flames die down.

3. Transfer the apples to a 6-cup, nonreactive charlotte or soufflé mold.

4. Scrape the seeds from the vanilla bean. Whisk together the eggs and the egg yolks in a medium-size bowl and then whisk in the vanilla seeds. Whisk in the remaining $^1/_2$ cup (100g) sugar and the cream until the mixture is combined. Pour the mixture over the apples, and bake in the center of the oven until the top is golden and puffed, about 35 minutes. Remove from the oven and present the dessert, then let it cool for about 20 minutes before serving.

4 TO 6 SERVINGS

ELEVEN

The Perfect Stove

ALL MY PROFESSIONAL LIFE I've cooked on the simplest of gas stoves, except for a brief period when I owned a six-burner professional stove with a "drive in" oven that was so large and inefficient it wouldn't brown anything. I've always preferred simple functionality over aesthetic drama, and I've always had a sense of responsibility to my readers not to cook on a stove that was any different from what I imagined they had in their kitchens.

Times have certainly changed. Many American cooks or aspiring cooks have kitchens that would put a simple French restaurant to shame, with gorgeous professional equipment, multiple ovens, acres of space and light. So as we began planning the kitchen at 1 rue Tatin I didn't feel I needed to worry about having a kitchen that might be more sophisticated than those of my readers. With that concern banished, I started thinking about what I really wanted to cook on. I knew I wanted something gorgeous, but aesthetics were not my first consideration as I started searching. I began by reading the want ads. A national want-ad sheet called the ARGUS offers professional equipment sold at auction and comes out each Thursday. I looked in it to see what was being offered and found everything from *chambres froides*—huge walk-in refrigerators—to croissant-makers and *baguette* shapers. The problem was that all the auctions were in distant cities like Lyon or Nantes and I wasn't interested in going to all that much trouble. So I searched the want ads closer to home, hoping to find my dream stove.

I began talking with friends—restaurateurs and others who'd done their own stove searches. I called kitchen equipment companies for their catalogues, went to stores that sold kitchen equipment, then eventually to professional equipment showrooms. I soon discovered that my choice was limited to either the run-of-the-mill stove that anyone can buy made by companies like Phillips, Brandt, Rosières, Dietrich, Gaggenau, or Bosch, or ultra-professional hunks of metal destined for restaurants made by Morice, Bonnet, or Ambassade. France wasn't like the United States with its wealth of semiprofessional stoves. Here it was the little guys or the big guns.

There was LaCornue, of course, which fits in a category all its own. Individually made to order, each one painstakingly constructed by a single artisan of the finest cast iron and enamel, the Rolls-Royce of the stove world, the LaCornue is so gorgeous you want to assemble the family around it and take its portrait. There were two things that held me back from the LaCornue, however, and the first was price. With the cost of labor in France and the time it takes to make and assemble a LaCornue we could have purchased another small house. The second was that I'd cooked on a LaCornue and while I enjoyed it, it wasn't the sublime experience I would have expected.

Nonetheless, I went to the LaCornue showroom in Paris to flirt with the possibilities. And there they all were, with names like Le Château, Le Petit Château, Le Castelet. They were stunning, sleek, old-world, with elegant brass hardware and beautiful oven doors that closed with a satisfying thud, forming a vacuum that ensured no heat could possibly escape. I discovered that LaCornue was just about to release a whole new line of stoves, intended, I suppose, for people with big dreams, smaller budgets, and limited space. I was excited and took the literature—there wasn't yet a stove to see. When I got home to study the brochure, however, I realized the baby LaCornues were made for Lilliputians. With their mini-burners and weensy ovens they would never do for me. Putting two pans on the stovetop at once without having one of them tumble to the floor would require a near-impossible feat of engineering. And the prices were still outrageous.

In leafing through professional catalogues, looking in show-rooms, and talking with professionals I had decided the most likely brand of stove for me was made by Morice. Sturdy, professional, and well-regarded, they had a certain sleekness to them. Of course I had not seen one up close but in the photographs they looked good. Morice also made a simple four-burner stove with a small oven and I figured two side-by-side would be perfect. The stoves were all gas, too, which is what I wanted. Not only is the cost of electricity in France impossibly high, but I don't trust electric heat for cooking—it's just not hot enough.

I went to a professional equipment showroom to look at a

THE PERFECT STOVE

Morice. The salesman said he didn't have the exact model I wanted but he showed me what he had. I was getting used to this. Showrooms in France aren't like showrooms in the United States. They usually don't have much in them, and the customer is required to place a great deal of faith in photographs and the salesperson. I'm not sure why but when you want to actually see a model of stove that is in a catalogue, nine times out of ten you can't. You have to imagine it.

The model the salesman did have to show was huge, an ultra-professional, hulking brute of a thing with stocky, unattractive legs. It didn't wow me. It didn't even make me excited, it just made me realize that my aesthetic demands were greater than I'd let on, even to myself. However, a problem worse than looks had presented itself. The all-gas ovens made by Morice had no broilers, and there was no way to have a broiler installed. The reasoning was simple. If a restaurant wants to produce dishes with a nice crusty brown top they simply stick it under the *salamandre*, an unwieldy piece of equipment that heats to approximately the same temperature as the surface of the sun and is very practical when producing food for forty to fifty people at a time.

Disappointed but not daunted, I tucked the Morice back in my file and continued my search, during the course of which I discovered that the era of beautiful home kitchens is arriving in France. Many of the professional stove manufacturers have begun to offer *mi-professionnels*, or semi-professional, stoves for the home, a step up from ordinary stoves but not quite in the league of professional stoves.

I became intrigued with a stove manufactured by a well-known company. From the dimensions in the catalogue there was one that would give me just what I wanted. I measured pots and pans and baking dishes, made three-dimensional drawings of the oven to see what would really fit in it, and calculated the cost, which fit within our budget. Now I just had to go see one. Michael and I took the train to Paris and found ourselves outside a promising-looking equipment store where stoves and refrigerators spilled out onto the sidewalk. We walked in and there was the stove sitting off to one side, looking just as good in real life as it did in the photographs. Graceful, it nonetheless looked well built and had many aesthetically pleasing features like brass knobs and a towel rack, and a lovely brushed metal finish. The closer I got, however, the less sturdy it looked and the brushed metal finish turned out to be paint. That in itself was no problem, I realized, because I knew they offered a plain, stainless steel façade.

I studied the burners; they were well placed with plenty of room for large saucepans. I could easily imagine a *pot au feu* simmering away on one of them. The brass handles were quaint, the brass bar across the front of the stove practical and attractive. The real test was yet to come, however. I opened the oven door. To my dismay it felt lightweight. I closed it and it kind of bounced once before really closing. Not a good sign. Michael did the same. He'd been examining other parts of the stove and I could tell from his look that he wasn't that impressed. My heart sank. I knew it was not as solid as what I was looking for. It certainly was attractive, however, and the price was decent.

Then I thought about the fact that for all the glories of French cuisine, most meals today cooked in a French home are prepared in kitchens the size of a large bathroom on the simplest of stoves with maybe four, but often just three, burners and one tiny oven.

THE PERFECT STOVE

The grandiose French kitchen belongs to a bygone era. It is Americans who have turned the contemporary kitchen into a palace where work and life intermingle. As France and French tastes change—and they are, as we could see with the fledgling selection of *mi-professionnels* stoves already available—choices will improve. For now, however, the selection was still limited.

I was becoming discouraged. I didn't want to wait for the evolution of the French kitchen. I wanted a stove I could use sometime in the next year. I continued to read the want ads and even went to several used equipment stores. I found what I thought was the stove of my dreams. True, it had six burners not eight and the oven was enormous, but it was painted a cobalt blue and in great shape, and it wasn't the least bit expensive. The salesman was really pressuring me, telling me he had seven clients who were desperate to have it but since I was *sur place*, on the spot, I could have it. I tried to bargain with him but the price was firm. He had me. I plunked down half the purchase price and arranged a delivery date.

But when the crew came to deliver it they couldn't fit it through the front door of our house. There they stood, the four *gaillards*, beefy men who had brought it, scratching their heads. Michael arrived home from an errand and looked at the stove, then got out his measuring tape. "We can't use this stove anyway," he whispered to me. "It's way too deep." At that exact moment the delivery crew had found a solution—they were proceeding to dismantle the stove and take it through the door piece by piece. I discouraged them, but they persisted. I told them they shouldn't do that, it was too bad but we'd live with our disappointment, that I didn't want them going to the trouble. I didn't tell them I'd made a mistake. They insisted in that frustratingly accommodating way people have when you really want them to just give up and give in, and finally I had to just come out and say I didn't want it.

They looked shocked and there was much head-shaking and a few phone calls back to the *patron*. With great huffing and puffing and more head-shaking they reloaded it onto the truck—it was incredibly awkward and heavy—and went off saying they didn't think I'd get my money back.

I called the store owner to explain that it was simply too big and that I hadn't realized it. He was very angry and didn't want to refund the money. I reminded him that the salesman had pushed me to buy it with the information that he had seven other people standing in line for it, and at that he relented. It took months, but I did get the down payment back.

With that experience I gave up entirely the idea of a used stove. My needs and desires were too specific and wouldn't be satisfied with just any old stove. So I kept looking. I got on the Internet and found an American company that was selling stoves in Europe, but they were obviously only doing it on paper because their salesman never did call me. I drooled over everything that was so easily available in the States, knowing I could get it shipped over but knowing also that it would cost as much as the stove to do it.

We finally decided we'd go look at a professional equipment place in Rouen that we'd avoided up until now, because everyone we knew said their prices were outrageous. We strolled around the showroom, which had a great selection of *mi-professionnels* in front, each of which we knew intimately, and a good selection of professional stoves in back. We admired a baby LaCornue that

THE PERFECT STOVE

was "on sale" for $5,000, and we drooled over a Smeg, which remained the best-designed stove we'd seen anywhere, except for its oven configurations, which were a mystery. It offered two electric ovens—I was ready to capitulate on that—but one oven was enormous, the other so narrow you couldn't fit a dinner plate into it. What was it for? No one could answer that question.

A salesman came to speak with us as we wandered and when we explained what we wanted he got a thoughtful, faraway look in his eye. He showed us what he had, listened to us talk, then sat us down.

"*Écoutez,*" he said. "I know what you want, and I can get it for you." I didn't believe him, but he started pulling out catalogues from a company called Cometto, which I'd never heard of.

Showing us photographs of the stoves, which were sturdy and beautiful in a very professional kind of way, he praised the workmanship comparing it with LaCornue but saying, very confidentially of course, that it was a much better stove because it was practical. He went on about all the European safety regulations that this stove met, about how they were made to order, and could thus be made in any configuration we wanted, about how the company had been in business for years but never made stoves for the home. They were just thinking about doing it, and he was sure they could give us what we wanted.

I started to get very excited. We talked more, going over all the stoves in his showroom and catalogues. He agreed with us on our assessments about them all, shaking his head in the most understanding way. "These companies are just beginning the *mi-professionnel* stove," he said. "I understand they don't suit your needs and, quite frankly, they aren't very good." Then he went through each brand of stove and told us why it had once been good and was no longer, or why it was good for some things but not for others. He was an excellent salesman, the first we had met who had given us good, solid information. He made a living selling equipment to food services and restaurants and we felt that our situation intrigued him and that he really wanted to find us a solution.

He gave us a Cometto catalogue and told us to go home and think about it, and that he would call us in a few days. The prices he had quoted were much more than we had planned to pay, but after all of the looking we'd done we knew they were fair.

We went home and got out our other catalogues and figures and compared them all, spreading everything on the dining room table. I re-drew diagrams of ovens so I could get a real sense of the dimension. The Cometto was looking better and better. We called the salesman before he could call us, to see if we could actually see a stove.

"Oh, I don't have a model to show you," he said, then paused. "There might be one you could go see, though it won't be exactly like what you want. I'll call the company and see about it."

One day he called us to say he had a Cometto in the showroom on its way out to a client. It wasn't the model we wanted, but it would show us the stove. We went to look at it and were impressed. It was way more stove than I needed in terms of its heft, but that was reassuring. It was attractive yet sensible. And we learned we could have it painted any color we wanted.

We hesitated, mostly because of the price. We looked around some more. We revisited runners-up to see if perhaps, in the light of what we now knew, they would work. Then we decided we'd buy it. It was going to cost us more than we'd paid for our car. It seemed ridiculous, but after a year's worth of looking it was either this or settle for something we knew wouldn't be right.

The salesman came to our house several times, first to show us more photographs of the Cometto, then to work out the details of its construction, as it, much like the LaCornue, was being built to our specifications. We had decided on a gas and an electric oven (to get the broiler). While I wanted eight burners that wouldn't be possible, so I settled for six. We opted for exterior thermostats. We drooled over the craftsmanship, the stainless steel pans that fit inside the burners and that could be removed and washed with ease, and the double-walled ovens.

When we'd decided on all the features we needed he calculated the price. It was well over what we'd discussed with him. He was very gentlemanly and discreet, and very firm. Finally he looked at me. "I'm going to write up what you want and give it to the *patron* of the company. When he's seen it, I'm going to have you call him to see about whether or not he can come down any further."

We got over that stumbling block—the owner met us halfway on the reduction we wanted, then the salesman returned to see where we were going to install it, then to see how the kitchen was coming along.

Finally all of the paperwork was finished and the salesman returned to present it to us so we could sign it and pay half the cost, and the company could begin to assemble our particular stove. The salesman was obviously excited. "*Vous savez*, I usually sell stoves to large companies who want a basic model," he said. "I visit them once, we strike our deal, and I return only for the installation. I would never make a living if I spent as much time with each client as I have spent with you. But I see lots of possibilities with this stove. Perhaps we can use it as a model and sell it to other individuals." We had driven him crazy with our requests and our negotiations and he had loved it.

The only thing we hadn't decided on was the color, because we needed a particular color wheel to choose from. "I have to get one from a garage, since the paint they use is car paint—it's sturdy and it lasts forever," the salesman said. That didn't seem difficult, but a month later I still hadn't seen a color wheel. I called him and he hemmed and hawed then finally just poured out his frustration. "The color wheels are impossible to get," he said. "No *garagiste* I've talked to will let me have one to bring you."

We went to our *garagiste* who shrugged and said he didn't dare give us his either, for if something happened to it he'd never be able to get another one.

"What a weird country," was all Michael could say.

Finally the salesman procured one and brought it by. We had 48 hours to look through it and decide our color. It was life and death, he assured us. So, we got the marble that was to line the counters of our kitchen and held every color up to it, finally choosing a rich pine green. With that decision made we forgot about the stove. I had to, otherwise I would have been so impatient and eager I wouldn't have been able to work and it would take several months to get it built and delivered.

I couldn't believe the decision-making process was over. No more trips to showrooms, no more perusing of catalogues. I hoped we'd made the right choice.

When the stove was delivered, it took three good-sized men to get it into the house—they had to unscrew the legs to get it through the door—set it up, and hook it to the gas. It was a regal piece of

THE PERFECT STOVE

equipment, so grand, so large, so imposing amidst the work site that was to be the kitchen. Once installed everyone, including the workmen, stood around to admire it. Its top was brushed stainless steel with a backsplash of stainless steel emblazoned with a gorgeous bronze medallion right in the center of it with the word Cometto and the logo of a crowing rooster. The pine green was a perfect match to the marble we'd chosen. I was itching to use it, absolutely dying to bake a cake, make a stew, sauté vegetables, even fry an egg, but I couldn't until the walls were protected behind it, for one splash of grease and they would have to be redone.

Michael covered the stove with a drop cloth and it was several more months before I turned it on. The kitchen still wasn't finished yet, but the pear and honey *clafoutis* and the herb roasted veal shank were better than any I'd ever made. I'm sure it was because they were cooked in such a gorgeous stove.

HERB ROASTED VEAL SHANK
JARRET DE VEAU RÔTI

Large, meaty, and flavorful veal shanks are one of the wonders of living in France, and they remain the focal point of many a repas de fête, *or holiday meal, in our home. I like to prepare them with plenty of herbs, so that after long, slow cooking they emerge laced with herbal flavor, and so tender the meat practically falls from the bone.*

I have no problem finding large veal shanks at my butcher's, but if you can't find large ones simply buy small ones. The cooking time will not differ substantially from that called for here. Serve this with a hearty Côtes du Rhône, or a wine from the Languedoc.

3 tablespoons/45ml extra-virgin olive oil

2 large veal shanks, preferably hind (3¾ pounds/1kg
   875g total), with bone

3 medium carrots, trimmed, peeled, and finely chopped

1 large onion, finely chopped

3 stalks celery, strings removed and finely chopped

2 garlic cloves, halved, green germ removed

Sea salt and freshly ground black pepper

3 long sprigs fresh rosemary plus 2 tablespoons fresh
   rosemary leaves

16 fresh sage leaves

¾ cup/180ml dry white wine such as Sauvignon Blanc

3½ to 4½ cups/875ml to 1½ liter rich beef or veal stock

1. Preheat the oven to 425° F/220° C/gas 8.

2. Heat the oil over medium-high heat in a heavy-bottomed, ovenproof dish that is just large enough to hold the veal shanks, liquid, and vegetables, until it is hot but not smoking. Brown the veal shanks on all sides in the hot oil. Add the vegetables and the garlic to the dish, placing them around the shanks, and stir so they are coated with oil. Roast the shanks and vegetables in the oven until they are golden, about 30 minutes. Remove the shanks from the oven and season them with salt and pepper. Add the rosemary sprigs and 10 of the sage leaves to the dish, and pour the wine and the stock over all. The liquid should come about halfway up the sides of the shanks.

3. Cover the dish and return to the oven to roast for 1 hour, turning the veal shanks once halfway through roasting. Remove

the cover and continue roasting until the veal shanks are deep golden, an additional hour, turning them once halfway through the roasting. Add additional stock if necessary to keep the level of liquid at least a third of the way up the sides of the shanks.

4. Remove the shanks from the oven. Mince the remaining 2 tablespoons rosemary and 6 sage leaves, pat them onto the meatiest part of the shanks, and return them to the oven to roast for an additional 15 minutes. Remove from the oven. Transfer the shanks to a warmed platter and cover them loosely with aluminum foil to keep them warm. Strain the juices, pressing hard on the herbs and vegetables. Return the cooking juices to the pan—if there are not enough cooking juices to sauce the meat, add additional stock. Bring the cooking juices to a gentle boil over medium-high heat, and boil until they are thickened, 4 to 5 minutes. Taste for seasoning, remove from the heat, and transfer to a warmed serving dish. Serve the shanks whole with the sauce alongside and carve them at the table.

6 SERVINGS

***

Sea Salt

I always use hand-harvested sea salt from Guérande, on the southwestern coast of Brittany. It comes in three varieties: coarse gray salt, which is used primarily in cooking and roasting; fine gray sea salt, which is used primarily at table; and pure white *fleur de sel*, which is used on certain delicate foods where its flavor and crunch will be appreciated. *Fleur de sel* is rare. Unlike the gray sea salts of Guérande, which are formed through carefully controlled evaporation, *fleur de sel* forms on top of the shallow water in the salt marshes only when the east wind blows. Then, its crystals sparkle and the *paludières* go into the marshes with their rakes and gently scrape the *fleur de sel* from the water—the men won't do it, for they claim they aren't careful enough.

PEAR AND HONEY CLAFOUTIS
CLAFOUTIS AUX POIRES ET AU MIEL

I was standing in line to buy pears at the market in Louviers from a handsome young pear grower. The elderly woman next to me was being very choosy about the state of her pears and their variety, and I asked her what she was going to do with them. "I'm going to make a clafoutis," *she said. I nodded appreciatively but perhaps not enthusiastically, for pear* clafoutis *is as common in Normandy as are cows in the rolling green pastures. "Oh, my* clafoutis *isn't any ordinary* clafoutis," *she said with a mischievous look. "Oh, no. Everyone who tastes it says it is the best they've ever eaten." "I don't suppose you'd be willing to share your recipe," I said to the woman. "Of course I would," she said. "I can't come to the market next weekend, but the weekend after that I will write it down and give it to you." I suggested she leave it with the pear grower. "I'd like a copy of it, too," he said eagerly.*

When I stopped by his stand two weeks later he had the recipe in hand. I took the beautifully handwritten recipe, bought several kilos

---

of both Williams and Comice pears as directed, and went home to make this lovely clafoutis. *The addition of honey makes it unique. I like the caramel on top but it isn't necessary if you think it's too much trouble.*

3 large pears/1½ pounds/750g, peeled, cored, and cut in
   sixths
⅓ cup/75ml mild but perfumed liquid honey, such as
   lavender
4 large eggs
¾ cup plus 2 tablespoons/115g flour
¼ cup plus 1 tablespoon/50g sugar
Pinch of fine sea salt
1 cup/250ml milk
4 tablespoons/60g unsalted butter, melted and cooled

1. Preheat the oven to 400° F/200° C/gas 6. Butter and flour an 11-inch/27½-cm round baking dish.

2. Arrange the pears in an attractive pattern in the baking dish. Drizzle them evenly with the honey.

3. Separate 3 of the eggs. In a large bowl mix the flour, all but 2 tablespoons (30g) of the sugar, and the salt. Make a well in the center and add the milk, 3 egg yolks, and 1 whole egg. Reserve the egg whites. Whisk together the ingredients in the well, then gradually whisk in the dry ingredients to make a smooth batter. Quickly but thoroughly whisk in the melted butter.

4. In another bowl, whisk the egg whites with a small pinch of salt until they are foamy. Add 1 tablespoon of sugar and continue whisking until soft peaks form. Fold the egg whites into the batter, then pour the batter over the pears. Bake in the center of the oven until the *clafoutis* is puffed and golden, about 30 minutes. Remove from the oven and place on a wire rack to cool.

5. To make the caramel, heat the remaining 1 tablespoon of sugar with 1 teaspoon water in a small, heavy saucepan over medium heat, shaking the pan occasionally to evenly distribute the sugar, until the mixture turns a deep golden brown, 3 to 5 minutes. Don't stir the sugar, which might encourage it to crystallize, just rotate the pan so the sugar and water caramelize evenly. When the sugar has caramelized, drizzle it over the top of the *clafoutis*. Wait about 5 minutes so the caramel hardens, then serve.

4 TO 6 SERVINGS

TWELVE

Notre Dame

THE YEAR JOE ENTERED CP, the equivalent of first grade, was a big one for us. Not only was it his entry into the world of *les grands*, or the big kids, but he went from a small village *maternelle*, or nursery school, to the much larger school in downtown Louviers, and from the public system to the private.

We'd chosen the only private establishment in Louviers, a Catholic school, after I'd visited the public school in our sector and met the principal, who basically discouraged me from sending Joe there. She was transferring out of the school at the end of the year and she said the teachers weren't very *sympa*. I had only to observe one class for five minutes to get a sense of what she was talking about, as the teacher verbally pummeled the children into doing their work.

We already knew the director of the Catholic school, a nun who passed our house often and was sweet and interested in Joe's progress. When I told her we would like to come speak with her about Joe's going to Notre Dame, she was visibly delighted.

I grew up in the American Catholic school system, so when, in the course of our meeting with her, she suggested I might want to volunteer for something, such as teaching English, I wasn't surprised. I remembered *my* mother's volunteer days and I told her I would consider it. I was surprised, however, on seeing that the curriculum included no formal catechism. In fact, the emphasis on religion was minor, which greatly reassured both of us, particularly Michael. He had only agreed to send Joe to Notre Dame because it was clearly the better of the choices available to us.

I couldn't believe the list of school supplies necessary to launch Joe into the French school system. Single-spaced on two sides of a sheet of paper, it included an astonishing array of specific *cahiers*, or workbooks with their dimensions and number of pages, the specific colors of protective folders required, and the exact number of pleats for the accordion folders that would, presumably, hold his work. There was also a daunting list of writing instruments and art supplies.

Convinced of the need to be prepared and to follow directions to the letter so that our son (or I) wouldn't be subject to that oh-so-French criticism of *travail mal fait*, or work poorly done, I set out first to the supermarket where I had been told I could find everything.

I entered the school supply aisle and checked my list. *Trois cahiers de travaux pratiques, sans spirales*, practical workbooks without spirals. I chose three, though they had more pages than called for. "Will he be reprimanded for that?" I wondered, understanding how important conformity is in this often frustratingly conformist country. I put them in the basket along with the *carnet, sans spiral format, 11 × 17 cm, 96 pages*—which also had too many pages.

Feeling uncertain, I spied a woman across the aisle and asked if she was buying supplies for her children. When she said she was, I showed her my list and asked her if I had chosen correctly. She was wonderfully tolerant, smiled in an understanding way, and looked through my basket and my list. I had made some errors and she set me straight. I thanked her profusely. *"Ne vous inquiétez pas,"* she said. "Don't worry—I had to go through this when my first one went to school. Each year teachers want specific things and they are always different from the year before."

Feeling confident, I moved on to multicolored plastic folders and large, imposing envelopes filled with sheets of heavy, ivory-colored drawing paper, a weekly *agenda,* or calendar, and three large spiral notebooks.

I went to the writing implement section and found the red, the blue, and the green pen, the twenty-centimeter ruler, the pencil sharpener in its box (*pas de fantaisie* was written on the list next to pencil sharpeners, which meant that I couldn't buy one shaped like an airplane or a truck, just something plain and workaday).

I put a *trousse* or leather pencil case in the cart and it fell next to the ruler, which was longer by several centimeters. Oh no. The ruler was meant to go in the pencil case. I returned the pencil case and measured all of the others with the ruler to see if one would fit. None were long enough. I double-checked the list. "Twenty-centimeter ruler." "Why would they want that?" I thought. There seemed to be no pencil case that existed to hold it. "Is it just to be difficult?" I wondered. "Do the public schools ask for this size? Is there something I don't understand?"

I continued down the list, picking out the colored markers and the easy-clean board they would write on. I opened one of the markers and just about passed out from its intense, petrol odor. "They let kids use these?" I thought. I was sure they were toxic, though nothing of the sort was written on them.

On the list was a rag for wiping the board clean, so when I got home I went to my linen armoire and pulled out a red and white checked napkin that had little lobsters dancing around it. I thought it was perfect for a six-year-old's school rag.

I found nearly everything on the list including the long ruler. Surely I would find a pencil case to fit. Indeed, at another supermarket I found one with a Dragonball Z logo on it that I knew would send Joe into a fit of ecstasy.

Joe, who seemed remarkably poised about this upcoming experience, which tugged my heart in all directions, was thrilled with the school booty. We carefully organized and labeled it all, checking off on the list the items I had found, marking in red the items still to find. We filled the pencil case and put the rest of the supplies directly into the blue leather satchel he would wear on his back when he walked to school. In went the math book I'd bought—its separate pages of pop-out cardboard coins, which I assumed the children would use to learn the currency, falling out and exciting Joe's interest. He immediately wanted to pop them all out and start playing *magasin*, or store.

"No," I said. "You must wait until the *maîtresse* tells you what to do with those." I was terrified he might use them before school and be the only child whose parents had allowed such a grave breach of discipline.

In went the reading book, whose stories Joe had already told me were *stupide*, and the writing book. I lifted the satchel and put it on his back. He straightened, looked at me, and said, "Mama, it's really heavy." And I still had things to add.

I put it all away, feeling nearly prepared. I would look for all the items marked in red at the local *papeterie*, or stationers. It was August and the *papeterie* was closed for a month so I would have to race in there the minute it opened to finish this laborious task in time for the first day of school. I could only hope they'd have everything I needed so that Joe could go to school with a full satchel. Imagine the shame if he didn't.

There was still more to do, for his clothes needed labeling because one of their weekly activities was to be a morning in the city swimming pool. My anxiety level about this whole thing was very high, mingled, I'm sure, with the anxiety of seeing our son go off into the big, grown-up world of real school. I could tell I was anxious by my dreams—in one I forgot to label his things and he lost them all the first day. In another I labeled them illegibly and everyone made fun of him.

As much as I worried, I was excited, too, for this year Joe would learn to read (by Christmas, we were told). Joe would probably also learn to pray at school. We both figure he will make his choice about religions when he's old enough to have thought about it. Until then it won't hurt him to be exposed to Catholicism, particularly in the land of Joan of Arc and St. Theresa, the little flower, where the history of religion is practically a part of daily life. Every time we go to Rouen we pass the Vieux Marché where

Joan of Arc was burned at the stake, and we've been to the cathedral in nearby Lisieux several times and seen the exhibit there about the life of the beautiful St. Theresa.

We'd been told that Joe would have homework every day, a novel experience.

In primary and middle school, students go to school Monday and Tuesday, have Wednesday off, then go back Thursday, Friday, and Saturday morning. This meant his school week would be four-and-a-half days long instead of the four-day week he had at the *maternelle*. The system was instituted long ago to give children a day during the week for religious education, and it holds true for Catholic as well as public schools. Today many teachers in the French school system would like to change it, for it leaves everyone with a very short weekend, but for the moment it holds. Michael and I have adjusted our work schedules to fit the school schedule, and we each work half a day on Wednesday so we can spend time with Joe, and take Saturday afternoon and Sunday off.

As the date approached I found myself becoming increasingly nervous. I recognized the symptoms. As a child I changed schools every two years as we followed my father's military career. All the first days at school were flashing before me. I was much more nervous than Joe, as though it were I, not he, who would be going to school. Michael rolled his eyes and thought I was overdoing it. He was right and I knew it, but some things you just can't control.

The night before the big day Joe polished his new leather shoes and set them out to wear. We laid out his clothes, checked his list of school supplies once again, folded and refolded the red and white cloth with the lobsters on it. He went to bed easily, excited about his first day at school.

NOTRE DAME

We were up early and at 8:45—a half hour later than the normal hour, the school administration's concession for the first day—all three of us left the house, Joe with his satchel on his back. After about ten steps he asked his father to take it for him. "It's really heavy, Papa," he said in a little voice. I looked at him. I could tell he was nervous, his face set in a serious look. But he eagerly walked the ten minutes through town, down a long narrow street and up to the double metal doors that opened into the school playground.

The school used to be a boarding school. I've met many adults my age who lived there during their early school years. Now there is a small handful of nuns who live there who have added a few homey touches like paintings and little doilies on the furniture in the entrance to the administrative offices, and a pretty little flower garden with a shrine to the Virgin Mary across from it, which the children aren't allowed to enter. The playground is huge and divided into three sections—one for the preschoolers in *maternelle*, who start as early as age 2½; one for the younger primary children, who included Joe; and one for the "big kids" ages nine and ten. I had noticed when visiting the school that there wasn't a toy, a painted line, a basketball hoop in sight. "What do these kids do during recess?" I wondered.

The playground was filling up with parents and their children who were starched and clean behind the ears. We didn't know a soul and weren't quite sure of the protocol. All we knew is that the children of Joe's age had to arrive by 9 A.M., so here we were.

The principal, a dour-looking woman, arrived and clapped her hands for attention. She took up a microphone and announced that she would call the name of the teacher then the name of each child in her class. I was excited about Joe's teacher, Brigitte, whom I'd met briefly years before when she taught Edith's children. A tiny woman with thick red hair and an angular face full of humor, she was the first teacher called.

She looked expectantly at the crowd, a smile twitching at the corners of her mouth. "That's your teacher," I whispered down to Joe, who was clutching and unclutching my hand and stepping on one foot with another. He was so nervous.

The principal started calling names and children walked up to Brigitte, offered their faces for a kiss, then got in line behind her. "Loomis, Joseph." Joe put his satchel on his back and without a backward glance strode up to the teacher, offered his cheek like everyone else, and got in line. He didn't look at us, nor give us a sign. We waited until all the children's names had been called and Brigitte had walked them off toward their classroom before we left the schoolyard. We walked home, both filled with a mixture of excitement and apprehension for Joe in his new world.

At 11:25 I was back at school to pick up Joe for lunch. The bell rang and he, along with several classmates, burst forth from the school. "Mama," he yelled as he flew toward me. "I love it!"

And that began his first year at Notre Dame. Every morning Joe and I left the house at 8:15, stepping outside into air redolent of the morning smells of France—butter, freshly baked bread, caramelized sugar. We would wander our way past bakeries, succulent-smelling *charcuteries*, and a handful of shops that include the *parfumerie*, the *graineterie*, a shoe store, then across the marketplace to school.

We usually arrived about five minutes early and would walk into the playground and wait together until the bell rang. Then Joe would put on his satchel, and line up with the other children behind his teacher. I would wait with the other parents until Brigitte led the children into school, then go home.

Standing in that playground in the early mornings made for good people-watching as parents arrived with their charges. I marveled at the well-dressed mothers who even if they wore jeans had high heels on their bare feet, perfect makeup and hair, and perfume trailing sweetly behind them. Many of the fathers wore the *bourgeois* uniform of olive green overcoat with yellow cashmere scarves, their shoes slightly scuffed in the way Frenchmen have of ignoring that one detail of their dress.

There was another fashion category among the parents which surprised me. Particularly on Saturday mornings many would come in shiny sweat suits with brand-new Nikes (pronounced "n-eye-ks") on their feet. I hadn't expected the French to dress so casually, though admittedly their sweat suits were starched and ironed, the shoes unblemished.

Children generally reflected their parents. Most of the girls wore dresses and sweet little empire-style overcoats, while the boys wore corduroy pants, button-down shirts, and wool sweaters or else the opposite extreme of sweatpants and sweatshirts. Joe was the trousers, shirt, and wool sweater type, though occasionally he asked to wear sweats, which we wouldn't allow.

Joe's ardor cooled as he realized that school involved work and discipline, that the teacher had expectations, that the day was long, and that he had to sit still in his seat for most of it. To

Brigitte's credit she had the kids do stretching and breathing exercises each morning to help them settle in. And she had a sense of humor, so it wasn't all hard work. But she was severe, too, with rigid ideas. One day during the second week Joe came home and handed me the lobster napkin I'd given him to wipe his slate. "It's too fancy," he said. "Brigitte says I need to bring a rag."

There were times when she yelled at the kids in a way that both Michael and I found astonishing. We had already noticed that French parents yell a great deal at their kids in general, so we weren't entirely surprised that this carried over into school. We didn't much like it and we spoke about it to the teacher. She took our comment well, though she was surprised at our observation, for she felt that in comparison with her colleagues she didn't yell much at all. Another one of her disciplinary tactics was to tear a page out of a child's workbook if the work wasn't done correctly or tidily enough. We found this harsh, but Joe accepted it as normal. He was adjusting to French ways, and we had to follow.

For the first half of the year we continued to pick up Joe each day for lunch at 11:30 and return him to school at 1:30. After eating we would trade off spending the lunch hour with him reading, playing a game, or otherwise occupying him. It took a big bite out of the workday, but we loved having him come home.

It dawned on us, however, that he wasn't really making friends. We realized the only time the kids had to get to know each other was during the long lunch break, so we decided that he should stay at school for lunch at least two days a week.

We decided to institute that after all of the CP classes went on their yearly outing, which was to be a week at the beach. There, during what was called the *classe de mer*, they would spend the mornings in a classroom and the afternoons outdoors either visiting an oyster farm, digging for clams, or inspecting tide pools.

The list of belongings necessary for that trip was almost as long as the list of school supplies, and it included stamped, self-addressed envelopes so the kids could write home. Parents weren't allowed to visit, call, or write letters.

We had expected to be delighted to have Joe off with his class for a week and had imagined rediscovering our life pre-Joe. Instead, we missed him so much that the house felt like an empty shell. Each morning one of us walked to school where the news of the *classe de mer* was posted on the front door in brief bulletins like "It's sunny, the kids went wading, all is well." That was enough to reassure us.

Friday rolled around and with it the return of the children. I called to verify when the bus was to arrive and was told 6 P.M. We arrived at 5:45 and found it already there. Most of the children had gone home. There was Joe talking to a teenage boy, one of the monitors from the trip. We were mortified to be late, but Joe wasn't upset in the least. Tanned and freckled, he threw himself in our arms then went back to kiss his teacher and say good-bye to the teenager. Brigitte came up to us, bubbling.

"Impeccable, c'était impeccable pour lui," she said. "It was perfect for him and he opened up, made friends, had fun. You'll see. He's changed."

Joe just smiled, proudly. As we walked home he told us what they'd done, talked about the oysters and the clams, the wading, and the sand. Then he talked about the *boom*, or dance. Apparently one night the teachers had installed a sound system in the dining room where they were all staying and after the kids were in their pajamas they turned up the music and everyone danced. We later saw a video and there was Joe right in amongst them doing his rendition of *Saturday Night Fever*.

The difference in Joe was remarkable. Less shy and reserved now, he had made friends and was eager to go to school. We instituted the two lunchtimes a week at the *cantine* and he hardly objected. Indeed, by the end of the year he was staying every day, and it was unthinkable to him that he eat lunch at home. Of course we missed having him come home but it was a relief, too, for now we could work full days and be much more available to him when he came home at 4:30 in the afternoon.

I had noticed that the weekly menu from the *cantine* was placed outside the front door of the school and I would read it and drool. Three courses were offered each day, including salads or the *entrée* or appetizer, meat or fish with two vegetables and a starch as the main course, and desserts, which were often flavored yogurts, but now and then might be something homemade like a poached pear in chocolate sauce or a cream-filled pastry.

Joe would come home rapturous after a lunch of *hachis Parmentier*, a blend of ground beef and onions topped with mashed potatoes. He also loved *cordon bleu*, a chicken breast wrapped around ham and cheese that is breaded and fried. He never talked about vegetables, but if there was a good dessert we always heard about it.

I decided I would investigate further and asked the principal if I could eat with the children one day. She agreed. We arranged a date and I showed up at the appointed hour of 11:45. I slipped in line behind Joe and we walked into the *cantine*. Joe and his friends got me my tray and set a glass on it, gallantly provided silverware, and led me straight past the *entrée* salads to desserts and fruit. There they spent a few minutes mulling over fruit yogurt or a chocolate and cream confection, with half of them choosing yogurt, the others going for the chocolate. The cheese selections sat next to the desserts and one of the boys gave me a wedge of Camembert and a square of Kiri, which resembles cream cheese.

I asked Joe and his friends if they were going to take salads and they all looked at me cross-eyed. "*Non*," they said in unison. I reached for a tempting sausage and potato salad then stood in front of the hot food while a cheery woman served slices of rosy roast beef with *jus*, a creamy potato gratin, steamed barley, and parsleyed carrots. It looked surprisingly good. No one in my group asked for the carrots, and several dolloped mustard on their plates to go with the roast beef.

In the dining area the school's principal and the head nun were busily cutting up beef for the smallest children, making sure water pitchers were filled, keeping the general peace. They graciously seated me and my party, which now included seven youngsters. We had forgotten napkins, so the principal rushed off to get some, returning with a handful that included two flowered ones, for me and for Joe. We were getting the royal treatment.

The children discussed food the entire time they were eating, and I learned that this was not their favorite meal. Their eyes sparkled when they talked about the hamburgers and French fries, or *hachis Parmentier*, or *cordon bleu*, or fried fish. One boy piped up that he liked it when the chef prepared *chinois*, or Chinese food.

Another said *"beurk,"* or yuck. They all agreed that they loved dessert whether it was fruit yogurt or homemade apple compote.

It took exactly one half hour for the group to finish the meal, which included time for a demonstration of one boy swallowing a Kiri whole, and another mashing his banana in his water glass and eating it with a spoon.

At the last bite they were all up like shots, rushing to empty their trays and stack their dishes, so they could go out and play. "See you later, Mama," Joe said, waving as he ran outside with his friends.

As school lunches go it was pretty good. I might have urged more vegetables on the kids, but then what mother wouldn't? What I'd enjoyed most was the detailed conversation about food. But when push came to shove what really interested these kids was *la récré*, or recess. Food was simply a hurdle to get over before getting outside!

By the end of his first year, Joe was completely integrated into school. The education he was receiving was strict and formal and steeped in basics, and he was flourishing. By mid-year he was reading well and writing in an elegant longhand. He memorized a poem every two weeks, and did lots of coloring (and was reprimanded if he ever went outside the lines). He was learning about Vikings and Gauls and Celts, and was making forays into science and biology. He was even learning a bit about art as we discovered well after the fact. We had taken Joe to an art opening of a painter friend of ours, and after going through the whole exhibit Joe couldn't contain himself.

"I hate this art," he said. "My favorite painter is Monet."

Not long after that we went to Monet's house and garden in

nearby Giverny and Joe was overcome with excitement as he discovered the *pont japonais* (Japanese bridge) and the water lilies in real life, and pointed out many things that he'd learned in class.

His class switched from swimming to ice skating when the weather turned cold, and they went on several outings toward the end of the year and spent a lot of time practicing a dance program to perform in front of the parents at the end of the year for the *kermesse*, or annual fair.

We sometimes shake our heads at what we perceive as the lack of creativity and imagination used in teaching children in the French school system, the general lack of art and music, the dourness of the administration. To its credit, however, Notre Dame has a less rigorous classification system than many schools. The children aren't given grades, so, while they all know who is best and worst among them, they aren't assigned a ranking in the class.

Since Joe's second year I've taught English to his class, so I get a close look at what happens in the classroom. We've mostly appreciated the individual teachers, though the yelling continues in varying degrees, which we don't like. However, time is set aside for the children to have fun, and each child's birthday is celebrated in class, so that on any given day they all burst from the classrooms with their mouths full of candy. We like the insistence on the fundamentals such as intense reading, penmanship, mathematics, biology, geometry, and ethics. The homework has not yet become onerous, and while Joe is not overjoyed with school—how many children are?—he does well.

I received a letter from a friend in the United States whose son is the same age as Joe. She described the Montessori school he attends. "The theme this year will be Stonehenge to Star Wars: A

Celestial Odyssey. They'll learn how different cultures regarded celestial bodies, with a focus on the Anasazi Indians."

I sighed as I looked at Joe's list of homework: mathematics, spelling, poetry, writing, and reading. It would be terrific for Joe to participate in a program like that, but it looks as though it will be up to us to teach him about celestial bodies and the Anasazi. At the very least, and aside from his fluency in two languages, he'll know how to recite poetry in French and understand the position of a cheese course in a meal.

AUDREY'S YOGURT CAKE
GÂTEAU AU YAOURT D'AUDREY

This is a cake that every French schoolgirl once learned to make, and many still do, though they now learn it at home rather than at school. Over the years I've collected dozens of recipes for this cake and never found one that was particularly good. Recently I was at Notre Dame, Joe's school, preparing to teach my weekly English lesson. The teacher came over to me and whispered that there was going to be a party for one of the girls who was leaving, and would I please stay to enjoy it after the lesson. At the stroke of 9:30 the girl's slightly harried mother arrived with a basket containing three cakes. I helped the teacher cut and distribute slices of cake while the mother poured glasses of Coca and Orangina.

When all the children were served I had a slice of cake. I took one bite and realized that I was eating something special. I asked the mother what kind of cake it was and she shrugged and said, "It's a gâteau au yaourt, nothing more." I told her it was the best yogurt cake I'd ever had. I think you will agree.

1½ cups/200g all-purpose flour

¾ teaspoon baking powder

Pinch of fine sea salt

3 large eggs

1 cup/200g sugar

½ cup/125ml plain, full-fat yogurt

1 teaspoon vanilla

8 tablespoons/125g unsalted butter, melted and cooled

3 ounces/90g bitter chocolate, preferably Lindt 64%,
    melted in a double boiler, then cooled

Confectioners' sugar, optional

1. Butter and flour one 9½-inch/24-cm round cake pan. Preheat the oven to 375° F/190° C/gas 5.

2. Sift together the flour, baking powder, and salt onto a piece of waxed or parchment paper.

3. In a large bowl, whisk together the eggs and the sugar until they are light and pale yellow. Sprinkle the dry ingredients over the eggs and sugar, whisking to incorporate them. Fold in the yogurt and vanilla, then the melted butter.

4. Pour half the batter into the prepared cake pan. Fold the melted chocolate into the remaining batter until it is thoroughly combined. Pour the chocolate batter on top of the plain batter that is already in the cake pan and run a rubber spatula through the batter several times to make a marble pattern.

5. Bake the cake in the center of the oven until it is slightly mounded and your finger leaves a very slight impression when you touch the top of it, about 35 minutes.

6. Remove the cake from the oven and let it cool in the pan for about 15 minutes, then turn it out onto a wire rack. Serve when it is fully cool, or the following day. If you like, dust the top with confectioners' sugar.

ABOUT 8 SERVINGS

THIRTEEN

The Beauty Around Us

THE OTHER DAY while I was walking home from taking Joe to school—a ten-minute trip each way through the center of Louviers—I became completely lost in the sky. It was a mosaic of mottled gray with pockets of pale blue, shadows of rose, pillows of billowy white, wavy edges of what I have to call yellow but were really simply pure, almost liquid, light. It was a sky that demanded attention—once I started looking at it I couldn't look away. It fascinated me as I tried to figure out how to describe it, what to call its colors.

When I was growing up my father, who was a pilot in the air force, described a pale blue sky dashed with pink as "sky blue pink," a term that I find perfect in its descriptive nature. This sky wasn't quite that, though it was similar, and I wished I could find a phrase as apt to describe it.

Since living in Normandy I've found myself reflecting a great deal on the sky, and on color and light. I didn't expect to do so. I've been in so many places where drama forced reflection, like Montana where the sky makes you feel tiny; in Maine where the play of color off of frigid, steely water and brittle sky pushes you to huddle near the fire; in Washington State's Skagit Valley where, when the tulips are in bloom, there is so much color you can't decide whether to embrace it or run from it; or on the ocean off the Alaskan coast where light beams not only from the heavens but from the cracks between the trees and up from the backs of the king salmon that glide through the water. In all of my previous visits to Normandy and its peaceful, bucolic landscape I had always felt a force that drew me back. I now think it was the sky, the color, the light.

I take great comfort from the lushness of Normandy, its green pastures that surround us and run down into the Vallée d'Auge with its low thatched farmhouses; the dark blue coastal waters off Honfleur and Houlgate, Fécamp, and Mont-St-Michel; the blushing reds of the apples that hang heavy in the graceful apple trees from June through September. The colors of land and sea are soothing, calming, constant. Light provides the edge, the excitement, the visceral emotion, a different but distinguishable palette of colors, sensations, and moods every single day.

We have a front row seat for the performance, because the sky and the light play out their daily drama on the church. I can't count the number of times while we've been eating—either outside in our small courtyard, where we are physically dwarfed by the church, or inside in the small dining room whose window looks out into the front yard and at the church—that either Michael or I have called everyone's attention to the light. It can be

THE BEAUTY AROUND US

breathtaking, too good to miss, too dramatic to overlook, too magical, sometimes, to believe.

Depending on the season, the church might be bathed in light so golden and rich it looks as if a jar of honey had been upended over its carved buttresses. At other times, usually around five o'clock in the afternoon, it looks like a lacy ballerina dressed in delicate pink, a reflection of the late afternoon sky. The other morning it was light and mottled like the sky, but toward the end of the afternoon on a day that became increasingly cold, it looked like brittle, chilly gray snow.

I frequently glance out the window, memorizing different things in the garden, using the moment away from the computer or pencil and paper for reflection. The other day my eye was pulled to one of the last roses of the season on the bush that climbs up the end of the house as high as the tiny window of Joe's room on the second floor. Brave and alone it stood out a deep pink, in dramatic contrast to the slice of gray sky behind it between the church's tower and the building that houses Le Progrès, the café kitty-corner from the house. Across the grass at the outside edge of the garden, on the hedge near the street at the foot of the church hung our last, bright orange *potimarron*, a pear-shaped squash whose plant valiantly climbed up and out of the garden to the very top of the hedge. The *potimarron* itself was so heavy it seemed to defy gravity, hanging there like a vivid, overgrown ornament on a Christmas tree. I knew I should pick it so we could enjoy its sweet, chestnut-flavored flesh, but if I did that I'd miss its brave spot of color.

Our modest patch of grass, which is about twenty feet square (except that it isn't quite square), is at its most gorgeous, engorged with rain and almost kelly green from the late autumn sun, which has been particularly abundant this year. I love its color now, in contrast to the deeper, darker green of summer when it is fed with sun but more starved for water. I do miss our summer flowers, however, which grow well in our soil, and so they should. For years—hundreds I believe—our front garden was cultivated by the Sisters of Mercy, and rows of vegetables went from the front door around the old lady of the garden—our apple tree—right to the edge of the property, which was once bordered by a high brick wall and is now bordered by a hedge and a metal fence.

Our neighbors the florists remember the sisters' vegetable garden in recent times. They also remember the gradual decrepitude that took over the garden after the house was purchased by the woman we bought it from. The trees withstood the neglect, though they grew droopy and sad. The soil itself seemed to wither, for it was nearly dead when we took over and the few things we planted in it had a hard time maturing. We collected compost from a farmer who lives in Surtauville, a village about fifteen minutes from us, and dug it into the garden the first winter. By spring and planting time the soil already had a new look to it, and that year vegetables and flowers were stronger, more vibrant. We have repeated the composting nearly every year, so that now whatever we plant thrives.

I indulge myself without hesitation in the bachelor buttons, *capucines* (nasturtiums), *soucis* (calendula), *nigella* (love-in-a-mist), dahlias (such generous plants), and cosmos that I love to pick for bouquets. The *hortensias*, or hydrangeas, planted on either side of the "holy stone" were malingering when we bought the house and they are now productively purple and white. The lilies of the val-

THE BEAUTY AROUND US

ley sprout up under them, waxy and pure, around the first of May and a variety of other lilies bloom later in the year. I planted white strawberry plants, which have run rampant, their lush, dark green leaves creating a bumpy blanket under the pear tree. Unfortunately they yield a mere handful of berries. Michael thinks they are a space waster and he's right, yet that handful of berries is so ethereally flavored, so tender and juicy, so unlike anything that can be purchased anywhere that I can't bear to give them up. I keep thinking one day I'll have space to let them really go, and time to tend them, so their production will increase.

We also have ruby chard, sorrel, *mesclun*, and a variety of other lettuces including butter lettuce and gorgeous red oak leaf lettuce, which I plant on the border of the garden. There they look like giant flowers against the black soil. We eat their leaves all summer and into the winter—I pick from them selectively the way a deer nibbles on plants, just the most tender leaves for salad, so that they provide for a long time. I also have domesticated and wild arugula growing up around the trunks of the espaliered apples, curly endive, tarragon, several sage varieties, and a whole garden full of different mints. I have sweet cicely and garlic chives, thyme and oregano, fennel and salad burnet, and other herbs that are essential for good eating. They and the flowers mix in the garden in a wonderful blend of colors and textures. Around mid-summer when the plants are healthiest the harsh summer sun bounces off them. That same sun a month later, in the fall, enfolds them at different times of the day to create innumerable and intense contrasts.

The espaliered apple trees we planted to shield us from our

neighbors are young and healthy, their leaves at this late autumn date a deep, even green. The leaves on the elderly apple and pear trees, however, are starting to turn pale, and it is only a matter of a few short weeks before they will be the first to denude themselves and show their graceful skeletons. Then the light plays around their gnarled bones like a squirrel running around the branches, and their shadows go from graceful to snaky.

During the Middle Ages when our church, Notre Dame de Louviers, was built—it took two hundred years to construct, so its architectural style meanders from the Romanesque to the Gothic—churches were painted gaily, like birthday cakes. Vestiges of the vivid colors that once covered it remain, and on cloudy days they are easiest to see, for bright sun makes them fade away. To see the colors I have just to look at the large door across from my window where a statue of the Virgin stands, hip cocked to hold the infant Jesus. Her robes are generous folds of corn yellow, her upper garments show pale blue, above and behind her head is a patch of pale rose, and next to that are hints of royal blue and gold.

Few people are aware of the whisper of colors still on the church, but how could they be? The colors are almost impossible to see unless you really search the statue and doorway in certain light, and we are the only people in town who have the luxury to do so from just the right perspective. To the casual observer the doorway in question is simply gray and black, lost to soot. We hope that some of the money available to shore up the church, which is sagging in parts and leaking in others, will be appropriated to bring back the rich old colors that remain. A costly laser process exists that magically uncovers old paint—we saw its results on the cathedral of Amiens to the north, and we hope it will be used one day in Louviers.

Normandy is known for being a rainy region, a reputation not entirely undeserved. For former Seattlites like us, however, the rain here is nothing. Even when it's a *temps de cochon*, or "pig weather," and the rain is tumbling from the sky, there is tangible light that minimizes the grayness. When it is soft and misty, walking in it is like getting a facial.

When the torrents fall and the temperature is truly bone-chillingly cold even the Norman light can't warm it up, and the best place to be is inside. January and February are the hardest months, for dark descends in mid-afternoon and the evenings are long and cold. A favorite way of warding off the chill is for Michael to build a fire in the dining room fireplace and for me to put chestnuts in a pan and set it over the flames. Then I serve soup—golden orange pumpkin, which looks like the sun in a bowl, or mixed vegetable potage redolent of bay leaf and thyme, or rich and subtle creamed turnip soup. Sometimes we have a loaf of Michael's bread with a vegetable frittata, or a goat cheese sauce over steamed vegetables and a fresh *baguette* and salad. For dessert I make *clafoutis*, just like a true Normande. This fruit-filled pan cake is the most common of winter desserts. I fill it with pears or apples or, like my friend and neighbor Nadine Devisme, raisins soaked in rum. If it is Tuesday night, which is like Friday night for us, since Joe doesn't have school on Wednesday, we either invite friends over for supper, sit near the fire and play cards or a *jeu de société*, a board game, or sit on the couch and read a book out loud.

Fortunately the dark days of winter don't last too long in Normandy. By March spring has arrived, the skies have cleared, and we're looking forward to another whole year of stunning Norman light and sky.

CREAM OF TURNIP SOUP
SOUPE DE NAVETS À LA CRÈME

I like to make this soup on cool early-winter evenings when dark descends early and we light a fire in the dining room fireplace. The soup is as comforting as it is delicious. Even Joe likes it! To keep the flavor subtle you must use baby turnips, and be sure to remove their skin.

2 tablespoons/30g unsalted butter

1 small onion, diced

2 pounds/1kg fresh baby turnips, trimmed, peeled, and diced

1½ cups/375ml light veal stock

1½ cups/375ml bottled water

2 dried, imported bay leaves

Fine sea salt

¾ cup/185ml *crème fraîche* or heavy cream, preferably not ultra-pasteurized

1. Place the butter, onion, and turnips in a large, heavy-bottomed saucepan over medium heat and cook until the onions

and the turnips are translucent, stirring occasionally so they don't stick, for about 15 minutes. Add the veal stock and the water, stir, and add the bay leaves and salt to taste. Increase the heat to medium-high and bring to a boil. Reduce the heat so the liquid is at a lively simmer and cook, covered, until the turnips are very tender, 25 to 30 minutes.

2. Remove the bay leaves and purée the soup. Whisk in the *crème fraîche* so the soup is slightly foamy (or use a wand blender to incorporate the cream), season to taste with salt, and serve.

4 TO 6 SERVINGS

SWISS CHARD FRITTATA
FRITTATA AUX BLETTES

I always plant ruby chard in my garden—I can't imagine a garden without its dramatic presence. Its stems are blood red, its generous, wavy leaves a deep green veined with the same vivid red, so intense it vibrates among the nasturtiums and lettuces, the tomatoes and the fennel. It is as delicious as it is ornamental. I pick the first, newest leaves to add to salads, then as it gets larger and more fleshy I cook it, using it in soups, stews, and often all on its own seasoned simply with garlic and toasted bread crumbs. This frittata is one of my favorite ways to use it, for it makes a wonderfully robust appetizer that pleases everyone—it is the only food, I think, that I have never had anyone of any age turn down. Joe loves it and comes back for serving after serving!

It is best served at room temperature, with a Languedoc red.

1 garlic clove, minced
2 tablespoons/30ml extra-virgin olive oil
1 pound/500g ruby or regular green Swiss chard, stems
    removed, leaves cut in ½-inch/1.3cm strips
6 large eggs
¼ teaspoon sea salt
¼ cup/1 ounce/30g finely grated Parmigiano-Reggiano
Generous pinch of hot paprika

1. Place the garlic and 1 tablespoon of the oil (15ml) in a 9 ½-inch/24-cm skillet over medium heat and cook until the garlic begins to brown, about 3 minutes. Add the chard, stir, cover, and cook until it is wilted and has turned a very dark green, about 25 minutes, stirring occasionally to be sure it doesn't stick to the bottom of the pan.

2. In a large bowl, whisk together the eggs with the salt, the cheese, and the paprika just until they are broken up. Preheat the broiler.

3. Add the remaining oil to the chard and stir, making sure that it doesn't stick to the bottom of the pan. Pour the eggs over the chard and let them cook until they are set on the bottom, 4 to 5

THE BEAUTY AROUND US

minutes. You will detect a somewhat toasty aroma, and the eggs will be set, except for about ¼ inch (.7cm) on the top.

4. Remove the pan from the heat and place it about 5 inches/12.5cm from the broiler. Cook until the top is just set and there is no uncooked egg, 1 to 2 minutes. Be careful not to over-cook.

5. Remove from the heat and place the serving platter on top of the pan. Reverse the pan and the platter so the frittata falls onto the platter. Allow to cool to room temperature before serving.

6 APPETIZER SERVINGS; 2 TO 4 MAIN-DISH SERVINGS

GOAT CHEESE SAUCE
SAUCE DE FROMAGE DE CHÈVRE

This light, delicate sauce, which I make with fresh goat cheese from the market in Louviers, is perfect with freshly steamed asparagus (preferably white, though it is wonderful with green as well). It is also delicious alongside freshly grilled fish or poultry, or a thick, tender steak.

1 cup/250ml fresh goat cheese curds (or ¾ cup/185ml fresh
goat cheese and ¼ cup/60ml either goat or cow's milk)
2 tablespoons/30ml extra-virgin olive oil

1 cup/about 10g mixed fennel fronds, sweet cicely, and
    chervil leaves, or fresh chives
Fine sea salt

1. Whisk the goat cheese until it is light. Whisk in the olive
oil until thoroughly incorporated and smooth.

2. Mince the herbs, and whisk them into the goat cheese mixture. Season to taste with salt.

1 GENEROUS CUP/250ML—ABOUT 6 SERVINGS

FOURTEEN

Paris

PARIS IS ONLY an hour from Louviers, and it beckons constantly. I go often, to meet editors for business, friends for lunch, to see the doctor, the dentist. Michael and I drive in at night to meet friends for dinner. Often I go to run errands for things I can't find anywhere else. At least I think I can't find them anywhere else, though Rouen, a good-sized city, is much closer and most things could probably be purchased there.

But I know Paris like my own backyard. And I love it. I step off the train at Gare St-Lazare, cross that scruffy station, emerge outside, and at once feel right with the world. I love walking down the steps, past the sculpture that is an assemblage of clocks, and across the street to the new FNAC, a bookstore that has made waiting for trains so much more pleasant. I try to arrange my trips so that I can stop at Ladurée, the early-nineteenth-century tea salon, which is a ten-minute walk from the station down the rue

Royale. It has the best *café crème* in Paris and atmosphere unequaled anywhere else.

I know because I've spent years sampling *cafés crèmes* in Paris. When I lived there in the early eighties I loved nothing better than to start out in the morning with my *Plan de Paris*, the indispensable guide to Paris streets, and explore, stopping frequently for a *crème* as I studied the map and the passersby. The very first newspaper article I ever wrote in Paris, for a publication called *Paris Passion*, was a roundup of *salons de thé* in Paris. To do the research I visited every single one in the city sampling more *crèmes*, teas, and pastries than I could count. I liked some of the tea salons better than others but what I loved most was the fact that searching them out took me places I might otherwise not have gone.

When Michael and I lived together in Paris we explored the city *arrondissement* by *arrondissement*. We would set out early on a weekend morning and go to a market to buy all the ingredients for a picnic, then make our way to a garden or a park to eat it. Afterwards we visited a museum or a gallery, or simply window-shopped and we wouldn't return home until after dark.

Our favorite market street was the one nearest our studio apartment, on rue Mouffetard in the fifth *arrondissement*. We went there regularly and always stopped at the Café Mouffetard at number 116. The *crèmes* there were good but what really drew us were the dense and yeasty homemade croissants and brioche. We liked the twice-weekly market at rue Monge, too, also in the fifth, for it offered more rustic fare like huge loaves of bread baked in wood-fired ovens, different honeys and spice breads, sausages, and other *charcuterie* from every region in France. We also loved rue Poncelet, a fast-paced and chic market street in the seventeenth where I had shopped regularly for nearly six months when I lived near it in a *chambre de bonne*. The best place for coffee there is a quaint Austrian tea salon and pastry shop called Le Stubli, and we would choose among little crescents filled with poppy seeds, miniature linzer-tortes, spice cookies, or butter cookies dusted in powdered sugar and have them in the dining room upstairs, where we could hear the bustle of the market over the hushed tones of the other guests.

Our studio apartment was equidistant between the Jardin des Plantes and the Jardin du Luxembourg and we spent a lot of time in both of them. They lack abundant shade, however, so when our studio was simply too unbearably hot in summer we would go to the Arènes de Lutèce, a small garden nearby, to sit in the shade and read. Evenings we walked along the banks of the Seine, which were crowded in summer and virtually empty in winter.

We had a handful of favorite restaurants and the one we went to most often was Polidor on rue Monsieur-le-Prince. We always be-gan with the same dish, a dozen fat, juicy, garlic- and parsley-sauced snails. Served blistering hot by the cheerful waitress, they were the most delicious I've tasted, before or since. We also loved a beer bar on the rue Mouffetard where we drank our first Morte Subite (a very high-alcohol beer in a liter-and-a-half bottle that practically knocks you dead on your feet, thus the name "Sudden Death") and another beer bar on the rue Soufflot that served dozens of varieties of beers, each with its own glass, and the best *moules frites* in Paris.

Chez René, a bistro on the Blvd. St-Germain whose lentils with smoked sausages and *coq au vin* are as delicious now as they were then, was where we took visiting guests. I remember going with my parents for dinner and while we entered as customers we left as friends, the en-tire staff seeing us out the door with handshakes and smiles.

ON RUE TATIN

We often went very far afield in our rambling about the city. Once we were deep in the heart of the eighteenth *arrondissement* and ended up at a tiny African restaurant tucked into an alley there, eating spiced meat and peanut sauce that we washed down with beer. Often we made our way to the first *arrondissement* and would always stop at a *pâtisserie/charcuterie* on rue St-Honoré called Gargantua, where the pastries were gigantic and excellent. In Chinatown we would have egg drop soup or dim sum, and very occasionally we would dress to the nines and go out for a meal at our truly favorite restaurant, Le Grand Véfour in the Palais-Royal.

I still try to walk wherever I'm going in Paris so that I can inhale as much Parisian air as possible. Walking allows for discovery of an as-yet untried café or restaurant, an unexplored antique shop or shoe store. In summer I always walk through the Tuileries and stop for an organic sorbet sold from a gaily colored little cart at the Louvre end. My French publisher is across the Seine and as often as not my business takes me there, so I cross the river and head down a tiny, choked street enjoying the rare antiques, artful flower arrangements, and chic handbags in the store windows on the way.

The decorous beat of the city infiltrates my bones so that I'm instantly at home. As I walk I relive other walks I've taken, simultaneously inhabiting the past and present. When we have friends or family visit I take them to Paris and lead them to all my favorite old places and some new ones, too. My life changes constantly but Paris remains the same even as it lives and thrives, a steady reference point.

Joe enjoys the train ride to Paris. And he loves the Meteor, the spanking, shiny, clean new metro line that cuts the city down to size. He goes wild with delight when we go to the aquarium at the Musée des Arts Africains. And he loves the hot chocolate and strawberry tarts at Ladurée. But other than that, Paris to Joe is mainly a pain in the neck.

Some things disappoint him. He dreamed of seeing the eternal flame under the Arc de Triomphe so we made that possible last Christmas. When we got there and he saw it burning bravely amidst the crowds he looked up and said, "This is all there is?" Others frighten him. The noise, the clank of the metro—he fears one or the other of us will get stuck between the doors. And still others bore him, including visits to the doctor or dentist, which means time in the waiting room.

Dissatisfied with medical and dental care in Louviers, we've established our medical relationships in Paris, which has its good and bad sides. The bad side is that a checkup is never simple for it implies a good part of the day away from home. The good part is that a visit to the doctor necessitates a day in Paris. I love it. Joe doesn't.

Not that he doesn't love our doctor, Pierre. He does. Anyone would. Pierre is a young, handsome, jolly homeopath and physician with a droll sense of the absurd. His dark office—he keeps the shades pulled—is stuffed with books about everything from I Ching to Babar. Toys are placed cleverly in the shelves here and there to tempt and surprise young patients. The examining couch and the stethoscope are incidental.

Most sessions with Pierre involve conversation during which he doodles on a thick pad with one of the dozens of colored pencils on his desk. He listens thoughtfully as he doodles, asking questions that appear to have no relevance to anything. He will suddenly look up and ask whoever among us is describing symptoms, "Do your feet get hot at night?" Or "Do your eyes itch when the sun comes out?" Or "Do you like spicy food?" As we continue he will look up and ask, "Do you like to drink hot drinks?" Michael is convinced that Pierre hears voices, which is why his questions are non sequiturs. I've learned to answer them without questioning, because Pierre is a crack analyst and nine times out of ten whatever treatment he prescribes, and he always prescribes *something* in true French fashion, cures the ill.

Pierre's office is right near the Jardin du Luxembourg, which we used to jog around regularly when we lived near it in the early eighties. We loved the French joggers we would meet, many of them women swathed in silk scarves and heavy clouds of perfume daintily running along, or gentlemen in simple sport shoes and shiny, color-coordinated sweat suits. Michael and I, dressed in shorts, t-shirts, and clunky jogging shoes, would pass them and giggle, imagining how much time it must have taken them to get ready to go do their morning "footing."

Within the Jardin du Luxembourg is a very luxurious playground with rubber flooring and colorful toys, and when Joe was much younger we went directly there from Pierre's office. It costs 30 francs to enter and once inside the jostle of kids, languages, and colors embraced us as Joe climbed, jumped, swung, and wiggled on and over everything. It kept him busy for hours and was an ample reward for the doctor visit.

There were ponies to ride, puppet shows to see, and beehives to visit in the Jardin, as well as tiny sailboats to rent on the central pond. Joe is too old for all of that now, though he is occasionally tempted by the boats, but we can always entice him with a movie

259

PARIS

or a museum geared to children so that, while he doesn't look forward to a day in Paris, it is usually a success.

A visit to the dentist is another story. Our dentist couldn't be nicer. A handsome young man who trained in the United States, he not only speaks good, slang-filled English, but his dentistry techniques are in line with what we expect. He treats Joe like a human being not a laboratory animal, as we found dentists in Louviers tended to do. "Oh, I never give novocaine to children. They don't feel pain, it never hurts them much," said one to me as I asked him to ease the obvious pain he was causing my screaming son. Needless to say, we never returned to him. Every effort is made to be gentle, quick, thorough. But it is, any way you look at it, time in the dental chair. And because Joe's teeth are weak, he's spent more of his share there than most children.

One warm July day I had to take him in to the dentist. He resisted. I was working on a story about sorbets and to sweeten the visit I asked if he would help me judge their flavors. That perked him up and we drove directly from home to the Île-St-Louis, home of Berthillon, the best ice cream shop in Paris.

I parked the car illegally on the Ile, in very good company since most of the cars around me were also parked illegally. As soon as I turned off the key Joseph and I were out of the car and walking briskly down the sidewalk to a restaurant whose windows boasted Berthillon Glaces et Sorbets. We walked in and the waiter informed us he could only sell us cones through the small window that gave out onto the street, not inside. We dutifully went outside and he came to the window to take our order.

There are always at least forty flavors of Berthillon ice cream and sorbet to choose from, which makes it tough. Joe reflected for a long time before weighing in for black currant, strawberry, and peach. The waiter prepared Joe's cone and handed it to him. His eyes lit up. "Mama, I've never had three flavors at once before," he said.

I received mine—red currant, apricot, and rhubarb—paid the bill, grabbed a handful of napkins, and we walked back toward the car. The air was warm so our tiny balls of sorbet were melting and we lapped at them studiously. I tried apricot first, and my mouth tingled at its tartness. The rhubarb, a gorgeous pink color, was also tart, and the red currant vivid and fresh. I almost hate to say this, but Berthillon sorbets are sometimes better than the ripe fruit itself.

Joe liked the black currant best, and when we switched cones to sample I had to agree with him. Exquisitely tart and tannic like a black currant, it had just the right amount of sweetness. It was so intense it was hard to appreciate the other flavors (though the strawberry was delicious and the peach delicately perfumed).

The car, mercifully undiscovered by a *oiseau bleu*, or parking policewoman—nicknamed bluebirds for their pale blue uniforms and hats—was parked right by two benches that overlooked the Seine, so we sat there to enjoy our cones, savoring intense hits of fruit flavor with every lick.

We finished, got back in the car, and went on our way to the dentist. I had bought Joe a delicious-smelling chicken sandwich for lunch, and he munched that as I threaded my way through traffic. "It was great eating dessert first, Mama," he said between bites. "But I just want you to know I'm not going to the dentist."

I didn't insist or cajole, I simply said fine. I had an appointment too, so I told him I'd just leave him on the sidewalk while I went up. He was quiet. "What will I do there, Mama?" he asked. "I don't know, Joe, but if you won't go there is nothing else I can do."

I parked and Joe went with me reluctantly, asking me if the dentist would drill and if it would hurt. His experience with the sadistic dentist in Louviers had left a bad memory.

It turned out the dentist had to pull his tooth, which he did painlessly thanks to novocaine. Joe emerged from his office, his face lopsided but smiling, a handful of plastic spiders clutched in his fist as consolation prizes. "It didn't hurt a bit," he said proudly. The dentist assured us both that Joe would be just fine, and the only thing he couldn't do was eat hot or hard food.

We got back into the car and headed out to the *autoroute*, around the place de la Concorde, up the Champs Elysées, around the Arc de Triomphe and on our way. The novocaine began to wear off, and Joe started to moan, then he fell asleep.

Another Parisian adventure, certain to make Joe hate the city even more. But we'll counter it soon with a visit to the Science Center at La Villette—a favorite spot—or some other event that will redeem the City of Light in the eyes of a young boy.

RUSTIC APRICOT SORBET
SORBET RUSTIQUE AUX ABRICOTS

When apricots are in season at the market the air is filled with their honeyed scent. We love to eat them fresh and in tarts and compotes, but I think our favorite way to eat them is like this—frozen with a hint of sugar and lemon juice. I often make an apricot tart and serve this apricot sorbet alongside.

NOTE: Chilling the poached and puréed apricots before freezing them makes for a better-textured sorbet.

> 1 cup/250ml bottled water
> ½ cup/100g sugar
> 1 pound/500g apricots, pitted
> 1 tablespoon freshly squeezed lemon juice

1. Place 1 cup/250ml bottled water and the sugar in a small saucepan over medium-high heat and bring to a boil, stirring all the while. When the sugar has dissolved, add the apricots, return to the boil, and reduce the heat so the liquid is simmering gently. Simmer the apricots just until they begin to turn tender, about 5 minutes. Remove from the heat and cool completely.

2. Purée the apricots and their poaching liquid in a food processor until smooth and slightly foamy. Strain the mixture if you like, through a fine-mesh sieve, to remove any bits of skin. (This isn't necessary, but it does produce a finer, more sophisticated sorbet.) Chill the mixture in an airtight container in the refrigerator for at least 1 hour and up to 24 hours.

3. Just before freezing, whisk in the lemon juice. Transfer to an ice cream maker and freeze according to the manufacturer's instructions.

ABOUT 6 SERVINGS

PEAR SORBET
SORBET AUX POIRES

Just this year a young grower has begun coming to the Saturday market with crates of pears and apples. While his apples are big, reddish to green, and beautiful, his pears are exquisite. He grows Comice, Louise Bonne, Beurré Hardy, William, and several other old-fashioned varieties, each with its distinct color, flavor, and texture. I have never tasted pears with such sweetness and perfume.

He handles the pears like eggs, placing each gently on the scale then in a bag so he is sure not to bruise them. Since his arrival at our market, pears have become a regular part of our diet. We eat them fresh for snacks and dessert and I've prepared them cooked just about every way I can think of.

I made this sorbet early on in pear season with Williams, which are fine and delicate with just the slightest tartness for balance. I recommend making it with any aromatic variety.

1½ pounds/750g ripe pears, peeled and cored
5 tablespoons/65g sugar
2 tablespoons/30ml freshly squeezed lemon juice
1 egg white

1. Purée the pears in a food processor until smooth. Add the sugar and lemon juice, process until combined, then add the egg white and process just until incorporated and the mixture becomes just the slightest bit foamy—this will take less than 1 minute.

2. Chill the mixture for at least 2 hours. Transfer to an ice cream maker and freeze according to the manufacturer's instructions.

4 TO 6 SERVINGS

FIFTEEN

Early Morning Swim

THE WEATHER in Normandy usually begins to turn fragrant and clear in May. Then, we get warm days with cool mornings, brilliant sun that outlines everything with a distinct clarity. Everything about May is magic after the gray months of February and March, and the tumultuously unpredictable wet month of April.

Edith and I start waiting for these fine days at the end of April, like a beggar waiting for a coin. I in Louviers and she in Le Vaudreuil watch the sky, check the forecasts (she looks in the paper, I talk to a local farmer—the most accurate weather source I know). Finally we remind our families that once again, it's time for us to go swimming.

Going swimming in and of itself doesn't require permission, of course. It's the hour we choose to do it that means everyone must be forewarned. Once we've deemed the weather fine enough we meet three mornings a week at 6:45 A.M. to get on bicycles, ride

266

ON RUE TATIN

through the villages of Le Vaudreuil, Val de Reuil, and Léry, until we get to the manmade lake called Lac des Deux Amants, Two Lovers' Lake. There we rest our bicycles against a willow tree and ease ourselves into the water. Fine weather is relative. For our needs it must not be raining, and the temperature must promise to reach into the high sixties during the day, so that it warms up the water just slightly.

I savor every moment of our early morning adventure, beginning with waking in the morning in our large bedroom whose walls we painted with such surprising success. Lying there warm and cozy under the down comforter, it is almost unthinkable to get up and dress and go out, yet there is a deliciousness to it, too. I tiptoe into my swimming suit and clothes then slip out of the house with my towel under my arm. Still half asleep, I fumble for my car keys and get in the car to drive through the empty streets to Edith's. The only people about at that hour in our town and her village are early morning workers. Even the bakeries aren't open yet, though the air is filled with the aroma of fresh bread.

Edith and I look at each other and shake our heads, agreeing that we are a little nuts to have left our respective beds. Then we get on the bicycles and head out for our ride, which is almost completely flat until right before we get to the lake when it rises and falls a bit. It is hardly a physical challenge, however, but instead pleasant exercise.

In May we still start out in the dusk of early morning, when the sky usually looks like the mottled skin of a purple eggplant. The bicycle ride takes about 20 minutes, so by the time we get to the lake the sky is almost all pale blue with traces of night sky still on the horizon. The vast lake is the central feature of the Base de Loisirs de Léry-Poses, a recreation area that includes picnic sites, mini-golf, a small animal farm, and a running and bicycling path. Beyond the lake on the horizon are lush green foothills punctuated by white clay cliffs, like the cliffs of Dover. The train to Paris runs by one side of the lake but other than that it is a haven of calm. When the weather is good it is, as the French say, *noir de monde*, so popular that it is black with people.

Save for a lone fisherman or two we're the only ones at the lake early in the morning. Often, there's a heavy mist shrouding the shrubs and trees and hovering over the water, which makes me feel like the Lady of the Lake risking all to walk in. We know there are no man-eating beasts in this lake that was once a quarry and is deep and cold, though Edith is continually coming up with stories about huge big-toothed fish, infestations of various noxious weeds, unusual algae blooms, all calculated to send a *frisson* up my spine. She knows I have an intense intellectual love of water, and a physical fear of its wetness. I am terrified of drowning, I hate feeling underwater plants against my skin, I worry about something pulling me under the water, yet I love to swim.

Once we've begun this spring and summer ritual we don't stop until the coldest days of October (except for the various vacation periods during the summer when one or the other of us is away). Not every morning is warm but we go anyway, unless the rain is falling too hard to see. There's a challenge in going, and the bike ride serves to warm us up, so even if the air and water are cold, it feels good to get wet.

We often start out in long pants with heavy scarves around our necks and we judge the temperature by the point at which one or the other of us begins to feel warm, pedaling for all we're worth. Usually, the middle of the village of Léry right before the *boulangerie*, which emits its mouthwatering aromas each morning, is where the blood gets going. That's about halfway through our trip, so we know that by the time we reach the water we'll be warm enough to go in.

Still, it's not always easy, once the bikes are parked, to peel down to the bathing suit and actually put a toe in the lake. The lake bottom is small stones that hurt the feet and it's a challenge to walk out far enough to dive in. Edith is always the first in the water, tiptoeing her way in as I cautiously follow. On mornings like these I ask myself, and we ask each other, why on earth we're not home in our cozy beds. Then she dives in. I wait a bit, certain I'll die of shock if I submerge myself too quickly, then finally jump in, too. It is so cold we shout and scream sometimes, laughing so hard, so hysterically, that if anyone were around they would think us crazy. Twenty strokes later we've convinced ourselves the water is warm. Sometimes it is, sometimes it isn't. At the start and toward the end of the season it simply isn't, but it still feels wonderful. It wakes you up to your toes yet your heart stays warm and beats fast, a reminder of all that is good and wonderful in life.

Often, a brace of ducks swim far out on the lake and their quacks filter through to us. We quack back, acting like kids for the quick twenty minutes we're in the water, swimming to our goal, which is a huge oak tree that leans out over the water. We reach it, and if there is time we go farther. My schedule is more restricted than Edith's, so I usually determine what we should do. Some mornings, those that herald a hot day, we both wish we could just unfold easel and writing tablet and stay at the lake all day.

EARLY MORNING SWIM

The goal of being home, cleaned, and dressed by 8 A.M., so that I can walk Joe to school governs the morning, however. I walk gingerly out of the water, bruising my feet on the stones. "I must talk to Bernard about these stones," Edith says each morning. "He should put sand in here, just for us." Bernard is the genius behind the development of this manmade lake, and he keeps a close eye on it, helping supervise the crews that maintain it. We don't really expect him to order sand for the lake bottom, though it would make our morning swims that much nicer.

Back on our bicycles, refreshed and invigorated, we speed home through the villages, waving at acquaintances on the way as they make their morning trip to the *boulangerie*, or head off to work in their cars, all dressed up. We imagine their lives, smugly thanking our lucky stars that we each work at home (Edith painting her canvases and me writing and cooking) so that we can be out at 7:30 in the morning bicycling instead of driving off to work.

When I return home after a swim, Michael and Joe are usually just finishing breakfast. I race upstairs, my skin still cool from the water even on the hottest of days, and change into my working clothes—usually a skirt, blouse, and sandals. A quick cup of tea and it's time to walk Joe to school. Everything seems brighter, clearer, more effervescent on swim mornings. Joe and I laugh as we walk along, and I return home after seeing him line up at the ring of the bell, hungry to start my day.

Sometimes Edith and I go swimming on a Wednesday, which is not a school day for Joe. Since he sleeps in on those mornings, I can take more time. We swim longer, and we often vary our route home to stop at our friend Michel's bakery, for a freshly baked *baguette de campagne*, a long sourdough loaf made with part whole wheat flour, which is still warm when we arrive there. We take it to Edith's, where I make the coffee and she assembles breakfast—butter, jam, and big bowls to sip our coffee from. We set ourselves up in her huge back garden under the apple trees. Her children are still asleep, the dog, César, is jumping to catch the fresh, warm figs that hang heavy on the tree in the corner of the garden, the few chickens Edith keeps are mercifully quiet. It's heaven. We always "remake the world" as the French call discussing and solving the current issues of the day. By 9 A.M. a pleasant drowsiness begins to take hold of both of us.

Tempted to stretch out on one of the *chaises longues* in the garden, I instead kiss Edith good-bye and head for home. These mornings are delicious but not geared for efficiency as once I've slowed down it's hard to pick up the pace again. But that doesn't really matter, since Wednesday is our weekend.

When I began swimming, Michael looked askance at this early morning ritual. He didn't quite understand why I would give up an hour or more of precious sleep to go swimming in a freezing lake.

But one morning last summer when Joe was staying with friends of ours in Burgundy for a week and the two of us were alone in the house, I convinced Michael to go to the lake with me. Instead of driving to Edith's as I do, to save time, we bicycled the entire way—about a half hour trip—met her, then continued on to the lake and plunged in. The water was relatively warm—if it hadn't been, Michael would never have gone. An early morning mist hung over it, and the ducks were out and quacking. By the time we had done half our swim the mist had evaporated and the sun was out. The three of us were alone in the lake. It was pure, peaceful heaven.

I looked at Michael. He was swimming and diving like a loon. "This is fabulous," he exhaled, water dripping from his head. He swam off, way out into the center of the lake, while Edith and I did our usual route. We stayed for an hour, swimming, talking, enjoying the peace and solitude.

Then we got on our bicycles and rode by Michel's to pick up a *baguette*. He and his wife, Chantal, think we're crazy and when they saw Michael with us they just shook their heads and laughed, "You too?"

We went to Edith's and prepared our usual breakfast, taking it out under the apple trees. It was bliss, and we lingered until midmorning, dunking lengths of *baguette* slathered with butter and jam into our bowls of coffee. Finally, Michael and I roused ourselves to get home, so we could get some work done. On arriving at the house Michael parked his bicycle and came in, ruffling his hair.

"That was fantastic," he said. "I'm not saying I'd do it every day, but I get it now."

RED PEPPER AND TOMATO SALAD
SALADE DE POIVRONS AUX TOMATES

This salad comes from the mother of a friend of ours, Michel Amsalem, a baker and pastry chef who is a French Algerian Jew. She came to France in the sixties when many French Algerians were repatriated, bringing with her family recipes for food that is colorful and savory. I had heard about her cooking long before I tasted it, particularly this salad, which Michel says he eats by the bowlful. It is traditionally served as an accompaniment to couscous, though I've found lots of other ways to serve it. One of my preferences is to warm it with slivers of air-cured ham and delicious black olives from Nyons, though I also like to simmer eggs in it, serve it simply with slices of fresh, crusty bread, or alongside roast chicken or lamb, where it lends a bright, flavorful counterpoint.

2½ pounds/1kg 125g red bell pepper, grilled
⅓ cup/75ml extra-virgin olive oil
1 large garlic clove, green germ removed, minced
1 pound/500g fresh tomatoes, peeled, cored, half the
    seeds removed, and diced
Fine sea salt, optional

1. Remove every speck of skin from the grilled bell peppers without rinsing them, because you don't want to rinse away any flavorful juices. Remove the core and white pith inside and scrape away all the seeds, then slice the flesh into strips that are about ¼ inch/.7cm wide. Reserve.

2. Heat 1 tablespoon of the oil and the garlic together in a medium-size skillet over medium heat. When the garlic is sizzling add the tomatoes, stir, and cook them until they have given up almost all of their liquid. They will still be a bit chunky, which is fine. Remove the tomatoes from the heat and stir in the peppers and the remaining

oil. You may season the salad lightly with salt if you like, though it really doesn't need it. Let cool to room temperature and serve.

4 TO 6 SIDE-DISH SERVINGS

Grilling Peppers

To grill a pepper, place it on a gas burner with the flame turned up high, and turn it frequently until its skin is black and blistered all over. Transfer it to a paper bag and close it, or to a tea towel and wrap it up, and let it cool to room temperature. Slide off the skin and remove the stem and the seeds from the interior.

Alternatively, place the pepper under the broiler—about 1 inch from the heat—and turn it frequently until the skin blackens.

MICHE'S APRICOT JAM
LA CONFITURE D'ABRICOTS DE MICHE

I thought I already had the best recipe for apricot jam until I tasted Miche's. Miche is Edith's aunt and she lives about five minutes away from us in Louviers. In her eighties, she is the voluntary grandmother to all of Edith's children and nieces and nephews, which numbered twenty-eight at last count, and in summer she buys kilos of apricots to make this jam for them. This is a favorite for spreading on buttered bread after one of our early morning swims.

Miche is categoric—she makes the jam in small batches, uses as little sugar as possible, and cooks fruit for as short a time as she can get away with. She also refuses to put apricot pits in her jam—a typical French custom—for in her mind, anything that interferes with the pure, fresh apricot flavor is blasphemy. She's right; her apricot jam is out of this world.

3 pounds/1½ kg apricots, pitted and halved
1 pound/500g sugar

1. Place the apricots and sugar in a nonreactive pan or bowl, stir, cover, and let macerate for at least 12 hours.

2. Transfer the fruit and sugar to a large, heavy saucepan and bring to a boil over medium-high heat. Reduce the heat so the mixture is boiling merrily and cook for 10 minutes, stirring occasionally. Remove from the heat and ladle the jam into sterilized canning jars, leaving ¼ inch (.7cm) headroom. Seal according to the jar manufacturer's instructions.

ABOUT 10 CUPS/2½ LITERS

SIXTEEN

Too Good to Be True

MICHAEL, JOE, AND I were walking to a neighbor's house for a Bastille Day party. It was hot and I was wearing a lightweight blue and white polka-dotted skirt with red and white buttons, my most patriotic item of clothing. I'd had the skirt for many years and it had always been on the large side. This day it felt tight, a phenomenon I'd noticed all too frequently recently.

A couple of days later we were driving to Paris to meet friends for a picnic on the Champ de Mars. I was suddenly struck with a headache and general malaise that lasted well into the picnic then disappeared as suddenly as it arrived.

Over the next several weeks I experienced the malaise more frequently and it always seemed to disappear as suddenly as it arrived. My clothes continued to feel tight, my head a bit light. I didn't think a lot about it except that it was odd and that the symptoms seemed a bit familiar, like when I'd been pregnant with Joe.

But I couldn't be pregnant. Michael and I had wanted a second child and had tried for nearly three years without success before I went to see a doctor and get some tests. The doctor told me I couldn't have more children because I was so advanced into menopause that pregnancy was virtually impossible. It didn't matter that I was young—facts were facts, and tests were tests. As a double check I went to see our family doctor who put it to me like this. "You are past child-bearing age. It is time for you to say good-bye to that phase and to prepare yourself for the second half of your life." While it broke my heart to hear that, I thought it a considerate way to tell me.

But I had these strange symptoms. Without saying anything to anyone I went to the pharmacy for a pregnancy test kit, a pharmacy where I knew no one, of course, as news travels fast in Louviers. The test was packaged with a tiny gold heart, which was, I guessed, for the happy mother. It was as if the makers of the test didn't envision the possibility that the test results could be negative. I imagined women hoping against hope for positive results, finding them negative, and hurling tiny golden hearts out of windows.

Unbelievably, my test results were positive. I bought another test to be sure and it was positive, too. Oh my goodness. Michael and I had wanted another child but after trying for such a long time we'd given up, put it behind us. I was forty-three, busy, satisfied to be a family of three. This was totally unexpected and I was ecstatic.

When I told Michael he looked at me, his brain working. "I'll be sixty-five when the baby goes to college," he said, then we threw our arms around each other. We were too old, over our heads in

TOO GOOD TO BE TRUE

every aspect of our lives, and just a year before we had finally given away all of Joe's baby things. We were deliriously happy.

I had a blood test to confirm the situation, then called a friend who had just given birth to ask her what was the protocol in terms of the clinic where she had had her baby. She told me I needed to reserve a space immediately, that the clinic was so popular it was booked for months in advance. I called right away and was told that there were no more rooms for the period when I thought my baby was due. I called another highly regarded clinic and was lucky to find a space there. The receptionist briefly described the clinic to me, informing me that midwives delivered the babies, though a physician was always on call, and that I would need to schedule a meeting with a midwife immediately, as well as with an anesthesiologist, if I thought I wanted anesthesia during the birth. I told her I was ready to schedule both appointments. She told me all the appointments were full for August, since most of the staff was on vacation, and the computer couldn't schedule anything yet for September.

She then told me I needed to see a doctor immediately to initiate the necessary paperwork, so I tried to make an appointment with one of the clinic's doctors. Same story. "You must see a doctor before the tenth of August, but we have no one here until mid-September."

I called our family doctors who were both on vacation. I called doctors suggested by friends and they were all on vacation. I called the few gynecologists in the area and they were gone. How was I supposed to schedule an appointment with a doctor if they were all on vacation? Finally I called another clinic and, miracle of miracles, their doctor was not only working but had time to see me.

Michael and I went together. The doctor was visibly shocked when I told him my age. He looked at me, scribbled a few things on a notepad, and said seriously, "Madame, you will have to have an amniocentesis you know." I said I did know that. He looked at me again then told me he had to give me an ultrasound because the paperwork required it. It seemed awfully soon to be doing that, but I was delighted.

"You are twelve weeks along," he said as we looked at the little form on the screen. "You didn't get here a minute too soon."

We were stunned. How could I have been pregnant for so long without realizing it? Both Michael and I paid rapt attention as the doctor measured every possible part of the fetus. "The neck is thin, this is a good sign," the doctor said. "It means there is little chance the baby has Down's syndrome, which is something we worry about in women of your age."

I then listened vaguely as he outlined what tests I would need to have—the amniocentesis, monthly blood tests for toxoplasmosis, regular sonograms.

We drove home in a daze. I hadn't wanted to tell anyone I was pregnant until the third month but we could announce it to whom we liked—it *was* the third month.

For at least three years Joe had begged me for a little sister. I hadn't explained why he didn't have a younger sibling, and now I wouldn't have to. While I couldn't guarantee him a sister, his wish for a sibling was about to come true.

His reaction to the news was shock. "Oh Mama, I don't want

you to get fat," he said. We laughed, hugged each other, and that was that.

My middle now grew exponentially. I went about my life and plans in the unique state of grace that pregnancy confers. I didn't care if it would complicate our lives. It was like a dream come true, more wonderful because of its unexpectedness. Of course I did occasionally think about all the paraphernalia we would need to collect: clothes, booties, hats, strollers, bassinet. But I had time.

I continued bicycle riding and swimming in the early mornings with Edith, though I was often so nauseated I could hardly see. I had chosen to tell few people, but I naturally told her and she was happy but incredulous. "Oh Suzanne, how will you manage? I tell you I couldn't do it," she said. Since she already had four children I sympathized with her sentiment—one more probably would have killed her. But I knew I had energy to spare.

I had settled on a gynecologist in a nearby town to follow the pregnancy and on my first visit she outlined what I could and couldn't do. "Do not eat salad or tomatoes because of the toxoplasmosis problem," she said firmly. "Ride as little as possible in a car—they are bumpy and can bring on contractions. Do not run. Bicycling is not encouraged. Walking and swimming are. Do not eat oysters, because they can transmit bacteria to the fetus. Other than that, you are free to live normally."

Come on, I said to myself. A warning not to eat salad but nothing about cigarettes or alcohol? And what was this about not riding in a car? But I drove home gingerly. Once a concern is planted in your mind, it's hard to shake it.

As the pregnancy progressed, I encountered the considerable

obligations imposed by the French medical system, which included the monthly blood test for toxoplasmosis. This disease is apparently transmitted by fecal matter from cats and unwashed vegetables and can harm the fetus but leave the mother unaffected. When I asked a doctor at the clinic why I had to have a test every single month he rolled his eyes. "It is a disease discovered by a Frenchman. We are very proud to have discovered it, thus we must test constantly for it. It is ridiculous."

Another obligation was regular visits to the clinic where the baby would be born, meeting the anesthesiologist, and a session with a genetic counselor. The anesthesiologist, a charming woman originally from Jordan, spoke a French so difficult to understand we practically ended up drawing pictures for each other. The genetic counselor was another story. Very French in his pinstriped designer shirt and color-coordinated tie, well-fitting navy blue trousers, and healthy summer tan, he was brisk and had a lively sense of humor. He welcomed Michael and me heartily into his office, which had several tasteful paintings on the wall. On his wrist he wore a diving watch, and for the first twenty minutes of our visit we discussed art and his passion for boating. A retired pediatrician, he was a genetic specialist, and when he finally gave us his speech on genetics his passion for the subject was obvious.

When he was finished he asked me if I wanted an amniocentesis. While I had eschewed it for Joe, I felt it was important this time, given my age. When I said I wanted it he assumed a grave expression. "You understand what we test for here," he said. "We do not test to see if your child will be a mass murderer, will have a drug addiction problem, will end up in prison. All we test for are

TOO GOOD TO BE TRUE

certain genetic irregularities, do you understand this?" When we said we did he looked relieved. "Good, I don't want you to think we are performing miracles."

He then went on to outline our options should we discover a problem. Actually, he only mentioned one option, which was to dispose of the fetus, and when he was finished I asked him what people did who decided to keep their children despite genetic irregularities.

He looked surprised. "Few people ask this," he said quietly. "Should you decide to keep a child with a problem I could advise you. But let me say that in France we are not well equipped for this situation. We like to hide such things here. It isn't like America. I hope that your child is normal."

The clinic required that I have at least four sonograms there. In addition my gynecologist administered a sonogram at each monthly visit. This would be a well-documented baby. I loved going to the clinic for all the pre-pregnancy tests and visits. In a graceful old building with a lovely chapel surrounded by gardens and woods, it had a friendly, homey air. Women in various states of pregnancy walked the halls as did new mothers and proud family members. Each time I went there was a knot of nervous young men outside the clinic door, smoking furiously, as well as one or two pregnant moms puffing heartily on cigarettes as well. I wanted to shake them, but resisted the urge. Most of the clinic's staff was female and each person I met with was cheerful, solicitous, genuinely interested in my state of health.

Michael and I both went for the first "official" sonogram. An attractive technician took us into the room where it would be administered and waited as I settled myself on the examining table.

She asked us lots of questions, some formal, others simply showing her interest.

As the image of the baby came on the screen the woman's face brightened. *"Ah, voilà, le bébé,"* she said with an air of satisfaction. Moving an apparatus slowly over my abdomen she showed us the body parts. *"Voici le coeur, voilà la nuque, et voilà! Deux petits reins,"* she said in her lovely singsong. "The heart, the top of the spinal column, two little kidneys." She was thrilled at every little part she saw. The hand went up and she laughed, then tried to get the baby to turn so we could see all of its parts. It wouldn't cooperate. *"Le bébé sait déjà ce qu'il veut,"* she said. "This baby already knows what it wants—usually I can get them to turn."

She spent at least a half hour examining the baby, as filled with awe as though it were the first time she'd done it. When we left I heard her cheerfully welcome her next patient. There, I thought, is a woman who loves her job.

For days I was unable to get her melody out of my mind and I would find myself singing *"Deux petits reins, deux petits reins."* A baby with two kidneys—it was a comforting thought!

The results of the amniocentesis not only showed that our baby was normal, but that it was a girl. Joe was going to have his little sister.

I told our neighbor Marie-Odile, one of the florists, that it was to be a girl. A smile spread across her face. *"Le choix des rois,"* she said. I smiled and nodded and walked off thinking it was a poetic thing to say but not really understanding what it meant. From then on I heard the same phrase over and over—everyone congratulating me on the *choix des rois*, the choice of kings. Then one day I was with a friend and decided to get to the bottom of it. "What is this *choix des rois* anyway?" I asked him. *"Mais Suzanne, c'est evident,"* he said to me with a laugh. "Kings always wanted an elder son to inherit their title, land, and wealth, and a daughter who would marry well and bring more titles, land, and wealth into the family." Of course. *Le choix des rois*.

I had a professional obligation in the United States and was gone for five weeks. When I returned home, twice the size I had been when I left, time raced so fast I could hardly believe it. I had received conflicting dates as to when the baby would arrive, somewhere between the end of January and the beginning of March. Given my size I was convinced they were all wrong and that she was bound to arrive sometime right after Christmas.

I always throw myself into holiday preparations with gusto, baking cookies and fruit cakes, decorating, buying, and making gifts, and up until this year we had had family with us so it was not only necessary but part of the celebration. But this year was different. There would be just the three of us, my energy was extremely limited (despite my grand ideas about all the excess energy I had), and I was happy to make just a couple batches of cookies. I took a poll of Joe and Michael to find out what I should make for our Christmas Eve meal and they both decided they wanted fresh pasta. I suggested we have it with black truffles (I had some frozen, which I had been saving for a special occasion), and that was unanimously agreed upon. Michael and I chose champagne, Joe opted for Perrier.

Christmas Eve afternoon I made the pasta dough, which Joe cranked through the pasta machine then carefully hung across the two broom handles balanced on the backs of chairs. I sliver-cut the truffle and blended it with butter to put on the pasta right after it was cooked, and I made a simple green salad. There had been no request for dessert and I had no energy to make one so we were going to have fruit and cookies. Late that afternoon, however, we heard a knock on the door. Edith's eighty-five-year-old aunt and our friend, Miche, was there with one of her legendary *bûches de Noël*. "I didn't think you'd have the energy to make dessert so I made you a small one," she said. She wished us a *Joyeux Noël* and went on her way.

That night we set the table with silver and lots of candles, then each dressed up to celebrate what would be our last Christmas as a family of three. We talked about what the baby would be like. "I just hope she's pretty," said Joe.

Though the subject of a name for the baby had been broached, we had made no decision, but this evening we discussed it earnestly, each arguing for our favorite. Mine was Fiona. Michael's was Emmanuelle. Joe's was Ruby. We were at a stalemate. From that day on the baby's name became a major topic of conversation. All of us held to our favorite. I secretly prepared myself for compromise, though I had my heart set on Fiona. Michael liked Fiona but he was sure she would be called Fi-Fi, which he couldn't abide. He didn't like Ruby at all. Joe liked Ruby and only Ruby.

The French give their children strings of names, so I suggested we do likewise and name our baby all three names, beginning (naturally) with Fiona. That wasn't acceptable. No one really wanted to give up his chosen name. I mentioned the situation to friends when they would ask what the name would be. Everyone said "Suzanne, it's the mother who decides." I guessed that was a French tradition, and since we were in France . . .

TOO GOOD TO BE TRUE

December melted into January. My doctor told me the baby was anxious to arrive but that it was too soon so I would need to stay in bed. I must have looked at her like I thought she was crazy. *"Non, madame, vous ne devez pas bouger,"* she said firmly. She was serious—I wasn't to walk, to use the stairs, to get up at all. Of course this was the doctor who'd told me not to eat salad or ride in a car. I listened, however, as I did feel something wasn't quite right. For three weeks I worked from a prone position as I wrote, edited, and organized myself to the end of a project. Michael assumed the household chores; friends came by to visit.

One day Michael ushered in Héloïse and Anne-Marie, two very good friends. They came with two huge plastic bags, which they set next to the bed and proceeded to empty. Out came baby clothes of every size and description, blankets, booties, bibs, many of them antique and each one lovelier than the last. "We've been collecting these things for you, Suzanne," Héloïse said. "We thought since you were in bed you would have the time to go through them."

I was speechless. Everything was so gorgeous. I had gone from having the bare minimum to being deluged. Héloïse and Anne-Marie, both of whom have grown children, were cooing and crowing like chickens in a particularly choice patch of grass. Anne-Marie held up a dusty pink velvet sleeper. "This is my favorite," she said until she found the pair of pink leather slippers that looked about a hundred years old and were in perfect condition. There were little lace bonnets, white hand-knit sweaters, tiny little *bodies*, or one-piece undergarments. There was a miniature maroon velvet dress with a lace collar, itsy-bitsy trousers, a selection of blue-and-white-checked gingham dresses, everything so perfect and oh so French!

All the clothes had come from the donations Héloïse receives as part of her volunteer services for the Catholic church. I had long ago stopped feeling guilty at being on the occasional receiving end of such bounty—Héloïse assured me that she collected so many things that no one went without.

Once we had gone through all the clothes, Héloïse and Anne-Marie brought in another huge bag. They opened it to reveal a gorgeous wicker baby basket completely lined with white lace, the frilliest, frothiest contraption I had ever seen. "This is for her to sleep in," Héloïse said, and I burst into tears. I was overwhelmed with the generosity of these two women.

And it wasn't over yet. Out of the bag came a small down comforter covered in antique chintz and a graceful, round white wicker basket lined with more white lace. "This," Anne-Marie said, looking at me with laughter in her eyes, "this is for your *produits*." What *produits*, or products, I wondered. I must have looked quizzical for she said, "You know, the creams and unguents and sprays and aspirins and salt water nasal spray, the antiseptics, all the things you have to have for a baby." I was nonplussed. Yes, of course I would have all those things. But it would never have occurred to me to outfit a basket to put them in. Anne-Marie assured me that all good French mothers had baskets like this for their *produits*.

As we sat talking and admiring the baby things, Michael brought us tea and lemon biscotti I'd made some weeks earlier. Then these guardian angels left, giving me kisses and telling me they would be back to visit. I spent a good couple of hours looking at all the clothes, the baskets, and coverlets. Our baby would enter a very well-provisioned and comfortable nest.

I had no fear and few worries during this pregnancy, in part, I'm sure, because I had already been through a successful pregnancy, and in part because of the care I was getting. Every time I went to the clinic I left feeling like a princess. The staff was completely oriented toward my physical and emotional well-being. They cared about the baby, of course, but they were determined to see to my comfort and to assure me that my stay with them would be the finest it could be. I was beginning to view it as a vacation. Occasionally I would remember that I would actually have to give birth before I could take advantage of it, but five days in a single room with an entire staff to see to my needs sounded pretty comfortable, and I was looking forward to it. A friend of mine who had given birth there told me it was one of her finest memories and that she almost hated to leave when her five days were up.

Patricia Wells, an American friend in Paris, had offered to give me a shower and we settled on a date in January. I hadn't known I would be confined to bed, of course, and I called my doctor to see about a release from the confinement. She told me to come in and after examining me said I was free to go, as long as I took the train. "The car will be too rough," she admonished.

The baby shower is not a French tradition, and in inviting French friends I wasn't sure what to call it. I couldn't call it *"une douche,"* for that signifies stepping under a faucet to get clean. I checked with Edith and she didn't have any ideas, since she had never heard of such a fête. I ended up calling it *une fête entre copines pour donner du courage à la femme enceinte*, a party among good women friends to encourage the pregnant mother!

The day arrived and Michael drove me to the train station. When I purchased my ticket I asked the young woman behind the counter if I could simply cross the tracks to get to the platform rather than climb up and down the momentous stairways, given my condition. "*Non, madame*, you must take the stairs. What you suggest is not permitted. We are not equipped for the handicapped." That made my blood boil, which was good because I forgot how tired I was and climbed the stairs in record time.

Though it was January, there was a brightness to the sky and the sun came out the moment I arrived at Patricia's apartment, shining warmly through her sloped glass ceiling. Flickering cinnamon-scented candles burned next to bouquets in my favorite color of blue. A bright baby toy was hung on the front door knocker and the centerpiece was another pile of baby toys. Heavenly aromas set my taste buds flickering right along with the candles.

Soon everyone had arrived, each dressed as if going to a fancy *soirée*. We began with glasses of champagne, which I sipped right along with everyone else. Champagne, I'd learned, is an integral part of a French pregnancy. Every single time I announced to friends that I was pregnant they broke out a bottle and insisted I drink a glass. "Champagne is good for pregnant mothers," they would say. I believed them and sipped completely free of guilt.

We sampled the luscious dishes that streamed from Patricia's kitchen—toasted almonds tossed with fresh mint and sea salt, tiny cups of rustic celery root and leek soup, discs of inky black truffle sandwiched between thin rounds of pristine white goat cheese and set on tiny, toasted croutons, and miniature rolls of smoked salmon filled with diced salmon and fresh dill. Bliss. Everything was finger food, so the table remained uncluttered except for the shower gifts of toys, miniature tennis shoes, a bright wooden music box. We laughed, we shared secrets, we relaxed into this most special of afternoons.

Michael and I had agreed that, despite the doctor's warnings about riding in the car it would be easier on me if he simply came into Paris to pick me up after collecting Joe from school. We decided to turn the experience into an evening out and planned dinner with Patricia and her husband, Walter. Afterward I arranged myself in the front seat and the ride home went off without incident.

Edith had been invited to the shower in Paris, but couldn't make it. The idea intrigued her enough so that she planned one of her own, for my friends in and around Louviers. We settled on an evening and she called to ask what she should do. I explained the idea of the shower and she seemed to understand. At about 8:30 on the designated evening six women showed up at our house and, with much gaiety and hilarity, entered the living room. I was no longer confined to bed simply because my due date was close enough that the baby was no longer in danger, and I was delighted to have yet another celebration among women friends. I settled down to see just how the evening would play out.

Since there is no taboo in France on alcohol during pregnancy, it didn't surprise me in the least when one friend set down a bottle of homemade prune brandy that was at least 90 proof. "We shall all drink to your baby," she said as I went out to the kitchen to boil water for herb tea. Champagne was one thing, moonshine another. One friend whose husband is a baker had brought petits fours, and each woman had brought a gift. Edith gave me hers first. It was a jacket big enough for a two-year-old, absolutely adorable. "I had to get it for you, Suzanne, it's just your colors," she said. Magaly, who owns an antique store, offered me a vintage turquoise ashtray. I must have looked stunned. "I admit it," she said. "I had no idea what we were doing and what this was about. I just picked this up off the shelf before I came." Lise-Marie gave me a little cookbook from New Caledonia, where she and her husband were about to move, and Chantal gave me tiny dance slippers filled with sugared almonds. Héloïse handed me a pink and white stuffed rabbit and a small truck for Joe, and Anne-Marie gave me a stack of bibs she had hurriedly made. They were all laughing and giggling and just the slightest bit ill at ease. Finally Anne-Marie turned to me and said, "What exactly is this all about, this fête you Americans have among women?"

"*C'est une fête entre copines pour donner du courage à la femme enceinte,*" I explained. I went on to give an entire cultural explanation about the solidarity of women in the United States. My friends looked blank. I could tell they didn't get it, and from my experience of pregnancy in France I understood why. First of all, the original point of a shower was to make sure the expectant mother had all she needed for the baby before it arrived, but in France that simply isn't necessary. For one thing, the state gives a sum of money to women in about the seventh month of pregnancy if they prove themselves financially eligible (i.e., middle class). This sum is enough to purchase almost everything needed for a baby including stroller, bassinet, bed, and changing table. If family members can't supply everything else, friends can.

TOO GOOD TO BE TRUE

From my point of view, showers are about friendship and solidarity among women. It is also a chance to spend time with friends knowing that once the baby arrives time will be the most rare of commodities. I'm sure this point of view is one result of age. Anticipating a baby at forty-three, I found, one needs all the courage, reassurance, and support one can get.

In any case, little of this made sense among my French friends. Here, the older mother is a rare breed. Times are changing, of course, but my friends are still the norm, and they had most of their children in their twenties. While I was pregnant they were looking forward to getting their youngest children out of the house, and some were even anticipating being grandmothers, yet we were all, except for Héloïse, within five years of the same age. We had a wonderful time, anyway.

Edith raised her glass and said, "Let's drink, to Suzanne, to the baby, to all of us who have no more babies and will watch Suzanne with hers and be thankful it isn't us!"

We all shared a laugh and spent the rest of the evening talking and laughing some more until Héloïse looked at me and said, "All right everyone, we need to go. Suzanne is tired." She was right, I was exhausted but I was sorry to see them go. Edith gave me a brisk hug and said, "OK, Suzanne, you can have the baby now. We've been here and given you your shower." Everyone left with hugs and kisses, wishing me the best.

The next day I was working in the living room and Joe and Michael were outside. Joe walked in, closed the door, and came over to me. "Mama," he said, seriously. "Papa and I have decided that we like the name Fiona for the baby. We want her to be called

Fiona." I looked at him and cried. I could tell my date was nearing as I cried at just about everything!

Less than forty-eight hours later I awoke at 5:30 in the morning with that telltale feeling that is akin to an inner earthquake. I got up, put the finishing touches on an essay I was writing, cleared off my desk, and wrote a note to Joe. I cleaned the bathroom and the kitchen and when I was certain that it was time to go to the clinic, I went upstairs to wake Michael and Joe.

Within an hour Joe was safely ensconced at a friend's house and Michael and I were threading our way through morning traffic to Mont-St-Aignan, just outside Rouen, where the clinic is. We'd practiced every possible route to get there and we knew the quickest way.

I had received a packet of information when I registered at the clinic six months earlier stating exactly what I should bring to the birthing room. Héloïse had helped me translate it—I hadn't been sure if I really needed a wool *body* or if cotton was all right, nor did I understand some of the other things on the list, but she set me straight. So I had my blue and white flowered bag with the little outfit the baby would wear after birth as well as my own pajamas and overnight things. I also had decided to read the collected short stories of F. Scott Fitzgerald while I was in the clinic, a tome that weighed about as much as a newborn, and that was tucked into the bag as well. Following directions, I had packed another bag for my stay with more clothes, bath towels, and additional baby clothes, all required by the clinic, and both were tucked in the car.

We arrived and checked into the clinic and I was immediately examined by a midwife I had never met who looked about sixteen.

TOO GOOD TO BE TRUE

"You are definitely on the way, but it's not immediate," she said. "I want you to wait two hours and I'll examine you again to see if we need to keep you or if you can go home."

We were shown to a pale blue bedroom with two beds and windows facing a garden and a courtyard. We both rested and read, then I went in for more tests. She didn't think the birth was imminent, but didn't want me to go home. "I'd rather you stayed here if you can," she said. "A drive in the car wouldn't be good for you." I inwardly groaned. She then looked at me seriously. "Madame Loomis, I must tell you two things," she said. "You may not get into the warm bath we have available because your waters have broken and it wouldn't be healthy for the baby. And I am sorry to say that our anesthesiologists are on strike so no epidurals are being administered."

I just looked at Michael. I hadn't fully decided on either a warm bath or anesthesia, but knowing both of these venues of comfort were closed to me was a bit disappointing.

A nurse came in to see if I needed anything and brought us both tea, then took our order for lunch. We ate cold salmon and salad off trays, then accepted the espresso and yogurt offered for dessert.

As the afternoon wore on I slept and Michael went home to check on Joe and the house. At four-thirty a knock on the door announced a matronly woman who asked if I wanted a *petit goûter*, a little snack. I wasn't hungry but I was curious so I ordered a hot chocolate. She brought in a big steaming bowl with several crackers alongside, and a yogurt. She set it by the bed, plumped my pillow, and whispered, *"Bon appétit."* I drank the chocolate and fell immediately back to sleep, as if I were in a warm cocoon. No one bothered me. I had a button to call the midwife if anything happened, and no responsibilities except to wait for the momentous event.

Afternoon turned to evening and I started having contractions. Michael hadn't returned and I called home, but he wasn't there either. I called the midwife and a new face appeared, one older and more confidence-inspiring. She was brisk and efficient, gave me a quick exam, and a knowing smile. "It won't be long now, I don't think. You just relax in here and call me if anything happens."

Michael returned and dinner was served. I nibbled, too nervous and excited to eat. There was no turning back now, the mechanisms were all en route.

After the dinner tray was removed we were chatting when suddenly a contraction shook me from head to toe. This was serious, and from then on they came regularly and hard. We didn't call the midwife, however, for they weren't often. An hour later, however, the floodgates broke and I called the midwife. I was about to give birth, and I was still fully dressed. She rushed in the room, took one look, and said, "Madame Loomis, can you walk?" In the throes of a contraction I shook my head, and she raced out to get a wheelchair, wheeling it in as if she were driving in the Indy 500. "MADAME LOOMIS, DON'T HAVE THE BABY HERE," she cried, helping me into the chair and racing me back down the hall with Michael running along beside us. "I BEG YOU, HOLD ON!!!" she said. I pause here to say to all doctors and midwives it is useless to counsel a woman to hold on when she is about to give birth for no urge is more primeval, more immediate, more unstoppable. It is wasted breath.

We did make it to the birthing room and somehow I got out of my clothes and onto a table. The room was attractive, a burgundy color on one wall, a gentle turquoise on another. The light was low, the ambience calm. An assistant midwife was there to help. Just getting settled was an immense relief and with the four of us working hard, talking some and laughing now and then the baby was born twenty minutes later. The midwife placed her immediately on my chest, a tiny, golden little thing with a halo of fuzz for hair. Fiona Rose Marie Alice Herrmann Loomis. The sister Joe had dreamed of. The daughter Michael and I had hardly dared hope for. She was perfect. She was beautiful. She had arrived very gently.

Sometime in the middle of the night I was released from the birthing room and Michael and the assistant midwife wheeled Fiona and me up to our pale pink room. There, awaiting me, was a full three-course meal, which I couldn't even look at. I was impressed, though. Everything had been thought of except for one important thing. There was no place for Michael to stay. I asked the nurse about a cot and she looked horrified. *"Oh non, le papa ne peut pas rester."* "Oh no, the father can't stay. That isn't allowed." Michael and I were shocked. He should have just slept in the armchair in the room—I'm sure no one would have thrown him out. But the nurse was so firm that he stayed for an hour or so then dragged himself home.

Other than missing Michael and Joe, the five days in the clinic remain the most pleasant of dreams. Fiona and I had a room to ourselves, she in a clear, Plexiglas crib, me in a very narrow, adjustable bed, and the staff of nurses were there for our comfort. Each day I had a lesson in how to bathe the baby, and how to care for her and myself. They urged me to leave Fiona with them at night so I would sleep—I wouldn't hear of it—and told me if I wanted to take a walk, or sleep, or telephone they would happily watch her. I was fed three delicious meals a day accompanied either by beer or by hard cider, and every morning a brisk efficient maid came in and cleaned the room from top to bottom. I was so thirsty I thought I would die and asked Michael to bring me Orangina, which I love. I was happily sipping some when one of the nurses came in and looked at it, horrified! *"Oh, madame, ce n'est pas bon pour le bébé. Non, il ne faut pas boire ça."* "Madame, this is very bad for the baby, oh no, you mustn't drink that." I was so disappointed. I'd remembered from nursing Joe that there were many foods that were potentially upsetting, but I would never have guessed Orangina was one. *"Oh oui, madame, tous les boissons gazeuses sont mauvaises."* She was telling me that all fizzy drinks were bad. Why then, I wondered, was hard cider one of the drink options on the menu?

Gym classes were offered twice a week to new mothers, so two days after Fiona was born I left her with the nurses and went downstairs to "work out" with a kinestherapist who demonstrated how to get back in shape. The rest of the time I slept, read, and looked at or fed Fiona.

Joe and Michael came every day, and visitors began arriving almost immediately. I was shocked when the first group arrived. I was barely awake and somewhat disheveled and in they walked, two children and their parents, bearing gifts. It was lovely to see them but the last thing I wanted. The stream was, however, unstoppable. Some of the people who came were close friends, others were simply acquaintances, and all were motivated by the sheer joy of seeing a new baby. It is, I learned, a French custom to visit a new mother in the clinic. It is also a custom for the new mother to call people she knows to announce the birth. How, I wondered, is a new mother supposed to work up the energy and concentration to call people and announce the birth? I certainly didn't have it. But then I thought about the way the French social security system is set up for new mothers and I figured perhaps that was how they had the energy. A pregnant woman gets six weeks paid leave before the baby arrives and two months minimum leave afterwards. If there are extenuating circumstances— the baby is still nursing or eating at irregular hours, the mother isn't feeling up to returning to work—the leave can be extended by two weeks. If the woman already has two children, she is allowed a three-year, partially paid leave for each successive child with the guarantee of a job when she returns.

My room filled with the baby clothes everyone gave as gifts, which Michael would cart home with him each day. I loved seeing people but was jealous of the peace and quiet of the clinic and was tempted to press the *occupé*, or busy, button at the side of my bed, which would cause a red light to go on outside my door. I didn't do that, but I did take the phone off the hook.

Joe was ecstatic over his sister, but even more excited about the bed, which he would raise and lower with the little button on my bedside table. I got out of it while he was in the room so he could play with it at will. Fiona, the little *crevette*, or shrimp, in the bassinet, was a real curiosity to him, but all she did was sleep or curl her fist and emit a squeak or two. She would have to become a lot more entertaining before he'd be ready to take an interest.

Nurses stopped in at all times during the day to check on me and the baby, and they met Michael and Joe. One of them started discussing stamps with Joe and the next day brought him an envelopeful for his collection. The following day he brought her some of his. They were all wonderful, cheerful, maternal women who were so experienced they transferred their confidence to every new mother. They couldn't get over how long Fiona was—twenty-three inches. I could hear them talking about it down the hall. Although that isn't particularly long for an American baby, it evidently is for the French variety.

The nursing wasn't going as smoothly as the midwife thought it should, so she looked at me seriously and said she would not let me go home until she was sure all was well, which might mean an extra couple of days in the clinic. I was torn. I wanted to be home but loved the comfort and peace of the clinic. We agreed to wait until day five to see how it was going. As it happened, all was going well, so I prepared myself to check out. The midwife came in and asked at what time I'd be leaving. "My husband will be here around noon," I said. "Well, then you'll be wanting to have lunch with us—I'll go order it for you."

I didn't protest, though I wasn't sure I'd be hungry, but when the nurse brought in a steaming bowl of fragrant *pot au feu* I couldn't resist. Each meal had been better than the last, from the lentils with garlicky sausages to the roast pork. My favorite day had been Sunday, though. Instead of the usual *baguette* and butter for breakfast I was served croissants and a *pain au chocolat* along with what had become my ritual rich and delicious bowl of hot chocolate. Lunch was perfectly roasted lamb with potatoes and green beans and a chocolate *éclair* for dessert, which I saved for Joe. He and Michael arrived in the afternoon with brioches and champagne—it was Valentine's Day—and we had a little party in our room. Dinner that night was fragrant *brandade* and a potato gratin, both delicious and comforting.

The midwife signed my release form and gave me my *livret de famille*, or family book, where Michael's and my marriage is registered and where there are ten pages reserved for registering children. I hadn't registered Joe in it because he was born in the United States, though I'd reserved a page for him. I flipped through it to see Fiona's page and realized that the official who had inscribed her names into the book had left one out. I mentioned it to one of the nurses who was aghast. "You'd better go to city hall across the street right now," she said. "Here, I will take the baby."

As I ran out I wondered if I really had to rush to do this or if she simply wanted to hold Fiona for a while, so happy had she been to take her from me!

It took less than a half hour to put things right and I was ready with all of my bags packed. Michael arrived with a huge bouquet of flowers, which he gave the nurses, and I shed a tear or two as I told them good-bye.

Michael tucked us into the car and we drove home, ready to begin our lives anew with our wonderful baby girl.

When we arrived home from the hospital I carried Fiona inside and Joe threw himself at us, so happy to have us home. My mother and father had just arrived that same day to stay for several weeks, and it was thanks to my mother's efforts that the house smelled temptingly of roast chicken and vegetables. They admired Fiona as I placed her in the lace-lined wicker *couffin*, the comfortable basket that would be her bed for the first several months.

My mother shooed us all to the table and served lunch. Fiona slept through the festivities—my parents are a cheerful couple and it was a lively meal. In fact, she was so silent it was hard to remember she was there, though Joe kept popping up from the table to look at her.

In the weeks that followed, my sister came to visit and friends stopped by continuously, flooding us with clothing and gifts for Fiona. Soon stuffed animals filled every available corner of the house. We had more people at the house in those first weeks after Fiona and I came home than we had had in our entire time in Louviers, as parents of Joe's schoolmates, neighbors, schoolteachers, several of the nuns from the convent down the street, shopkeepers and friends came to see the baby. In general, we had noticed that acquaintances, such as parents who drop their children off to play, were reluctant to come into the house. Fiona's arrival changed all that, as people came, admired, and stayed.

It became apparent quite early on that, as Joe had been the neighborhood toddler, Fiona was to become the neighborhood baby, growing up at ease with the shopkeepers and characters of our life in Louviers.

My life had come together seamlessly—house, children, Michael, friends and neighbors, the markets, the shops, the customs, and the food. I felt wonderfully at home on rue Tatin.

TARTE TATIN

Living on rue Tatin, which is named after a general in Napoleon's army and has nothing to do with the tart, I nonetheless feel a tremendous responsibility to have an exceptional Tarte Tatin in my repertory. After years of tasting Tartes Tatin all over France and making them at home, I came up with this recipe, a version of which was first published in French Farmhouse Cookbook *(Workman, 1996). It is simple to make, and simply delicious, a perfect Tarte Tatin.*

One 10½-inch/26.5-cm tart shell (use the pastry from the
    Apple and Thyme Tart, page 80)
1½ cups/300g vanilla sugar
10 tablespoons/150g unsalted butter, cut in thin slices
5 pounds/2.5kg tart apples such as Cox's Orange Pippins
    or Boskoop, peeled, halved, and cored

1. Line a baking sheet with parchment paper or lightly flour it.

2. Roll out the pastry on a lightly floured work surface to form an 11-inch/29-cm round. Transfer the pastry to the prepared baking sheet and refrigerate for at least 1 hour.

3. Spread the sugar evenly over the bottom of a very heavy 10½-inch oven-proof skillet or flame-proof baking pan. Place the butter slices evenly over the sugar, then arrange the apple halves on top of the butter. Begin at the outside edge and stand the halves on their sides, facing in one direction with stem ends toward the center. Pack the apples as close together as possible, gently pushing them together so they are held standing by pressure. Make a second circle of apple halves inside the first, packing them in on their edges as well. Place one apple half right in the center of the second circle to fill in the small space that remains. The idea is to get as many apples into the pan as possible, while keeping them nicely arranged.

4. Place the skillet over medium-low heat and cook the apples in the butter and sugar, uncovered, until the sugar turns golden brown; this will take at least 1 hour. Watch the apples closely to be sure they don't stick; you may want to adjust the heat now and then, to slow down or speed up the cooking. As the sugar and butter melt and the apples give up some of their juices, baste the apples occasionally with a turkey baster. Gradually, the sugar will caramelize the apples nearly all the way through, though they will remain uncooked on top.

5. Preheat the oven to 425° F/220° C/gas 8.

6. When the cooking juices are deep golden and the apples are nearly cooked through, remove the pastry from the refrigerator and quickly and carefully place it over the apples, gently pushing it down around them, simultaneously easing it toward the center so that if it shrinks on the sides there will still be enough of it to cover the apples. Using a sharp knife, trim off and discard any extra pastry.

7. Place the skillet on a baking sheet. Bake in the center of the oven until the pastry is golden, 25 to 30 minutes. Don't be concerned if the juices bubble over; the tart will be more or less juicy, depending on the variety of apple you've used.

8. Remove the skillet from the oven. Immediately invert a serving platter with a slight lip over the skillet. Quickly but carefully invert the two so the crust is on the bottom, the apples are on top and the juices don't run off onto the floor. Remove the

TOO GOOD TO BE TRUE

skillet. Should any apples stick to it, gently remove them and reinsert them into their rightful place in the tart.

9. Serve generous slices as soon as the tart has cooled slightly, but is still very warm.

6 TO 8 SERVINGS

Recipe Index

RECIPE INDEX

SUSAN HERRMANN LOOMIS, journalist and professionally trained chef, is the author of five cookbooks: *The Great American Seafood Cookbook, Farmhouse Cookbook, Clambakes and Fishfries, French Farmhouse Cookbook*, and *Italian Farmhouse Cookbook*. She is the proprietor of On Rue Tatin, a cooking school she operates from her fifteenth-century home in Louviers, France, where she lives with her husband, Michael, and their two children, Joseph and Fiona Rose. She can be reached at her website, *www. susanloomis.com.*